THE BHOYS

<u>of all</u> To Aid in the winning of all, arguments!! Statto!

Enjoy bro'!

Brian Mc

THE BHOYS

DAY-TO-DAY LIFE AT PARKHEAD

RICHARD LERMAN AND DAVID BROWN

MAINSTREAM
PUBLISHING

EDINBURGH AND LONDON

First published in Great Britain in 1998 by
MAINSTREAM PUBLISHING COMPANY (EDINBURGH) LTD
7 Albany Street
Edinburgh EH1 3UG

ISBN 1 84018 031 5

A catalogue record for this book is available from the British Library

Typeset in Times
Printed and bound in Great Britain by Butler & Tanner Ltd

The long and proud history of Celtic Football Club has been recorded several times as the club evolved from humble origins to take its place today amongst the elite of European football.

Most football club history books are laid out chronologically from past to present, developing chapter by chapter the story of the journey to prominence (or in some cases oblivion) and the characters that shaped the destiny of the club and the team. Alternatively, a player-by-player analysis or a 'who's who' will attempt to list, in alphabetical order, all or sometimes just the key participants who have taken part in the building of the organisation or the events on the field.

We believe that *The Bhoys* introduces a third, and new, concept to the study of football clubs. Simply, by using a diary format, we have attempted to catalogue the important events, the landmarks along the way for both the club and its players and the highs and lows as they occurred on a daily basis from formation to the present.

Obviously in a topic as large as the one we have attempted to cover there will be a debate about what material should be included and what should be left out. It would not have been practical to have included details on every player that has ever worn the green and white hoop shirt that is Celtic. We have had to establish criteria that only those who have played a minimum number of games, or have been recognised for some other aspect of their career, be included. If, as we suspect, this has led to the omission of many fine players who for one reason or another did not make it into these pages, we apologise to them, their families and their supporters.

It has not been our policy to be contentious; we have desired to present a factual account of the history of this great club and, in so doing, some subjective decisions have had to be made. However, if any reader considers we have made a glaring omission or a factual inaccuracy, we should be glad to address these matters with correspondence via our publisher, so that we might include any changes in a future edition of this book.

Finally, it has been our privilege to work on this subject. Several clubs stake a claim for the mantle of the biggest club in Britain but of these only Celtic has been through a roller-coaster ride of uncertainty over the last few years. A change of ownership, managerial comings and goings, a question mark over stadium redevelopment and a period when performances on the field were less than the standard required were finally laid to rest during season 1997–98. Of the teams pretending to be at the summit, few if any would have emerged from similar events with the support that Celtic can muster.

Quite simply we understand that, for many, Celtic is more than a football club, it is a way of life.

ABOUT THE AUTHORS

This is the first time that Richard Lerman and David Brown have worked together. This book, and three other titles from the same partnership, form part of a series on football that Mainstream Publishing are issuing where the material is organised in diary format.

Richard Lerman is married with three sons (all keen football enthusiasts) and lives in North London.

David Brown is married with two daughters (who care more for music than football) and lives in Kent.

Both men travel the length and breadth of Great Britain and Europe in pursuit of their obsession with football and are avid collectors of football memorabilia and statistics.

ACKNOWLEDGEMENTS

Authors Richard Lerman and David Brown would like to thank the following who have helped us in the research and for providing us with the material to make this book possible; Bob Goodwin, Les Easterbrook, Steve Connor, Michael Bolam, John Allen, Derek Taylor and Andrew Miller. We would also like to thank the many readers of *Boot Magazine*, which specialises in football memorabilia (6 Denmark Road, London, N8 0DZ) who have provided us with material for this publication.

Last, but not least, we would very much like to thank Graham Betts for his efforts in organising this project together with all the staff at Mainstream Publishing.

BIBLIOGRAPHY

Whilst we have used many sources of material including various Celtic hand guides, programmes, autobiographies, the majority of the material has been gained from the following two excellent books which we would recommend to any true fan.

An Alphabet of the Celts: A Complete Who's Who of Celtic FC by Eugene MacBride and Martin O'Connor with George Sheridan published by ACL & Polar Publishing UK Ltd.
Celtic: A Complete Record published by Breedon Books.

| 1894 | Rangers | H | Friendly | 2–3 |

The very first New Year's Day meeting between the two great rivals of Glasgow saw Rangers win 3–2 at Celtic Park in front of a crowd of 15,000.

1895	Rangers	A	Friendly	3–2
1896	Rangers	H	Friendly	3–3
1898	Rangers	H	Scottish League First Division (match abandoned after 70 minutes due to spectator encroachment)	1–1
1900	Rangers	H	Scottish League	3–2

Celtic's victory at Celtic Park was Rangers first defeat in the League since February 12th 1898, a run that had taken in 35 matches, with 31 victories and only four draws. John Divers scored two of the goals.

1901	Rangers	A	Scottish League	1–2
1902	Rangers	H	Scottish League	2–4
1903	Rangers	A	Scottish League	3–3
1904	Rangers	H	Scottish League	2–2
1906	Rangers	H	Scottish League	1–0
1907	Rangers	A	Scottish League	1–2
1908	Rangers	H	Scottish League	2–1
1909	Rangers	A	Scottish League	3–1
1910	Rangers	H	Scottish League	1–1
1912	Rangers	H	Scottish League	3–0
1913	Rangers	A	Scottish League	1–0
1914	Rangers	H	Scottish League	4–0
1915	Rangers	A	Scottish League	1–2
1916	Rangers	H	Scottish League	2–2
1917	Rangers	A	Scottish League	0–0
1918	Rangers	H	Scottish League	0–0
1919	Rangers	A	Scottish League	1–1
1920	Rangers	H	Scottish League	1–1
1921	Rangers	A	Scottish League	2–0
1923	Rangers	A	Scottish League	0–2
1924	Rangers	H	Scottish League	2–2
1925	Rangers	A	Scottish League	1–3
1926	Rangers	H	Scottish League	2–2
1927	Rangers	A	Scottish League	1–2
1929	Rangers	A	Scottish League	0–3
1930	Rangers	H	Scottish League	1–2
1931	Rangers	A	Scottish League	0–1
1932	Rangers	H	Scottish League	1–2
1934	Rangers	H	Scottish League	2–2
1935	Rangers	A	Scottish League	1–2
1936	Rangers	H	Scottish League	3–4

Willie McGonagle played his last game for the club. In 10 years' service he made 325 appearances and won 2 Scottish Cup winners' medals, in 1931 and 1933.

| 1937 | Rangers | A | Scottish League | 0–1 |

1938	Rangers	H	Scottish League	3–0

According to most record books, the visit of Rangers attracted Celtic Park's biggest ever attendance of 92,000. However, other sources give a figure of only 83,500 for the traditional New Year's Day match, although all sources agree that this was Celtic Park's record attendance. Two goals from Divers and a penalty by Macdonald gave Celtic the thoroughly deserved victory.

1940	Rangers	A	League – Western Division	1–1
1941	Rangers	A	League – Southern Division	3–2
1942	Rangers	H	League – Southern Division	0–2
1943	Rangers	A	League – Southern Division	1–8

When the Second World War broke out in 1939 and football was reorganised on a regional basis, both Celtic and Rangers found their crowds restricted to a mere 15,000, although this figure was later relaxed for both clubs (not surprisingly, since clashes between the two have always attracted big crowds). This Southern League meeting was witnessed by 30,000 at Ibrox, with Rangers scoring eight times through Torry Gillick (3), Willie Waddell (2), George Young (2, one from the penalty spot) and Jimmy Duncanson. Celtic's cause was not helped by having two players sent off, Malcolm MacDonald and Matt Lynch, both of whom were dismissed for dissent when Rangers were leading 4–1. MacDonald was later suspended until August and fined £10, while Lynch was suspended until March and fined £5. A game to forget for more than just the scoreline.

1944	Rangers	H	League – Southern Division	1–3
1945	Rangers	A	League – Southern Division	1–0
1946	Rangers	H	League – 'A' Division	0–1
1947	Rangers	A	Scottish League	1–1
1949	Rangers	A	Scottish League	0–4
1951	Rangers	A	Scottish League	0–1
1952	Rangers	H	Scottish League	1–4
1953	Rangers	A	Scottish League	0–1
1954	Rangers	H	Scottish League	1–0
1955	Rangers	A	Scottish League	1–4
1957	Rangers	A	Scottish League	0–2
1958	Rangers	H	Scottish League	0–1
1959	Rangers	A	Scottish League	1–2
1960	Rangers	H	Scottish League	0–1
1963	Rangers	A	Scottish League	0–4
1964	Rangers	H	Scottish League	0–1
1965	Rangers	A	Scottish League	0–1
1966	Clyde	A	Scottish League	3–1
1968	Clyde	A	Scottish League	3–2
1969	Clyde	H	Scottish League	5–0

1969	Club Chairman Robert Kelly was awarded a knighthood in the New Year's Honours List.

1970	Clyde	A	Scottish League	2–0
1972	Clyde	A	Scottish League	7–0
1974	Clyde	A	Scottish League	2–0

1974	Billy McNeill was awarded the MBE by the Queen.

1975	Clyde	H	Scottish League	5–1
1976	Rangers	A	Scottish League Premier Division	0–1
1981	Kilmarnock	A	Scottish League Premier Division	2–1

1981 Bobby Lennox was awarded the MBE by the Queen for his services to the game.

1983	Rangers	A	Scottish League Premier Division	2–1
1985	Rangers	A	Scottish League Premier Division	2–1
1986	Rangers	H	Scottish League Premier Division	2–0
1987	Rangers	A	Scottish League Premier Division	0–2
1992	Rangers	H	Scottish League Premier Division	1–3
1994	Rangers	H	Scottish League Premier Division	2–4

JANUARY 2ND

1893	Third Lanark	H	Scottish Cup quarter-final	5–1
1897	Rangers	A	Glasgow League	0–3
1899	Rangers	A	Scottish League	1–4

Sandy McMahon scored his 100th League goal for the club, becoming the first player to achieve this milestone.

| 1903 | Hibernian | H | Scottish League | 0–4 |
| 1905 | Rangers | A | Scottish League First Division (match abandoned |

after 65 minutes due to spectator encroachment)   0–0

This match effectively stopped Rangers winning the League title in 1904–05 and gave Celtic the chance to overtake them in the title race. Both sides were neck and neck at the top of the table at the time of the match and a tense game had ensued for some 65 minutes when part of the crowd of 60,000 encroached onto the field and caused the game to be abandoned. When the match was replayed on February 18th, Rangers lost 4–1 and finished the season level on points, with Celtic subsequently losing in a championship play-off.

1906	Kilmarnock	H	Scottish League	2–0
1907	Hamilton Academical	H	Scottish League	2–0
1908	Aberdeen	H	Scottish League	3–0
1909	Kilmarnock	A	Scottish League	1–3
1911	Rangers	A	Scottish League	1–1
1912	Clyde	A	Scottish League	1–1
1913	Clyde	H	Scottish League	3–0
1915	Clyde	H	Scottish League	2–0
1917	Clyde	H	Scottish League	0–0
1918	Clyde	A	Scottish League	4–1
1919	Clyde	H	Scottish League	2–0
1922	Rangers	H	Scottish League	0–0
1923	Clyde	H	Scottish League	0–0
1924	Clyde	A	Scottish League	0–0
1926	Queen's Park	A	Scottish League	4–1
1927	Rangers	H	Scottish League	1–0
1930	Queen's Park	A	Scottish League	1–2
1932	Queen's Park	A	Scottish League	3–0
1933	Rangers	A	Scottish League	0–0

1937	Queen's Park	A	Scottish League	0–1
1939	Rangers	A	Scottish League	1–2

The attendance of 118,567 is the highest for a League game played in Britain. It was claimed that the gates were shut with a further 30,000 still trying to gain admittance!

1943	Partick Thistle	H	League – Southern Division	3–3
1946	Queen of the South	A	League – 'A' Division	0–0
1947	Aberdeen	H	Scottish League	1–5
1948	Rangers	H	Scottish League	0–4
1950	Rangers	H	Scottish League	1–1
1952	Hearts	A	Scottish League	1–2
1954	Aberdeen	A	Scottish League	0–2
1956	Rangers	H	Scottish League	0–1
1957	Kilmarnock	H	Scottish League	1–1
1958	Queen's Park	A	Scottish League	3–0
1959	Motherwell	H	Scottish League	3–3
1960	Hearts	A	Scottish League	1–3
1961	Rangers	A	Scottish League	1–2
1964	Third Lanark	A	Scottish League	1–1
1965	Clyde	H	Scottish League	1–1
1968	Rangers	H	Scottish League	2–2
1969	Rangers	A	Scottish League	0–1
1971	Rangers	A	Scottish League	1–1

The game will unfortunately be remembered in history as the Ibrox disaster. A tense Glasgow derby had only really woken from its slumbers in the final minutes of the match, with Celtic's Jimmy Johnstone heading what appeared to be the winning goal in the 89th minute after a Bobby Lennox shot had hit the crossbar. The goal was a signal for thousands of Rangers fans to begin streaming from the ground, although Colin Stein was on hand to hit the ball home for a dramatic equaliser in literally the last moments of the game. It has often been said that the roar of the Rangers crowd greeting the equaliser caused many on Stairway 13 to turn around and try to return to the terraces, but the facts, established by the Fatal Accident Inquiry, are somewhat different. A part of the crowd leaving on Stairway 13 stumbled and caused a domino effect down the huge gangway, creating an enormous crush at the bottom that left 66 people dead and 145 injured. The Inquiry later put the time of disaster as being at least five minutes after Colin Stein's equaliser, thus clearing him of any blame. Instead, it was Rangers' directors who came in for most of the criticism, although no action was taken against them.

1978	Motherwell	H	Scottish League Premier Division	0–1
1988	Rangers	H	Scottish League Premier Division	2–0
1990	Rangers	H	Scottish League Premier Division	0–1
1991	Rangers	A	Scottish League Premier Division	0–2
1993	Rangers	A	Scottish League Premier Division	0–1
1997	Rangers	A	Scottish League Premier Division	1–3
1998	Rangers	H	Scottish League Premier Division	2–0

JANUARY 3RD

1899	Clyde	H	Glasgow League	2–1
1905	Airdrie	H	Scottish League	2–3
1910	Clyde	A	Scottish League	1–0
1911	Clyde	H	Scottish League	2–0
1914	Partick Thistle	A	Scottish League	0–0
1916	Clyde	A	Scottish League	3–1
1920	Raith Rovers	A	Scottish League	3–0
1921	Clyde	H	Scottish League	1–0
1922	Clyde	A	Scottish League	1–1

Paddy Connolly made his debut.

1925	Airdrie	A	Scottish League	1–3
1927	Queen's Park	H	Scottish League	2–3
1928	Queen's Park	A	Scottish League	3–1
1931	Hibernian	A	Scottish League	0–0
1938	Queen's Park	A	Scottish League	3–0
1939	Queen's Park	H	Scottish League	0–1
1942	Clyde	A	League – Southern Division	1–2
1944	Third Lanark	H	League – Southern Division	4–0
1948	Hearts	A	Scottish League	0–1
1949	Hearts	H	Scottish League	2–0
1950	Raith Rovers	A	Scottish League	1–1
1955	Raith Rovers	H	Scottish League	4–1
1966	Rangers	H	Scottish League	5–1
1970	Rangers	H	Scottish League	0–0
1972	Rangers	H	Scottish League	2–1

1974 Ex-player and manager Jimmy McStay died aged 79.

1976	Dundee	H	Scottish League Premier Division	3–3
1981	Morton	H	Scottish League Premier Division	3–0
1983	Dundee	H	Scottish League Premier Division	2–2
1987	Hamilton Academical	H	Scottish League Premier Division	8–3

Anton Rogan made his debut for the club.

1989	Rangers	A	Scottish League Premier Division	1–4
1996	Rangers	H	Scottish League Premier Division	0–0

JANUARY 4TH

1892	Rangers	H	Friendly	2–0
1902	Hibernian	A	Inter City League	1–0
1913	Partick Thistle	H	Scottish League	1–0
1915	Kilmarnock	H	Scottish League	2–0
1919	Third Lanark	A	Scottish League	3–2
1926	Partick Thistle	H	Scottish League	3–0
1930	Aberdeen	A	Scottish League	1–3
1936	St Johnstone	H	Scottish League	2–0
1941	Clyde	A	League – Southern Division	1–1
1947	Queen of the South	H	Scottish League	2–0

| 1958 | Falkirk | H | Scottish League | 2–2 |
| 1964 | Falkirk | H | Scottish League | 7–0 |

Steve Chalmers scored a hat-trick and John Divers grabbed a brace. Chalmers's hat-trick was the 7th scored by a Celtic player in the last 13 games.

1969	Dunfermline Athletic	H	Scottish League	3–1
1975	Rangers	A	Scottish League	0–3
1986	Dundee United	A	Scottish League Premier Division	2–4
1992	Hearts	H	Scottish League Premier Division	1–2
1995	Rangers	A	Scottish League	1–1
1997	Motherwell	H	Scottish League Premier Division	5–0

JANUARY 5TH

1907	Falkirk	H	Scottish League	3–2
1914	Clyde	A	Scottish League	1–0
1918	St Mirren	A	Scottish League	0–0
1920	Clyde	A	Scottish League	2–0
1924	Hamilton Academical	H	Scottish League	1–0
1925	Third Lanark	H	Scottish League	7–0
1929	Ayr United	H	Scottish League	3–0
1935	St Johnstone	A	Scottish League	1–0
1946	Partick Thistle	A	League – 'A' Division	3–3
1957	Queen's Park	A	Scottish League	0–2
1963	Aberdeen	A	Scottish League	5–1

Tommy Gemmell made his debut.

1974	Rangers	H	Scottish League	1–0
1980	Dundee United	H	Scottish League Premier Division	1–0
1991	Hibernian	H	Scottish League Premier Division	1–1

JANUARY 6TH

1906	Falkirk	H	Scottish League	7–0
1912	Hearts	H	Scottish League	1–1
1917	Motherwell	H	Scottish League	1–0
1923	Aberdeen	H	Scottish League	1–2

Johnny McMaster after 10 years and 220 appearances played his last game for the club.

1934	Kilmarnock	H	Scottish League	4–1
1940	Airdrie	A	League Western Division	1–0
1945	Morton	H	League – Southern Division	6–1
1951	Motherwell	A	Scottish League	1–2

Alex Rollo made his debut.

1962	Kilmarnock	H	Scottish League	2–2
1973	Rangers	A	Scottish League	1–2
1990	St Mirren	A	Scottish League Premier Division	2–0

Roy Aitken made his final appearance for the club after 15 years' service. He made a total of 667 appearances scoring 55 goals in that time. He won 6 Championships, 5 Cups and 1 League Cup and was the captain of the Centenary Double-winning team in 1988. He won 50 caps for Scotland during his time at Parkhead.

1996	Motherwell	H	Scottish League Premier Division	1–0

JANUARY 7TH

1893	Third Lanark	H	Glasgow Cup semi-final	5–2
1899	Dundee	H	Scottish League	4–1
1905	Port Glasgow Athletic	H	Scottish League	3–0
1911	Partick Thistle	H	Scottish League	2–0
1922	Third Lanark	H	Scottish League	2–0
1928	Falkirk	A	Scottish League	3–1
1933	Morton	A	Scottish League	1–0
1939	Raith Rovers	A	Scottish League	0–4
1950	Motherwell	H	Scottish League	3–1
1956	Aberdeen	A	Scottish League	0–1
1961	Third Lanark	H	Scottish League	2–3
1965	Jim Craig signed pro forms for the club.			
1967	Dundee	H	Scottish League	5–1
1984	Motherwell	A	Scottish League Premier Division	2–2
1989	Hamilton Academical	H	Scottish League Premier Division	2–0
1995	Dundee United	H	Scottish League	1–1

JANUARY 8TH

1898	Arthurlie	A	Scottish Cup	7–0
1910	Airdrie	A	Scottish League	2–0

Peter Somers played his last game before leaving the club to join Hamilton Academical. He played in 219 games and scored 62 goals. He was an integral part of the 6 in-a-row team 1904–5 to 1909–10 and he also won 3 Scottish Cup winners' medals.

1916	Dumbarton	A	Scottish League	2–1
1921	Clydebank	A	Scottish League	2–0
1927	Morton	A	Scottish League	6–2
1938	Hearts	A	Scottish League	4–2
1944	Hearts	H	League – Southern Division	4–0
1949	Morton	A	Scottish League	0–0
1955	Kilmarnock	A	Scottish League	2–1
1964	Third Lanark	H	Glasgow Cup semi-final	1–1
1966	Dundee United	H	Scottish League	1–0
1972	Morton	A	Scottish League	1–1
1977	Dundee United	A	Scottish League Premier Division	2–1
1983	St Mirren	A	Scottish League Premier Division	1–0
1992	St Johnstone	A	Scottish League Premier Division	4–2
1994	Partick Thistle	A	Scottish League Premier Division	0–1
1997	Kilmarnock	H	Scottish League Premier Division	6–0

JANUARY 9TH

1897	Arthurlie	A	Scottish Cup	2–4

Maybe one of the biggest shocks ever in the Scottish Cup even today some 100 years on, when Celtic lost to the non-League part-timers of Arthurlie. Several reasons were given – players suspended, injured, bad pitch etc.

1904	Airdrie	A	Scottish League	3–4
1909	Hearts	H	Scottish League	1–1
1915	Partick Thistle	H	Scottish League	6–1
1926	Raith Rovers	H	Scottish League	1–0
1932	Aberdeen	H	Scottish League	2–0
1937	Kilmarnock	A	Scottish League	3–3
1943	Hibernian	A	League – Southern Division	0–4
1954	Falkirk	H	Scottish League	1–0
1960	Raith Rovers	H	Scottish League	1–0
1965	Dundee United	A	Scottish League	1–3
1971	Hibernian	H	Scottish League	2–1

1981 Alan Sneddon was sold to Hibernian for £60,000 where he helped them win the First Division, therefore qualifying for two championship medals in one season.

1982	Rangers	A	Scottish League Premier Division	0–1
1988	St Mirren	A	Scottish League Premier Division	1–1
1993	Clyde	A	Scottish Cup	0–0
1996	Raith Rovers	A	Scottish League Premier Division	3–1

JANUARY 10TH

1882 'Sunny' Jim Young was born in Kilmarnock.

1914	Dumbarton	H	Scottish League	4–0
1920	Morton	H	Scottish League	1–1
1925	Aberdeen	H	Scottish League	3–1
1931	East Fife	H	Scottish League	9–1
1942	Motherwell	A	League – Southern Division	1–2
1948	Aberdeen	H	Scottish League	1–0
1953	Motherwell	A	Scottish League	2–4
1962	Third Lanark	A	Scottish League	1–1
1976	Motherwell	A	Scottish League Premier Division	3–1
1981	Dundee United	H	Scottish League Premier Division	2–1
1987	Dundee United	A	Scottish League Premier Division	2–3

1995 Dutch international Pierre Van Hooijdonk joined the club from NAC Breda for £1.5 million.

1998	Motherwell	A	Scottish League Premier Division	1–1

JANUARY 11TH

1902	Thornliebank	H	Scottish Cup	3–0
1908	Clyde	H	Scottish League	5–1
1913	Queen's Park	H	Scottish League	1–0
1919	Clydebank	H	Scottish League	3–1

1924 John Bonnar was born.

1936	Queen of the South	H	Scottish League	5–0
1941	Airdrie	H	League – Southern Division	2–0
1947	Queen's Park	A	Scottish League	3–1

1958	Motherwell	A	Scottish League	3–1
1964	Eyemouth United	H	Scottish Cup	3–0
1967	Clyde	H	Scottish League	5–1
1969	Aberdeen	A	Scottish League	3–1
1975	Motherwell	H	Scottish League	2–3
1977	Rangers	H	Scottish League Premier Division	1–0
1986	Aberdeen	H	Scottish League Premier Division	1–1
1992	Motherwell	A	Scottish League Premier Division	0–0
1994	Motherwell	A	Scottish League Premier Division	1–2
1995	Hearts	H	Scottish League	1–1

1995 Pierre Van Hooijdonk scored on his full debut.

| 1997 | Hearts | A | Scottish League Premier Division | 2–1 |

JANUARY 12TH

| 1889 | Dumbarton | A | Scottish Cup semi-final | 4–1 |
| 1901 | Rangers | H | Scottish Cup | 1–0 |

1901 Jimmy Quinn signed professional forms with the club.

1907	Clyde	A	Scottish League	2–0
1918	Falkirk	H	Scottish League	0–0
1924	Third Lanark	A	Scottish League	3–1
1929	Partick Thistle	A	Scottish League	0–3
1935	Hamilton Academical	H	Scottish League	3–1
1946	Third Lanark	H	League – 'A' Division	3–2
1952	Raith Rovers	A	Scottish League	0–1
1957	Motherwell	H	Scottish League	2–1
1966	Dinamo Kiev	H	Cup-Winners' Cup quarter-final 1st leg	3–0
1980	Hibernian	A	Scottish League Premier Division	1–1
1994	St Patrick Athletic	A	Opening of floodlights	4–1

JANUARY 13TH

1875 Bernard Battles was born in Springburn.

1894	St Bernards	H	Scottish Cup quarter-final	8–1
1900	Bo'ness	H	Scottish Cup	7–1
1904	St Bernards	A	Scottish Cup	4–0
1906	Airdrie	A	Scottish League	5–2

1906 R.G. Campbell was sold to Rangers for £350.

1912	Motherwell	H	Scottish League	2–0
1917	Hearts	A	Scottish League	1–0
1923	Lochgelly Utd	A	Scottish Cup	3–2
1934	Hearts	A	Scottish League	1–2
1940	Ayr United	H	League Western Division	1–3
1945	Partick Thistle	A	League – Southern Division	3–0
1951	Aberdeen	H	Scottish League	3–4
1962	Dundee United	A	Scottish League	5–4
1973	Dundee	H	Scottish League	2–1
1990	Dundee United	A	Scottish League Premier Division	0–2

JANUARY 14TH

	Sixth Galloway Rovers	A	Scottish Cup	8–1
1905	Dundee	A	Scottish League	1–2
1911	Aberdeen	A	Scottish League	0–1
1922	Clydebank	A	Scottish League	2–0
1928	Dunfermline Athletic	H	Scottish League	9–0

Another milestone in the career of Jimmy McGrory as he scored 8 of the goals (and probably assisted in the other), a record that still stands today.

1933	Falkirk	H	Scottish League	0–1
1950	Aberdeen	A	Scottish League	0–4
1961	Aberdeen	A	Scottish League	3–1
1967	St Johnstone	A	Scottish League	4–0
1989	St Mirren	H	Scottish League Premier Division	2–1

1993 Jackie Dziekanowski was sold to Bristol City for £250,000. In his 30 months at the club he scored 22 goals in 66 appearances.

1995	Kilmarnock	H	Scottish League	2–1
1996	Aberdeen	A	Scottish League Premier Division	2–1
1997	Raith Rovers	A	Scottish League Premier Division	2–1

JANUARY 15TH

1898	Dundee	H	Scottish League	2–1
1910	Port Glasgow Athletic	H	Scottish League	4–0
1916	Hibernian	H	Scottish League	3–1
1921	Morton	A	Scottish League	1–1
1927	Clyde	H	Scottish League	7–0

Jimmy McGrory scored 5 goals in a single match for 3rd time in the season.

1938	Aberdeen	H	Scottish League	5–2
1944	Albion Rovers	A	League – Southern Division	1–2
1949	Albion Rovers	H	Scottish League	3–0
1966	Aberdeen	A	Scottish League	1–3
1972	Airdrie	H	Scottish League	2–0
1983	Motherwell	A	Scottish League Premier Division	1–2
1986	Motherwell	H	Scottish League Premier Division	3–2

JANUARY 16TH

1897	Clyde	H	Glasgow League	2–0
1904	Motherwell	H	Scottish League	6–0
1915	Falkirk	A	Scottish League	1–0
1926	Hibernian	A	Scottish League	4–4
1932	Falkirk	H	Scottish Cup	3–2
1937	Hamilton Academical	H	Scottish League	3–3
1943	St Mirren	A	League – Southern Division	2–0

John Paton made his debut.

1954	Raith Rovers	A	Scottish League	0–2
1960	Clyde	A	Scottish League	3–3
1965	Hearts	H	Scottish League	1–2

| 1971 | Dundee | A | Scottish League | 8–1 |
| 1988 | Hibernian | H | Scottish League Premier Division | 2–0 |

JANUARY 17TH

1914	Dundee	A	Scottish League	1–0
1917	Adam McLean signed pro forms with the club.			
1920	Kilmarnock	A	Scottish League	3–2
1925	Motherwell	A	Scottish League	0–1

Charlie Shaw played his last game between the posts for the club. In 12 years of outstanding brilliance he played in over 490 senior games, a club record for a goalkeeper, keeping a clean sheet in more than half of them. He was one of the main reasons why he won 6 Championship medals and 2 Scottish Cup winners' medals. He never made a full international appearance for Scotland, to which a reasonable explanation could never be given.

1931	East Fife	A	Scottish Cup	2–1
1942	Hibernian	H	League – Southern Division	2–1
1948	Morton	A	Scottish League	0–4
1953	Clyde	H	Scottish League	2–4
1970	Hibernian	A	Scottish League	2–1
1976	St Johnstone	A	Scottish League Premier Division	4–3
1996	Hearts	A	Scottish League Premier Division	2–1

JANUARY 18TH

1896	Queen's Park	H	Scottish Cup	2–4
1902	Hibernian	H	Inter City League	0–0
1908	Motherwell	A	Scottish League	2–2
1913	Hibernian	A	Scottish League	0–1
1919	St Mirren	A	Scottish League	4–0
1930	Inverness Caledonian	A	Scottish Cup	6–0
1936	Albion Rovers	A	Scottish League	3–0
1941	Falkirk	A	League – Southern Division	1–0
1947	Third Lanark	A	Scottish League	0–0
1958	Aberdeen	H	Scottish League	1–1
1964	St Mirren	H	Scottish League	3–0
1969	Dundee United	A	Scottish League	3–1
1973	Lou Macari was sold to Manchester United for a Scottish record fee of £200,000. The little striker had scored 57 goals in 102 appearances for the club.			
1975	Ayr United	A	Scottish League	5–1
1986	Hibernian	A	Scottish League Premier Division	2–2
1992	Dunfermline Athletic	A	Scottish League Premier Division	1–0
1994	Lee Martin was signed from Manchester United for £350,000 (fee set by tribunal some 2 months later)			
1997	Hibernian	H	Scottish League Premier Division	4–1

JANUARY 19TH

| 1895 | Dundee | A | Scottish Cup quarter-final | 0–1 |

1901	St Mirren	A	Scottish League	4–3

The legendary Jimmy Quinn made his debut and scored.

1907	Morton	H	Scottish League	2–1
1924	Aberdeen	H	Scottish League	4–0
1929	Arthurlie	H	Scottish Cup	5–1

Peter Scarff made his debut for the club.

1935	Aberdeen	A	Scottish League	0–2
1946	St Mirren	A	League – 'A' Division	2–1
1952	Dundee	H	Scottish League	1–1
1957	Queen of the South	A	Scottish League	3–4
1974	St Johnstone	H	Scottish League	3–0
1980	Aberdeen	A	Scottish League Premier Division	0–0
1991	Aberdeen	H	Scottish League Premier Division	1–0
1994	Aberdeen	H	Scottish League Premier Division	2–2

JANUARY 20TH

1894	St Bernards	A	Scottish League	2–1
1900	Queen's Park	H	Inter City League	3–2
1906	Partick Thistle	H	Scottish League	4–1
1912	St Mirren	A	Scottish League	1–1

Davie Hamilton played his last game for the club. A regular in the 'six in a row' team he also won 3 Scottish Cup winners' medals. He made over 260 appearances, scoring 60 goals. Amazingly, he never won a cap for Scotland.

1917	Dumbarton	H	Scottish League	1–1

Adam McLean made his debut for the club.

1923	Third Lanark	A	Scottish League	0–1

Jimmy McGrory made his debut.

1934	Dalbeattie Star	A	Scottish Cup	6–0
1945	Hibernian	A	League – Southern Division	4–2
1951	Dundee	A	Scottish League	1–3
1962	Falkirk	H	Scottish League	3–0
1968	Hibernian	A	Scottish League	2–0
1973	Ayr United	A	Scottish League	3–1
1990	Forfar Athletic	A	Scottish Cup	2–1
1993	Clyde	H	Scottish Cup	1–0
1996	Kilmarnock	A	Scottish League Premier Division	0–0

JANUARY 21ST

1898	Third Lanark	A	Scottish Cup	2–3
1899	Queen's Park	H	Glasgow League	2–2
1901	Hibernian	N	Glasgow Exhibition Trophy	1–0
1905	Hibernian	H	Scottish League	2–0
1911	Falkirk	H	Scottish League	0–0
1922	Aberdeen	H	Scottish League	2–0
1928	Bathgate	H	Scottish Cup	3–1
1933	Dunfermline Athletic	A	Scottish Cup	7–1

McGrory and Hugh O'Donnell scored a hat-trick apiece in this one-sided game.

1939	Burntisland Shipyard	A	Scottish Cup	8–3
1950	Dundee	H	Scottish League	2–0
1956	Raith Rovers	A	Scottish League	1–1
1959	Kilmarnock	H	Scottish League	2–0
1961	Airdrie	H	Scottish League	4–0
1964	Third Lanark	A	Glasgow Cup semi-final	3–0
1967	Hibernian	H	Scottish League	2–0
1987	Hibernian	H	Scottish League Premier Division	1–0
1989	Hibernian	A	Scottish League Premier Division	3–1
1995	Partick Thistle	A	Scottish League	0–0

JANUARY 22ND

1910	Dumbarton	A	Scottish Cup	2–1
1916	Third Lanark	A	Scottish League	4–0
1921	Motherwell	A	Scottish League	1–1
1927	Queen of the South	A	Scottish Cup	0–0
1938	Third Lanark	A	Scottish Cup	2–1
1944	Partick Thistle	A	League – Southern Division	2–1
1949	Dundee Utd	A	Scottish Cup	3–4
1955	Queen of the South	A	Scottish League	2–0
1962	Motherwell	H	Scottish League	1–1
1966	Motherwell	H	Scottish League	1–0
1972	St Johnstone	A	Scottish League	3–0
1977	Kilmarnock	A	Scottish League Premier Division	3–1
1983	Hibernian	H	Scottish League Premier Division	4–1
1992	Montrose	H	Scottish Cup	6–0

Gerry Creaney and Tommy Coyne helped themselves to a hat-trick each.

1994	Dundee United	H	Scottish League Premier Division	0–0
1997	Bayern Munich	H	Peter Grant testimonial	1–2

JANUARY 23RD

1892	Cowlairs	H	Scottish Cup quarter-final	4–1
1904	Morton	H	Scottish League	5–1
1909	Leith Athletic	A	Scottish Cup	4–2
1918	Airdrie	H	Scottish League	3–3

1923 John Gilchrist was sold to Preston North End for £4,500, a record fee at the time.

1926	Kilmarnock	A	Scottish Cup	5–0
1932	Hamilton Academical	A	Scottish League	0–1

Frank O'Donnell made his debut.

1937	Aberdeen	A	Scottish League	0–1
1943	Third Lanark	H	League – Southern Division	3–2

1950 Davie Hamilton died aged 68 in Glasgow.

1954	Queen of the South	H	Scottish League	3–1
1960	Arbroath	H	Scottish League	4–0
1965	Morton	A	Scottish League	3–3

| 1971 | Queen of the South | H | Scottish Cup | 5–1 |
| 1982 | Queen of the South | H | Scottish Cup | 4–0 |

Paul McStay made his debut.

| 1993 | Airdrie | A | Scottish League Premier Division | 0–1 |

JANUARY 24TH

| 1891 | Vale of Leven | A | Scottish League | 1–3 |

Sandy McMahon made his debut.

1903	St Mirren	H	Scottish Cup	0–0
1914	Airdrie	H	Scottish League	1–0
1920	Clydebank	A	Scottish League	0–2
1925	Third Lanark	A	Scottish Cup	5–1
1931	Aberdeen	A	Scottish League	1–1
1948	Partick Thistle	H	Scottish League	1–2
1953	Eyemouth Utd	A	Scottish Cup	4–0
1959	Queen of the South	A	Scottish League	2–2
1970	Dunfermline Athletic	H	Scottish Cup	2–1

1973 Ally Hunter was signed from Kilmarnock for £40,000.

1976	Motherwell	A	Scottish Cup	2–3
1981	Berwick Rangers	A	Scottish Cup	2–0
1987	Falkirk	A	Scottish League Premier Division	2–1
1998	Greenock Morton	H	Scottish Cup 3rd round	2–0

JANUARY 25TH

| 1902 | Arbroath | A | Scottish Cup | 3–2 |

1905 Joe Kennaway was born in Montreal.

| 1908 | Peebles Rovers | H | Scottish Cup | 4–0 |
| 1913 | Airdrie | H | Scottish League | 1–1 |

1916 Alexander 'Duke' McMahon died aged 45 in Glasgow.

1919	Motherwell	H	Scottish League	0–0
1930	Clyde	A	Scottish League	3–2
1939	Albion Rovers	H	Scottish League	4–1
1941	Motherwell	H	League – Southern Division	4–1
1947	Dundee	A	Scottish Cup	1–2
1958	Raith Rovers	A	Scottish League	2–1
1964	Morton	A	Scottish Cup	3–1
1969	Partick Thistle	A	Scottish Cup	3–3
1975	Hibernian	A	Scottish Cup	2–0
1986	St Johnstone	H	Scottish Cup	2–0

JANUARY 26TH

1924	Kilmarnock	A	Scottish Cup	0–2
1927	Queen of the South	H	Scottish Cup	4–1
1929	Hearts	A	Scottish League	1–2
1935	Montrose	H	Scottish Cup	4–1
1946	Falkirk	A	League – 'A' Division	2–4

1957	Falkirk	H	Scottish League	4–0
1966	Dinamo Kiev	A	Cup-Winners' Cup quarter-final 2nd leg	1–1
1980	Raith Rovers	H	Scottish Cup	2–1
1991	Forfar Athletic	A	Scottish Cup	2–0

1994 Gerry Creaney sold to Portsmouth for £600,000. He made over 140 appearances for the club scoring 55 goals but couldn't persuade the manager Liam Brady to offer him a new contract.

1997	Clydebank	A	Scottish Cup	5–0

JANUARY 27TH

1900	Port Glasgow	A	Scottish Cup	5–1
1906	Dundee	A	Scottish Cup	2–1
1912	Dunfermaline	H	Scottish Cup	1–0
1917	Third Lanark	A	Scottish League	0–0
1923	Hurlford	H	Scottish Cup	4–0
1934	St Johnstone	H	Scottish League	0–0

1938 Joe McLaughlin signed for the club.

1945	St Mirren	H	League – Southern Division	2–1
1951	East Fife	A	Scottish Cup	2–2
1962	Morton	A	Scottish Cup	3–1
1968	Dunfermline Athletic	H	Scottish Cup	0–2

1971 Scotland beat an Old Firm Select XI 2–1 at Hampden in front of 81,500 people in aid of the Ibrox Disaster fund.

1973	Airdrie	A	Scottish League	1–2

Ally Hunter made his debut.

1974	Clydebank	H	Scottish Cup	6–1
1990	Motherwell	H	Scottish League Premier Division	0–1
1998	Dundee United	A	Scottish League Premier Division	2–1

JANUARY 28TH

1893	Leith Athletic	A	Scottish League	1–0
1898	Partick Thistle	H	Scottish League	3–1
1905	Dumfries	A	Scottish Cup	2–1

1909 John Thomson was born in Buckhaven.

1911	St Mirren	A	Scottish Cup	2–0
1922	Montrose	H	Scottish Cup	4–0
1928	Kilmarnock	A	Scottish League	2–2
1933	Kilmarnock	A	Scottish League	2–2
1939	Queen of the South	A	Scottish League	1–1
1950	Brechin City	A	Scottish Cup	3–0
1956	Hearts	H	Scottish League	1–1
1961	Falkirk	A	Scottish Cup	3–1
1963	Falkirk	A	Scottish Cup	2–0
1967	Arbroath	H	Scottish Cup	4–0
1983	Clydebank	A	Scottish Cup	3–0
1984	Berwick Rangers	A	Scottish Cup	4–0

1989	Dumbarton	H	Scottish Cup	2–0
1995	St Mirren	A	Scottish Cup	2–0
1996	Whitehill Welfare	A	Scottish Cup	3–0

JANUARY 29TH

1896	Third Lanark	A	Scottish League	2–1
1910	St Mirren	A	Scottish League	1–2
1916	Ayr United	H	Scottish League	3–1
1921	Aberdeen	H	Scottish League	3–1
1938	Clyde	A	Scottish League	6–1
1944	Airdrie	H	League – Southern Division	3–1
1948	David Hay was born in Paisley.			
1949	Queen of the South	A	Scottish League	0–1
1955	Hearts	H	Scottish League	2–0
1966	Hearts	A	Scottish League	2–3
1969	Partick Thistle	H	Scottish Cup	8–1
1972	Hibernian	H	Scottish League	2–1
1977	Airdrie	A	Scottish Cup	1–1
1994	Motherwell	A	Scottish Cup	0–1
1997	Dunfermline Athletic	A	Scottish League Premier Division	2–0

JANUARY 30TH

1892	Cambuslang	A	Scottish League	4–0
1904	Dundee	A	Scottish League	1–2
1909	Falkirk	H	Scottish League	2–0
1915	Hearts	H	Scottish League	1–1

Jimmy Quinn, one of the greatest ever players to have played for Celtic, played his last game for the club before retiring through injury. He played over 330 games scoring 216 goals. He won 6 consecutive Championship medals and 5 Scottish Cup winners' medals.

1926	Motherwell	H	Scottish League	3–1
1932	St Johnstone	A	Scottish Cup	4–2
1937	Stenhousemuir	A	Scottish Cup	1–1
1943	Airdrie	H	League – Southern Division	2–3
1952	Third Lanark	H	Scottish Cup	0–0
1965	Aberdeen	H	Scottish League	8–0
1971	Dunfermline Athletic	H	Scottish League	1–0
1982	Aberdeen	A	Scottish League Premier Division	3–1
1985	Hamilton Academical	A	Scottish Cup	2–1
1988	Stranraer	H	Scottish Cup	1–0
1991	Motherwell	A	Scottish League Premier Division	1–1
1993	Motherwell	H	Scottish League Premier Division	1–1

JANUARY 31ST

| 1903 | St Mirren | A | Scottish Cup | 1–1 |
| 1914 | St Mirren | A | Scottish League | 3–0 |

| 1920 | Dundee | A | Scottish League | 1–2 |

Jimmy McColl played his last game for the club. Despite not scoring in his last 9 games the diminutive striker scored over 120 goals in under 170 appearances for the club, which amazingly failed to find him international recognition for Scotland. He was the club's centre-forward during the great spell of Championships between 1915 and 1919.

1923	Hibernian	H	Scottish League	0–0
1925	Hibernian	H	Scottish League	1–1
1934	Jim Kennedy was born in Johnstone.			
1942	St Mirren	H	League – Southern Division	3–0
1948	Clyde	H	Scottish League	0–0
1951	East Fife	H	Scottish Cup	4–2
1953	Queen of the South	A	Scottish League	1–2
1959	Albion Rovers	H	Scottish Cup	4–0
1968	John Collins was born in Galashiels.			
1970	Dunfermline Athletic	H	Scottish League	3–1
1976	Dundee United	H	Scottish League Premier Division	2–1
1979	Montrose	A	Scottish Cup	4–2
1981	Hearts	A	Scottish League Premier Division	3–0

FEBRUARY 1ST

1896	Queen's Park	A	Glasgow League	2–1
1908	Partick Thistle	H	Scottish League	4–1
1913	Third Lanark	H	Scottish League	2–0
1919	Kilmarnock	H	Scottish League	2–1
1930	Arbroath	H	Scottish Cup	5–0

Jimmy McGrory scored another hat-trick.

1936	Hearts	A	Scottish League	0–1
1941	Hibernian	A	League – Southern Division	0–2
1958	Airdrie	A	Scottish Cup	4–3
1964	Dunfermline Athletic	A	Scottish League	0–1
1969	Hearts	H	Scottish League	5–0
1986	Dundee	A	Scottish League Premier Division	3–1
1987	Aberdeen	A	Scottish Cup	2–2
1992	Falkirk	H	Scottish League Premier Division	2–0
1997	Dundee United	A	Scottish League Premier Division	0–1

FEBRUARY 2ND

| 1889 | Third Lanark | Hampden Park | | |
| | | Friendly (Scottish Cup final originally) | | 0–3 |

What was meant to be the first major landmark in playing terms for Celtic turned out to be a non-event. Just a few months after being formed, Celtic reached the Scottish Cup final. Very bad weather hit Glasgow and a freak snowstorm made conditions very poor, resulting in both teams complaining. It was agreed that the match be deemed a friendly with the final itself to be played a week later. However, the 18,000 crowd, a record for Scottish football at the time, had paid record receipts and were completely unaware that the game was not for the cup. Third Lanark, after winning 3-0, had tried to get the result to stand but were obviously refused.

1907	Clyde	H	Scottish Cup	2–1
1918	Queen's Park	A	Scottish League	2–0
1924	Morton	A	Scottish League	0–1
1927	Hibernian	H	Scottish League	2–3
1929	East Stirling	H	Scottish Cup	3–0
1935	Albion Rovers	H	Scottish League	5–1
1946	Hibernian	H	League – 'A' Division	0–1
1952	Hibernian	A	Scottish League	1–3
1957	Forres Mechanics	A	Scottish Cup	5–0
1974	Motherwell	A	Scottish League	2–3
1977	Airdrie	H	Scottish Cup	5–0
1982	Hibernian	H	Scottish League Premier Division	0–0
1985	St Mirren	A	Scottish League Premier Division	2–0
1991	Dundee United	H	Scottish League Premier Division	1–0
1998	Aberdeen	H	Scottish League Premier Division	3–1

FEBRUARY 3RD

1894	Third Lanark	A	Scottish Cup semi-final	5–3
1906	Dundee	A	Scottish League	0–1
1912	Third Lanark	H	Scottish League	3–1
1917	Raith Rovers	H	Scottish League	5–0
1923	Kilmarnock	A	Scottish League	3–4
1934	Ayr United	A	Scottish Cup	3–2
1937	Stenhousemuir	H	Scottish Cup	2–0
1945	Airdrie	A	League – Southern Division	2–1
1951	Hibernian	H	Scottish League	0–1
1962	St Johnstone	H	Scottish League	3–1
1968	Partick Thistle	H	Scottish League	4–1
1973	East Fife	H	Scottish Cup	4–1
1990	Dundee	A	Scottish League Premier Division	0–0
1993	St Johnstone	H	Scottish League Premier Division	5–1
1996	Hibernian	H	Scottish League Premier Division	2–1

FEBRUARY 4TH

1899	St Bernards	H	Scottish Cup	3–0
1905	Morton	H	Scottish League	5–2
1911	Motherwell	A	Scottish League	1–2
1922	Partick Thistle	A	Scottish League	0–0
1928	Keith	A	Scottish Cup	6–1

McGrory and McInally scored a hat-trick apiece.

1931	Dundee	A	Scottish Cup	3–2
1933	Falkirk	H	Scottish Cup	2–0
1939	Montrose	A	Scottish Cup	7–1
1950	Hibernian	A	Scottish League	1–4

1952	Third Lanark	A	Scottish Cup	1–2
1956	Morton	A	Scottish Cup	2–0
1961	St Mirren	A	Scottish League	1–2
1967	Airdrie	A	Scottish League	3–0
1984	Aberdeen	A	Scottish League Premier Division	0–1
1987	Aberdeen	H	Scottish Cup	0–0
1992	New Zealand XI	H	Friendly	0–1
1995	Motherwell	A	Scottish League	0–1

FEBRUARY 5TH

1916	Aberdeen	A	Scottish League	4–0
1921	Vale of Leven	A	Scottish Cup	3–0
1927	Brechin City	A	Scottish Cup	6–3

Jimmy McGrory scored 4 goals.

1930	Airdrie	H	Scottish League	1–2
1938	Arbroath	H	Scottish League	4–0
1944	Falkirk	A	League – Southern Division	2–3
1955	Alloa	A	Scottish Cup	4–2
1966	Stranraer	H	Scottish Cup	4–0
1972	Albion Rovers	H	Scottish Cup	5–0
1977	Hibernian	H	Scottish League Premier Division	4–2
1983	Dundee United	A	Scottish League Premier Division	1–1
1994	Raith Rovers	A	Scottish League Premier Division	0–0

FEBRUARY 6TH

1892	Rangers	H	Scottish Cup semi-final	5–3
1904	Port Glasgow Athletic	A	Scottish League	3–2
1909	Port Glasgow Athletic	H	Scottish Cup	4–0
1915	St Mirren	H	Scottish League	2–1
1926	Hamilton Academical	H	Scottish Cup	4–0
1932	Falkirk	A	Scottish League	0–2
1937	Hearts	H	Scottish League	3–2
1943	Falkirk	A	League – Southern Division	0–6
1954	Hearts	A	Scottish League	2–3
1960	Aberdeen	A	Scottish League	2–3

1963 Pat Crerand was sold to Manchester United for £56,000. In his time at the club he made over 120 appearances and scored 5 goals.

1965	St Mirren	A	Scottish Cup	3–0
1971	St Johnstone	A	Scottish League	2–3
1978	Dundee	H	Scottish Cup	7–1

Alan Sneddon made his debut.

| 1982 | Dundee | A | Scottish League Premier Division | 3–1 |
| 1988 | Motherwell | H | Scottish League Premier Division | 1–0 |

1992 Tommy Boyd was signed in a swap deal with Tony Cascarino from Chelsea. Cascarino hardly proved he was worth his £1 million transfer fee, managing only 4 goals in 30 appearances for the club.

| 1993 | Falkirk | A | Scottish Cup | 0–2 |
| 1997 | Raith Rovers | H | Scottish League Premier Division | 2–0 |

FEBRUARY 7TH

1891	St Mirren	H	Scottish League	3–2
1914	Clyde	A	Scottish Cup	0–0
1920	Dundee	A	Scottish Cup	3–1
1925	Alloa	H	Scottish Cup	2–1
1931	Morton	A	Scottish League	1–0
1942	Third Lanark	A	League – Southern Division	1–1
1948	Cowdenbeath	H	Scottish Cup	3–0
1953	Stirling Albion	A	Scottish Cup	1–1
1959	Falkirk	A	Scottish League	2–3
1967	Dynamo Zagreb	H	Friendly	0–1
1970	Dundee United	H	Scottish Cup	4–0
1973	Kilmarnock	A	Scottish League	4–0
1976	Hearts	H	Scottish League Premier Division	2–0

Kenny Dalglish scored 2 goals in this match, the middle of a run that saw him score 16 goals in 11 games.

1977	Hearts	H	Scottish League Premier Division	5–1
1978	Rangers	A	Scottish League Premier Division	1–3
1987	St Mirren	H	Scottish League Premier Division	3–0

FEBRUARY 8TH

1908	Rangers	A	Scottish Cup	2–1
1913	Arbroath	H	Scottish Cup	4–0
1919	Airdrie	A	Scottish League	2–1
1930	Dundee	A	Scottish League	2–2
1936	St Johnstone	H	Scottish Cup	1–2
1941	Partick Thistle	H	League – Southern Division	5–1

Joe McLaughlin made his debut.

1946 Jimmy Delaney was sold to Manchester United for £4000. One of Celtic's all-time greats, he scored 160 goals in over 300 appearances during his 13 years at the club. He won 2 Championship medals and 1 Cup winners' medal.

1964	Aberdeen	A	Scottish League	3–0
1975	Arbroath	A	Scottish League	2–2
1986	St Mirren	H	Scottish League Premier Division	1–1
1992	Airdrie	H	Scottish League Premier Division	2–0

Tommy Boyd made his debut for the club.

| 1998 | Hearts | A | Scottish League Premier Division | 1–1 |

FEBRUARY 9TH

| 1889 | Third Lanark | Hampden Park | | |
| | | Scottish Cup final | 1–2 |

After the shambles a week earlier, Celtic finally attempted to win their first major honour. Despite a goal from Neil McCallum they had to wait for the moment. Their total of 37 goals in the season's competition is still a club record.

1901	Kilmarnock	H	Scottish Cup	6–0
1905	Bernard Battles died in Glasgow aged 30.			
1907	Morton	A	Scottish Cup	0–0
1918	Hearts	H	Scottish League	3–0
1929	St Mirren	A	Scottish League	1–0
1935	Partick Thistle	H	Scottish Cup	1–1
1946	Motherwell	A	League – 'A' Division	3–1
1957	Raith Rovers	A	Scottish League	1–3
1972	Dynamo Kiev	H	Friendly	1–0
1980	Partick Thistle	A	Scottish League Premier Division	1–1
1985	Dundee	A	Scottish League Premier Division	0–2
1987	Aberdeen	A	Scottish Cup	1–0
1994	Willie Falconer was signed from Sheffield United for £350,000.			

FEBRUARY 10TH

1894	St Mirren	H	Scottish League	5–1
1906	Bo'ness	H	Scottish Cup	3–0
1912	East Stirlingshire	H	Scottish Cup	3–0
1914	Clyde	H	Scottish Cup	2–0
1917	Morton	A	Scottish League	1–0
1923	East Fife	H	Scottish Cup	2–1
1926	Kilmarnock	A	Scottish League	1–2
1940	Morton	H	League Western Division	0–3
1945	Motherwell	H	League – Southern Division	1–1
1951	Duns	H	Scottish Cup	4–0
1962	Stirling Albion	A	Scottish League	0–1
1968	Motherwell	A	Scottish League	1–0
1973	Partick Thistle	H	Scottish League	1–1
	Andy Lynch made his debut after coming on as sub for Bobby Lennox.			
1974	Dundee	H	Scottish League	1–2
	History was created when the club played its first League game on a Sunday.			
1990	Hibernian	H	Scottish League Premier Division	1–1
1996	Falkirk	A	Scottish League Premier Division	0–0

FEBRUARY 11TH

1893	Abercorn	A	Scottish League	2–4
1899	Clyde	A	Glasgow League	5–2
1905	Lochgelly Utd	H	Scottish Cup	3–0
1911	Galston	H	Scottish Cup	1–0
1922	Third Lanark	A	Scottish Cup	1–0
1925	Ayr United	A	Scottish League	2–0
1928	Clyde	A	Scottish League	1–0
1933	Hearts	H	Scottish League	3–2
1939	Clyde	H	Scottish League	3–1
1953	Stirling Albion	H	Scottish Cup	3–0

1956	Motherwell	A	Scottish League	2–2
1961	Montrose	H	Scottish Cup	6–0
1967	Ayr United	A	Scottish League	5–0
1975	Dumbarton	H	Scottish League	2–2
1976	Leeds United	H	Friendly	1–3
1984	St Johnstone	H	Scottish League Premier Division	5–2
1989	Motherwell	H	Scottish League Premier Division	1–2
1992	Dundee United	H	Scottish Cup	2–1
1995	Hibernian	H	Scottish League Premier Division	2–2

FEBRUARY 12TH

1898	St Mirren	H	Scottish League	3–0
1910	Third Lanark	H	Scottish Cup	3–1
1916	Dumbarton	H	Scottish League	6–0
1921	St Mirren	H	Scottish League	6–0

Willie McStay made his international debut for Scotland in the 2–1 victory over Wales in Aberdeen.

| 1927 | Dundee | A | Scottish League | 2–1 |

John Thompson made his debut in goal for the club.

1929	Cowdenbeath	H	Scottish League	1–0
1938	Nithsdale Wanderers	H	Scottish Cup	5–0
1944	Hibernian	H	League – Southern Division	2–2
1949	Hibernian	H	Scottish League	1–2
1955	Falkirk	A	Scottish League	1–1
1966	Falkirk	H	Scottish League	6–0
1969	Clyde	A	Scottish Cup	0–0
1977	Partick Thistle	H	Scottish League Premier Division	2–0
1983	Aberdeen	H	Scottish League Premier Division	1–3
1994	Hearts	A	Scottish League Premier Division	2–0

FEBRUARY 13TH

1909	Port Glasgow Athletic	A	Scottish League	4–1
1915	Morton	A	Scottish League	2–0
1924	Motherwell	A	Scottish League	1–0
1926	Falkirk	A	Scottish League	1–1
1932	Motherwell	A	Scottish Cup	0–2
1935	Partick Thistle	A	Scottish Cup	3–1
1937	Albion Rovers	A	Scottish Cup	5–2
1943	Hearts	A	League – Southern Division	3–5
1960	St Mirren	A	Scottish Cup	1–1
1965	St Mirren	A	Scottish League	5–1
1971	Dunfermline Athletic	H	Scottish Cup	1–1
1982	Aberdeen	A	Scottish Cup	0–1
1983	Peter Wilson died in Beith shortly before his 78th birthday.

| 1988 | Dundee | A | Scottish League Premier Division | 2–1 |
| 1993 | Aberdeen | A | Scottish League Premier Division | 1–1 |

FEBRUARY 14TH

1893	St Bernards	H	Scottish Cup semi-final	5–0
1903	St Mirren	H	Scottish Cup	4–0
1914	Morton	H	Scottish League	3–0
1920	Albion Rovers	H	Scottish League	3–0

Jimmy McMenemy played what was to be his last game for the club.

1922	St Mirren	A	Scottish League	2–0
1923	Albion Rovers	H	Scottish League	1–1
1925	St Johnstone	H	Scottish League	2–1
1928	Dundee	H	Scottish League	3–1
1931	Morton	A	Scottish Cup	4–1
1942	Airdrie	A	League – Southern Division	2–2
1948	Queen of the South	A	Scottish League	0–2
1953	Hearts	H	Scottish League	1–1
1968	Stirling Albion	H	Scottish League	2–0
1978	Aberdeen	A	Scottish League Premier Division	1–2
1981	Stirling Albion	H	Scottish Cup	3–0
1984	St Mirren	H	Scottish League Premier Division	2–0
1987	Hearts	H	Scottish League Premier Division	1–1

FEBRUARY 15TH

1897	Woolwich Arsenal	A	Friendly	5–4

Celtic staged a remarkable recovery after being 1–4 down at half-time to rattle the Englishmen with 4 second-half goals.

1902	Hearts	H	Scottish Cup quarter-final	2–1
1908	Port Glasgow Athletic	A	Scottish League	3–0
1913	Aberdeen	A	Scottish League	0–3
1919	Hamilton Academical	H	Scottish League	4–1
1930	St Mirren	H	Scottish Cup	1–3
1936	Kilmarnock	H	Scottish League	4–0
1941	St Mirren	A	League – Southern Division	0–1
1950	Third Lanark	A	Scottish Cup	1–1
1958	Stirling Albion	H	Scottish Cup	7–2
1964	Airdrie	H	Scottish Cup	4–1
1975	Clydebank	H	Scottish Cup	4–1
1986	Queen's Park	H	Scottish Cup	2–1

FEBRUARY 16TH

1895	Hearts	A	Scottish League	0–4
1901	Dundee	A	Scottish Cup quarter-final	1–0
1907	Morton	H	Scottish Cup	1–1
1918	Hamilton Academical	A	Scottish League	2–1
1924	Queen's Park	A	Scottish League	1–0

Peter Wilson made his debut.

1927	Hamilton Academical	A	Scottish League	3–3
1929	Arbroath	H	Scottish Cup	4–1

1931	Bobby Collins was born in Govanhill.			
1935	Queen of the South	A	Scottish League	4–3
1946	Kilmarnock	H	League – 'A' Division	1–1
1952	Stirling Albion	H	Scottish League	3–1
1957	Rangers	H	Scottish Cup	4–4

Apart from 15 minutes at the beginning and 15 minutes at the end, this match was as tight as one would imagine whenever these two great foes clashed. The opening quarter of an hour, however, had produced four goals, two for each side, to set up the game for the next hour as play ebbed and flowed. Fifteen minutes from the end it exploded into life again, with Celtic scoring twice in eight minutes, pushing themselves into a 4–2 lead and surely a passage into the next round. As Rangers' attacks became more desperate, so did Celtic's defending, and Rangers grabbed two lucky late goals to force a replay.

1970	Partick Thistle	A	Scottish League	5–1
1980	St Mirren	H	Scottish Cup	1–1
1985	Inverness Thistle	H	Scottish Cup	6–0
1992	Lossiermouth	A	Highland Tour	7–1
1998	Dunfermline	A	Scottish Cup 4th round	2–1

FEBRUARY 17TH

1894	Rangers	Hampden Park		
			Scottish Cup final	1–3
1900	Kilmarnock	H	Scottish Cup quarter-final	4–0
1906	St Mirren	A	Scottish League	3–1
1912	Queen's Park	H	Scottish League	2–1
1917	Dundee	H	Scottish League	2–0
1923	Falkirk	A	Scottish League	0–0
1931	Bobby Collins was born in Govanhill.			
1934	Falkirk	H	Scottish Cup	3–1
1940	Kilmarnock	A	League – Western Division	2–3
1945	Falkirk	H	League – Southern Division	2–1
1948	Jock Weir was signed for £7000 from Blackburn Rovers.			
1951	Falkirk	A	Scottish League	2–0
1954	Falkirk	A	Scottish Cup	2–1
1962	Hearts	A	Scottish Cup	4–3
1968	Newcastle United	H	Friendly	2–3
1971	Dunfermline Athletic	A	Scottish Cup	1–0
1973	East Fife	A	Scottish League	2–2
1974	Stirling Albion	H	Scottish Cup	6–1
1990	Aberdeen	A	Scottish League Premier Division	1–1
1996	Raith Rovers	H	Scottish Cup	2–0
1997	Hibernian	A	Scottish Cup	1–1

FEBRUARY 18TH

1893	Rangers	N	Glasgow Cup final	1–3
1911	Queen's Park	H	Scottish League	2–0

1922	Clyde	H	Scottish League	1–0
1928	Alloa	H	Scottish Cup	2–0
1930	Ayr United	H	Scottish League	4–0
1931	Clyde	H	Scottish League	0–1
1933	Partick Thistle	H	Scottish Cup	2–1
1939	Hearts	A	Scottish Cup	2–2
1950	Stirling Albion	H	Scottish League	2–1
1956	Ayr Utd	A	Scottish Cup	3–0
1959	Clyde	H	Scottish Cup	1–1
1961	Hibernian	H	Scottish League	2–0
1967	Elgin City	H	Scottish Cup	7–0
1969	Patrick Connolly died in Hairmyres hospital aged 68.			
1984	East Fife	A	Scottish Cup	6–0
1989	Clydebank	H	Scottish Cup	4–1
1992	Peterhead	A	Highland Tour	1–0
1995	Meadowbank Thistle	H	Scottish Cup	3–0

This was the first time Meadowbank had been the opposition.

FEBRUARY 19TH

1898	Queen's Park	A	Glasgow League	2–4
1910	Aberdeen	H	Scottish Cup quarter-final	2–1
1916	Queen's Park	A	Scottish League	1–0
1921	East Fife	A	Scottish Cup	3–1
1927	Dundee	A	Scottish Cup	4–2
1929	Hamilton Academical	H	Scottish League	3–0
1938	St Johnstone	A	Scottish League	2–1
1939	Pat Crerand was born in Glasgow.			
1940	Ex-player Jimmy McStay was appointed manager and had the unenviable task of succeeding Willie Maley.			
1944	Motherwell	A	League – Southern Division	2–1
1955	Kilmarnock	A	Scottish Cup	1–1
1964	Dundee United	H	Scottish League	1–0
1969	AC Milan	A	European Cup quarter-final 1st leg	0–0
1972	Dunfermline Athletic	H	Scottish League	1–0
1977	Ayr United	A	Scottish League Premier Division	4–2
1983	Dunfermline Athletic	H	Scottish Cup	3–0
1985	Morton	H	Scottish League Premier Division	4–0
1991	Queen's Park	A	Closed doors match	4–1

FEBRUARY 20TH

1897	Dundee	H	Scottish League	0–1
1904	Dundee	H	Scottish Cup quarter-final	1–1
1909	Airdrie	H	Scottish Cup quarter-final	3–1
1915	Dumbarton	H	Scottish League	1–0
1926	Hearts	A	Scottish Cup	4–0
1932	Clyde	A	Scottish League	1–2

1932   Jimmy Kelly former player and Chairman between 1909 and 1914 died aged 67 in Blantyre.

1937	Dundee	H	Scottish League	1–2
1943	Albion Rovers	A	League – Southern Division	4–0
1950	Third Lanark	H	Scottish Cup	4–1
1954	Dundee	H	Scottish League	5–1
1957	Rangers	A	Scottish Cup	2–0

After the excitement of the first match four days previously came the reality of the replay. Celtic had let Rangers off the hook in the last eight minutes at Parkhead, this time around they made no mistake, scoring twice through Higgins and Mochan in the first half and then frustrating all of Rangers' attempts to get back on level terms.

1965	Queen's Park	A	Scottish Cup	1–0
1971	Airdrie	H	Scottish League	4–1
1980	St Mirren	A	Scottish Cup	3–2
1981	Paul McStay signed professional forms with the club.			
1982	Partick Thistle	H	Scottish League Premier Division	2–2
1993	Partick Thistle	H	Scottish League Premier Division	0–0

Packy Bonner made his 600th appearance for the club.

FEBRUARY 21ST

1891	Dumbarton	A	Scottish League	2–2
1903	Port Glasgow Athletic	H	Scottish Cup	2–0
1914	Forfar Athletic	A	Scottish Cup	5–0
1920	Partick Thistle	H	Scottish Cup	2–0
1925	Solway Star	H	Scottish Cup	2–1
1928	St Mirren	A	Scottish League	2–0
1931	St Mirren	A	Scottish League	3–1
1942	Falkirk	H	League – Southern Division	2–0
1948	Motherwell	H	Scottish Cup	1–0

Jock Weir made his debut.

1953	Falkirk	A	Scottish Cup	3–2
1959	Third Lanark	A	Scottish League	1–1
1962	Hearts	H	Scottish League	2–2
1970	Rangers	H	Scottish Cup quarter-final	3–1
1976	Aberdeen	A	Scottish League Premier Division	1–0
1981	Rangers	H	Scottish League Premier Division	3–1
1987	Hearts	A	Scottish Cup	0–1
1988	Hibernian	H	Scottish Cup	0–0
1998	Kilmarnock	H	Scottish League Premier Division	4–0

FEBRUARY 22ND

1908	Raith Rovers	A	Scottish Cup quarter-final	3–0
1913	Peebles Rovers	H	Scottish Cup	3–0
1919	Partick Thistle	H	Scottish League	2–1
1930	Falkirk	A	Scottish League	1–0
1936	Queen's Park	A	Scottish League	3–2

1939	Hearts	H	Scottish Cup	2–1
1941	Third Lanark	H	League – Southern Division	4–3
1947	St Mirren	H	Scottish League	2–1
1958	Kilmarnock	A	Scottish League	1–1
1964	Airdrie	A	Scottish League	2–0
1975	Hibernian	A	Scottish League	1–2

Peter Latchford made his debut.

1977	Partick Thistle	A	Scottish League Premier Division	4–2
1984	Aberdeen	A	League Cup semi-final	0–0
1986	Hearts	H	Scottish League Premier Division	1–1

Derek Whyte made his debut at the age of 17.

| 1992 | Hibernian | A | Scottish League Premier Division | 2–0 |
| 1997 | Motherwell | A | Scottish League Premier Division | 1–0 |

FEBRUARY 23RD

1895	Third Lanark	A	Scottish League	4–4
1907	Morton	H	Scottish Cup	2–1
1918	Morton	H	Scottish League	2–0
1921	Third Lanark	A	Scottish League	2–1
1927	Falkirk	H	Scottish League	3–1
1929	Hibernian	A	Scottish League	1–2
1935	Partick Thistle	H	Scottish League	3–1
1946	Queen's Park	A		

Southern League Cup ('A' Division – Section D)   1–3

1952	Raith Rovers	H	Scottish League	0–1
1955	Kilmarnock	H	Scottish Cup	1–0
1957	Aberdeen	H	Scottish League	2–1
1959	Clyde	A	Scottish Cup	4–3

After the game ended 3–3 Celtic finally won in extra-time. This was only the 3rd time in their history (at that point) they had done so.

1966	Dundee	A	Scottish Cup	2–0
1974	Hibernian	A	Scottish League	4–2
1980	Dundee	H	Scottish League Premier Division	2–2
1985	Aberdeen	H	Scottish League Premier Division	2–0
1993	Dundee	A	Scottish League Premier Division	1–0

FEBRUARY 24TH

| 1894 | Rangers | H | Scottish League | 3–2 |

2 goals by Jimmy Blessington sealed the clubs 2nd consecutive Championship.

1900	Rangers	A	Scottish Cup semi-final	2–2
1906	Hearts	H	Scottish Cup quarter-final	1–2
1909	Aberdeen	H	Scottish League	2–0
1912	Aberdeen	A	Scottish Cup quarter-final	2–2
1917	Kilmarnock	A	Scottish League	2–2
1923	Raith Rovers	H	Scottish Cup quarter-final	1–0
1925	Hamilton Academical	A	Scottish League	4–0

1931	Hamilton Academical	H	Scottish League	2–1
1934	Aberdeen	H	Scottish League	2–2
1940	Raith Rovers	H	War Emergency Cup	4–2
1945	Clyde	A	Southern League Cup (Section B)	0–0

Joe McCulloch who played 12 games as left-back was tragically killed in action at the tender age of 27.

1951	Hearts	A	Scottish Cup	2–1
1960	St Mirren	H	Scottish Cup	4–4
1962	Dunfermline Athletic	A	Scottish League	3–0
1969	Clyde	H	Scottish Cup	3–0
1973	Motherwell	A	Scottish Cup	4–0
1988	Hibernian	A	Scottish Cup	1–0
1990	Rangers	H	Scottish Cup	1–0

Earlier the previous month Rangers had come to Parkhead in the League and won 1–0 to register their first New Year's day win at Celtic for 20 years. That undoubtedly gave them confidence for the cup tie, but in a stop-start type of match Celtic outplayed Rangers and were not going to suffer the same fate. Tommy Coyne scored the winning goal.

| 1996 | Partick Thistle | H | Scottish League Premier Division | 4–0 |

FEBRUARY 25TH

1899	Queen's Park	H	Scottish Cup quarter-final	2–1
1905	Partick Thistle	H	Scottish Cup quarter-final	3–0
1905	Rangers	A	Scottish League	4–1
1906	Hearts	H	Scottish Cup semi-final	1–2
1911	Clyde	H	Scottish Cup quarter-final	1–0
1922	Hamilton Academical	H	Scottish Cup	1–3
1928	Aberdeen	H	Scottish League	1–1

1928 Jimmy McGrory made the first of his 7 appearances for Scotland in the 0–1 defeat by Ireland in Glasgow. His next appearance was to be 3 years later.

1933	St Johnstone	A	Scottish League	0–1
1939	Partick Thistle	H	Scottish League	3–1
1950	Aberdeen	H	Scottish Cup	0–1
1956	Clyde	H	Scottish League	4–1

1956 John McFarlane died aged 57.

1961	Raith Rovers	A	Scottish Cup	4–1
1967	Stirling Albion	A	Scottish League	1–1
1970	Raith Rovers	A	Scottish League	2–0
1978	St Mirren	H	Scottish League Premier Division	1–2
1984	Hearts	H	Scottish League Premier Division	4–1
1986	Manchester United	H	Friendly	0–3
1989	Dundee	A	Scottish League Premier Division	3–0
1995	Hearts	A	Scottish League	1–1
1998	Dunfermline	H	Scottish League Premier Division	5–1

FEBRUARY 26TH

1916	Dundee	H	Scottish League	3–0
1921	Queen's Park	A	Scottish League	2–0
1924	Hearts	H	Scottish League	4–1
1927	St Mirren	H	Scottish League	6–2

Jimmy McGrory, whose goalscoring feats are legendary, scored his 24th goal in the last 10 games.

1938	St Mirren	H	Scottish League	5–1
1944	St Mirren	A	League – Southern Division	2–2
1946	Willie Orr died.			
1949	East Fife	A	Scottish League	2–3
1955	St Mirren	H	Scottish League	5–2
1964	Slovan Bratislava	H	Cup-Winners' Cup quarter-final 1st leg	1–0
1966	Stirling Albion	A	Scottish League	0–1
1972	Dundee	H	Scottish Cup	4–0
1979	Berwick Rangers	H	Scottish Cup	3–0
1983	Kilmarnock	H	Scottish League Premier Division	4–0

1986 Tom McAdam was given a free transfer after 9 years' service. He made 362 appearances for the club, scoring 48 goals. At the time he held the record of scoring the most goals (8) in Old Firm matches since the war.

1991	St Mirren	H	Scottish Cup	3–0

1993 Frank McAvennie was signed by the club for the second time in his career.

1994	Kilmarnock	H	Scottish League Premier Division	1–0
1997	Hibernian	H	Scottish Cup	2–0

FEBRUARY 27TH

1892	Third Lanark	H	Scottish League	5–1
1897	Third Lanark	H	Glasgow League	3–1
1904	Dundee	A	Scottish Cup quarter-final replay	0–0
1915	Partick Thistle	A	Scottish League	2–0
1923	St Mirren	H	Scottish League	1–0
1932	Dundee	H	Scottish League	0–2
1937	East Fife	A	Scottish Cup	3–0
1943	Hibernian	H	Southern League Cup (Section D)	2–1
1952	Airdrie	A	Scottish League	1–2
1954	Stirling Albion	A	Scottish Cup	4–3
1961	Clyde	H	Scottish League	6–1
1965	Kilmarnock	H	Scottish League	2–0
1971	Hearts	A	Scottish League	1–1
1974	FC Basel	A	European Cup quarter-final 1st leg	2–3
1977	Ayr United	H	Scottish Cup	1–1
1978	Kilmarnock	H	Scottish Cup	1–1
1982	Hibernian	A	Scottish League Premier Division	0–1
1988	Morton	H	Scottish League Premier Division	1–0
1993	Falkirk	A	Scottish League Premier Division	3–0

FEBRUARY 28TH

1891	Hearts	H	Scottish League	1–0
1903	Rangers	H	Scottish Cup quarter-final	0–2

Sandy McMahon made his last appearance for the club. He played over 200 games and scored 171 goals including 45 Scottish cup goals in 43 games. He won 4 Championship medals and 3 Scottish Cup winners' medals in his 13 years' service to the club.

1914	Falkirk	A	Scottish League	0–1
1920	Hamilton Academical	H	Scottish League	2–0
1925	Dundee	H	Scottish League	4–0
1931	Aberdeen	H	Scottish Cup quarter-final	4–0
1942	Queen's Park	A	Southern League Cup (Section Two)	2–1
1948	Falkirk	A	Scottish League	1–0
1953	Third Lanark	A	Scottish League	3–1
1959	Rangers	H	Scottish Cup	2–1
1966	Dundee	H	Scottish League	5–0
1970	Airdrie	H	Scottish Cup final	4–2
1973	St Johnstone	H	Scottish League	4–0
1976	Hibernian	H	Scottish League Premier Division	4–0
1981	Morton	A	Scottish League Premier Division	3–0

1983 Danny McGrain was awarded the MBE by the Queen.

1987	Dundee	A	Scottish League Premier Division	1–4
1995	Real Madrid	N	Friendly	0–2
1998	Hibernian	A	Scottish League Premier Division	1–0

FEBRUARY 29TH

1908	Third Lanark	H	Scottish League	1–1
1936	Clyde	A	Scottish League	4–0
1960	St Mirren	H	Scottish Cup	5–2

Neil Mochan scored all 5 of Celtic's goals.

1964	East Stirlingshire	H	Scottish League	5–2
1992	Hearts	A	Scottish League Premier Division	2–1

MARCH 1ST

1902	Rangers	A	Inter City League	5–0
1919	Vale of Leven	H	Victory Cup	2–0
1922	Hamilton Academical	H	Scottish League	4–0
1924	Partick Thistle	A	Scottish League	1–1
1930	Dundee United	H	Scottish League	7–0
1941	Airdrie	A	Southern League Cup	2–1

1949 George Connelly was born.

1952	Queen of the South	H	Scottish League	6–1
1958	Clyde	H	Scottish Cup	0–2
1967	Vojvodina Novi Sad	A	European Cup quarter-final 1st leg	0–1
1969	St Johnstone	H	Scottish Cup quarter-final	3–2
1975	Partick Thistle	H	Scottish League	3–2

1978	Hearts		Hampden Park	
			League Cup semi-final	2–0
1980	Morton	A	Scottish League Premier Division	1–0
1989	Tommy Coyne was signed from Dundee.			
1997	Hearts	H	Scottish League Premier Division	2–0

MARCH 2ND

1907	Aberdeen	A	Scottish League	2–2
1912	Dundee	H	Scottish League	2–0
1918	Clydebank	A	Scottish League	2–1
1935	Clyde	H	Scottish League	0–2
1940	Raith Rovers	A	War Emergency Cup	0–3
1940	Billy McNeill was born in Bellshill.			
1946	Clyde	H	Southern League Cup	4–0
			('A' Division – Section D)	
1957	St Mirren	H	Scottish Cup quarter-final	2–1
1963	Airdrie	H	Scottish League	3–1
1968	Kilmarnock	A	Scottish League	6–0
1974	Hearts	H	Scottish League	1–0
1977	Ayr United	A	Scottish Cup	3–1
1985	Dundee United	A	Scottish League Premier Division	0–0
1988	Dunfermline Athletic	A	Scottish League Premier Division	4–0
1991	St Johnstone	H	Scottish League Premier Division	3–0
1996	Hearts	H	Scottish League Premier Division	4–0

MARCH 3RD

1900	Hibernian	H	Inter City League	4–1
1903	Alec McNair made his international debut for Scotland in the 0–2 defeat by Wales in Edinburgh.			
1906	Aberdeen	A	Scottish League	0–1
1913	Andy McAtee won his only Scottish cap in the 0–0 draw with Wales in Wrexham.			
1917	Queen's Park	H	Scottish League	3–2
1923	Alloa	H	Scottish League	1–0
1926	Hearts	A	Scottish League	2–1
1928	Motherwell	A	Scottish Cup quarter-final	2–0
1934	St Mirren	A	Scottish Cup quarter-final	0–2
1945	Falkirk	H	Southern League Cup (Section B)	3–2
1951	Third Lanark	A	Scottish League	0–2
1951	Andy Lynch was born.			
1956	Airdrie	H	Scottish Cup quarter-final	2–1
1962	Dundee	H	Scottish League	2–1
	Bobby Lennox made his debut.			
1973	Aberdeen	H	Scottish League	2–0
1976	Sachsenring Zwickau	H	Cup-Winners' Cup quarter-final 1st leg	1–1
1979	Aberdeen	H	Scottish League Premier Division	1–0
1982	Morton	H	Scottish League Premier Division	1–0

1984	Dundee United	A	Scottish League Premier Division	1–3
1990	Dundee United	H	Scottish League Premier Division	3–0
1992	Morton	H	Scottish Cup quarter-final	3–0
1993	Shelbourne	A	Friendly	4–0
1996	Celtic All Stars	H	Mike Galloway Benefit Match	3–1

MARCH 4TH

1905	Motherwell	A	Scottish League	6–2
1916	Kilmarnock	A	Scottish League	3–0
1922	Third Lanark	A	Scottish League	0–0
1924	Clydebank	H	Scottish League	1–2
1931	Motherwell	H	Scottish League	4–1
1933	Albion Rovers	A	Scottish Cup quarter-final	1–1
1939	Motherwell	A	Scottish Cup quarter-final	1–3
1944	Hamilton Academical	H	Southern League Cup (Section B)	8–1
1950	Falkirk	H	Scottish League	4–3

1951 Kenny Dalglish was born in Dalmarnock.

1959	Dundee	H	Scottish League	1–1
1961	Ayr Utd	A	Scottish League	3–1
1964	Slovan Bratislava	A	Cup-Winners' Cup quarter-final 2nd leg	1–0

1966 Owen Archdeacon was born in Greenock.

1967	St Mirren	A	Scottish League	5–0
1970	Fiorentina	H	European Cup quarter-final 1st leg	3–0
1972	Ayr United	H	Scottish League	2–0
1978	Dundee United	A	Scottish League Premier Division	1–0

MARCH 5TH

1904	Dundee	H	Scottish Cup quarter-final 2nd replay	5–0
1921	Hearts	H	Scottish Cup quarter-final	1–2
1927	Bo'ness	A	Scottish Cup quarter-final	5–2

Jimmy McGrory scored his 9th Cup goal in 4 games in the season.

1932	Ayr United	A	Scottish League	3–2
1938	Kilmarnock	H	Scottish Cup	1–2
1952	Morton	H	Scottish League	2–2
1955	Hamilton Academical	H	Scottish Cup quarter-final	2–1
1958	East Fife	H	Scottish League	4–0

Alec Byrne scored a hat-trick.

1960	Elgin City	A	Scottish Cup	2–1
1966	Hearts	A	Scottish Cup quarter-final	3–3
1969	Arbroath	H	Scottish League	7–1

Willie Wallace scored a hat-trick and Steve Chalmers continued his recent scoring run with a brace.

1977	Aberdeen	A	Scottish League Premier Division	0–2
1980	Real Madrid	H	European Cup quarter-final 1st leg	2–0
1983	Morton	A	Scottish League Premier Division	3–0
1988	Falkirk	H	Scottish League Premier Division	2–0

| 1994 | St Johnstone | A | Scottish League Premier Division | 1–0 |
| 1995 | Aberdeen | H | Scottish League | 2–0 |

MARCH 6TH

1909	Falkirk	A	Scottish League	1–1
1915	Hibernian	H	Scottish League	5–1
1920	Rangers	A	Scottish Cup quarter-final	0–1
1926	Dumbarton	H	Scottish Cup quarter-final	6–1
1928	Hamilton Academical	H	Scottish League	4–0
1929	Motherwell	H	Scottish Cup quarter-final	0–0
1937	Hibernian	A	Scottish League	2–2
1943	Rangers	A	Southern League Cup (Section D)	0–3
1948	Montrose	H	Scottish Cup quarter-final	4–0
1954	East Fife	H	Scottish League	4–1
1956	Willie Loney, the great centre-half of the six-in-row team, died aged 77 in Glasgow.			
1957	Dundee	H	Scottish League	1–1
1963	Hearts	H	Scottish Cup	3–1
1965	Kilmarnock	H	Scottish Cup quarter-final	4–1
1968	Aberdeen	H	Scottish League	4–1
	David Hay made his debut.			
1971	Raith Rovers	H	Scottish Cup quarter-final	7–1
1973	Morton	H	Scottish League	1–0
1978	Kilmarnock	A	Scottish Cup	0–1
1991	Dunfermline Athletic	A	Scottish League Premier Division	1–0
1994	Sligo Rovers	A	Opening of floodlights	1–0
1997	Rangers	H	Scottish Cup	2–0

MARCH 7TH

1891	Cambulsang	A	Scottish League	1–3
1903	Port Glasgow Athletic	A	Scottish League	1–1
1912	Willie Lyon was born in Birkenhead.			
1914	Motherwell	A	Scottish Cup quarter-final	3–1
1925	St Mirren	A	Scottish Cup quarter-final	0–0
1931	Partick Thistle	A	Scottish League	0–1
1936	Airdrie	A	Scottish League	3–2
1942	Hibernian	H	Southern League Cup (Section Two)	4–2
1953	Partick Thistle	H	Scottish League	3–1
1956	Dunfermline Athletic	A	Scottish League	1–1
1959	Dunfermline Athletic	H	Scottish League	3–1
1960	Hibernian	H	Scottish League	1–0
1964	Rangers	A	Scottish Cup quarter-final	0–2
1970	Dundee United	A	Scottish League	2–0
1978	Jimmy McColl died in Edinburgh aged 86.			
1987	Motherwell	H	Scottish League Premier Division	3–1

MARCH 8TH

1913	Hearts	H	Scottish Cup quarter-final	0–1
1919	Morton	A	Scottish League	0–0
1924	Kilmarnock	H	Scottish League	2–1
1930	Hibernian	A	Scottish League	2–0

Peter Scarff scored his 10th goal in 4 games.

1933	Albion Rovers	H	Scottish Cup quarter-final replay	3–1
1939	Third Lanark	A	Scottish League	2–0

1940 John Divers (son of John Divers who played in the '30s) was born in Clydebank.

1941	Motherwell	H	Southern League Cup	3–2
1952	Partick Thistle	A	Scottish League	4–2
1958	St Mirren	A	Scottish League	1–1
1967	Vojvodina Novi Sad	H	European Cup quarter-final 2nd leg	2–0
1969	Raith Rovers	A	Scottish League	3–1
1972	Ujpesti Dozsa	A	European Cup quarter-final 1st leg	2–1
1975	Dumbarton	A	Scottish Cup quarter-final	2–1
1980	Morton	H	Scottish Cup quarter-final	2–0
1981	East Stirlingshire	H	Scottish Cup quarter-final	2–0
1986	Hibernian	A	Scottish Cup quarter-final	3–4
1994	LoI Select/Limerick	A	Friendly	2–0
1998	Dundee United	A	Scottish Cup 5th round	3–2

MARCH 9TH

1895	Dumbarton	A	Scottish League	2–0
1907	Rangers	H	Scottish Cup quarter-final	3–0
1912	Aberdeen	H	Scottish Cup quarter-final replay	2–0
1918	Partick Thistle	A	Scottish League	0–0
1921	Dundee	H	Scottish League	2–0
1926	St Mirren	H	Scottish League	6–1
1927	Aberdeen	A	Scottish League	0–0
1929	Raith Rovers	A	Scottish League	4–1

David Prentice scored a hat-trick on his debut, the only goals of his short Celtic career.

1935	Aberdeen	A	Scottish Cup quarter-final	1–3
1940	Partick Thistle	H	League Western Division	1–1
1946	Third Lanark	A	Southern League Cup	4–3

('A' Division – Section D)

1955	Stirling Albion	A	Scottish League	3–2
1957	East Fife	A	Scottish League	0–2
1963	St Mirren	H	Scottish League	1–1

Ex-Celt Richard Beattie captained St Mirren on his return to Parkhead.

1965 After 20 years in the job as manager Jimmy McGrory stepped aside as Jock Stein took over. He took up the post of public relations officer immediately. In his time as boss, he won the Double, one FA Cup win and two successive League Cups.

1966	Hearts	H	Scottish Cup quarter-final replay	3–1
1977	Partick Thistle	H	Scottish League Premier Division	2–1

| 1985 | Dundee | A | Scottish Cup quarter-final | 1–1 |
| 1991 | Hibernian | A | Scottish League Premier Division | 2–0 |

MARCH 10TH

1894	Hearts	H	Scottish League	2–3
1900	Rangers	H	Scottish Cup semi-final replay	3–2
1906	Queen's Park	A	Scottish League	6–0
1917	Hamilton Academical	H	Scottish League	6–1
1923	Motherwell	Ibrox	Scottish Cup semi-final	2–0
1925	St Mirren	H	Scottish Cup quarter-final replay	1–1
1934	Motherwell	H	Scottish League	3–0
1945	Partick Thistle	A	Southern League Cup (Section B)	1–0
1951	Aberdeen	H	Scottish Cup quarter-final	3–0
1956	East Fife	A	Scottish League	0–3
1959	Airdrie	H	Scottish League	1–2

Steve Chalmers made his debut.

| 1962 | Third Lanark | H | Scottish Cup quarter-final | 4–4 |
| 1965 | Airdrie | A | Scottish League | 6–0 |

Jock Stein made his first signing as manager when he paid £5,000 for goalkeeper John Kennedy.

1970	Morton	H	Scottish League	4–0
1971	Ajax Amsterdam	A	European Cup quarter-final 1st leg	0–3
1973	Dundee United	A	Scottish League	2–2
1974	Motherwell	H	Scottish Cup quarter-final	2–2
1979	Aberdeen	A	Scottish Cup quarter-final	1–1
1984	Aberdeen	H	League Cup semi-final	1–0
1987	Partick Thistle	A	Glasgow Cup semi-final	1–0
1990	Hearts	H	Scottish League Premier Division	1–1
1993	Hearts	H	Scottish League Premier Division	1–0
1995	Kilmarnock	H	Scottish Cup quarter-final	1–0
1996	Dundee United	H	Scottish Cup	2–1

MARCH 11TH

1893	Queen's Park	Ibrox	Scottish Cup final	1–2
1899	Port Glasgow	H	Scottish Cup semi-final	4–2
1911	Aberdeen	H	Scottish Cup semi-final	1–0
1916	Hamilton Academical	H	Scottish League	5–1
1922	Kilmarnock	H	Scottish League	1–0
1933	Motherwell	A	Scottish League	2–4
1939	Ayr United	A	Scottish League	4–1
1944	Falkirk	A	Southern League Cup (Section B)	3–1
1950	Third Lanark	A	Scottish League	0–1
1961	Hibernian	H	Scottish Cup quarter-final	1–1
1964	Partick Thistle	A	Scottish League	2–2
1967	Queen's Park	H	Scottish Cup quarter-final	5–3
1972	Aberdeen	A	Scottish League	1–1

1978	Ayr United	H	Scottish League Premier Division	3–0
1980	Frank McGarvey was bought from Liverpool for £325,000.			
1989	Hearts	A	Scottish League Premier Division	1–0
	Tommy Coyne made his debut.			
1993	Tommy Coyne was sold to Tranmere Rovers after nearly 4 years at Parkhead, where he managed to score over 52 goals in 132 appearances.			
1997	Kilmarnock	A	Scottish League Premier Division	0–2

MARCH 12TH

1892   Ibrox hosted the Scottish Cup final between Queen's Park and Celtic, with a crowd estimated at 40,000 packing into the ground, a further 20,000 being locked outside and at least 5,000 clambering over the gates once they had been locked. Not surprisingly this was a recipe for disaster, and the game was subject to numerous interruptions and after 20 minutes the two captains approached the referee and complained that they would protest to the Scottish Football Association after the game. The referee had every sympathy with the players and it was therefore agreed that the match would continue as a friendly. The crowd were unaware of this arrangement and left for home at the end of the game, convinced Celtic had won 1–0 since the presentation of the cup and medals usually took place in the pavilion away from public eyes. The SFA agreed to a replay, which was also scheduled for Ibrox on 9th April, but in an attempt to reduce the crowd figure and avoid similar disruptions announced a doubling of the admission price.

1904	St Mirren	H	Scottish League	3–1
1910	Clyde	A	Scottish Cup semi-final	1–3
1921	Ayr United	A	Scottish League	1–3
1927	Cowdenbeath	A	Scottish League	1–2
1932	Motherwell	H	Scottish League	2–4
1938	Partick Thistle	A	Scottish League	6–1
1949	Falkirk	A	Scottish League	1–1
1955	Partick Thistle	H	Scottish League	0–0
1960	Partick Thistle	H	Scottish Cup quarter-final	2–0
1966	St Johnstone	H	Scottish League	3–2
1969	AC Milan	H	European Cup quarter-final 2nd leg	0–1
1975	Aberdeen	A	Scottish League	2–3
1980	St Mirren	H	Scottish League Premier Division	2–2
	Frank McGarvey made his debut for the club after his signing from Liverpool.			
1983	Hearts	H	Scottish Cup quarter-final	4–1
1988	Partick Thistle	A	Scottish Cup quarter-final	3–0
1991	St Mirren	A	Scottish League Premier Division	2–0

MARCH 13TH

1897	St Mirren	A	Scottish League	0–2
1909	Rangers	H	Scottish League	2–3
1920	Queen's Park	A	Scottish League	2–1
	Johnny McKay scored on his debut.			
1929	Motherwell	A	Scottish Cup quarter-final replay	2–1
1941	John Clark was born in Bellshill.			

1943	St Mirren	H	Southern League Cup (Section D)	2–0
1948	St Mirren	H	Scottish League	0–0
1954	Hamilton Academical	A	Scottish Cup quarter-final	2–1
1963	Gala Fairydean	H	Scottish Cup	6–0
1965	St Johnstone	H	Scottish League	0–1
1968	Airdrie	H	Scottish League	4–0
1971	Cowdenbeath	A	Scottish League	5–1
1974	Motherwell	A	Scottish Cup quarter-final replay	1–0
1977	Queen of the South	H	Scottish Cup quarter-final	5–1
1982	St Mirren	A	Scottish League Premier Division	5–2
1985	Dundee	H	Scottish Cup quarter-final replay	2–1

MARCH 14TH

1891	Cowlairs	H	Scottish League	2–0
1903	Morton	A	Scottish League	2–0
1908	Partick Thistle	A	Scottish League	3–0
1923	Hamilton Academical	A	Scottish League	1–1
1925	Cowdenbeath	A	Scottish League	0–3
1931	Kilmarnock	Hampden Park	Scottish Cup semi-final	3–0
1936	Motherwell	H	Scottish League	5–0

Some reports state that Jimmy McGrory's hat-trick was scored in 3 minutes.

1942	Hamilton Academical	H	Southern League Cup (Section Two)	1–0
1953	Rangers	A	Scottish Cup quarter-final	0–2
1958	Hearts	A	Scottish League	3–5
1962	Third Lanark	Hampden Park	Scottish Cup quarter-final replay	4–0
1964	Hibernian	H	Scottish League	5–0
1970	Dundee	Hampden Park	Scottish Cup semi-final	2–1
1979	Aberdeen	H	Scottish Cup quarter-final replay	1–2
1981	St Mirren	H	Scottish League Premier Division	7–0
1987	Aberdeen	A	Scottish League Premier Division	0–1
1992	Aberdeen	H	Scottish League Premier Division	1–0

MARCH 15TH

1902	Third Lanark	H	Inter City League	2–0
1913	Motherwell	A	Scottish League	0–1

Joe Cassidy made his debut.

1919	Queen's Park	H	Scottish League	2–0
1919	Albion Rovers	H	Victory Cup	3–1
1922	Motherwell	H	Scottish League	2–0
1924	Falkirk	A	Scottish League	1–3
1930	Motherwell	H	Scottish League	0–4
1941	Partick Thistle	H	Southern League Cup	2–4
1952	St Mirren	A	Scottish League	1–3

1961	Hibernian	A	Scottish Cup quarter-final replay	1–0
1969	Partick Thistle	H	Scottish League	1–0
1975	Dundee United	H	Scottish League	0–1
1976	John Doyle was signed from Ayr United.			
1980	Kilmarnock	A	Scottish League Premier Division	1–1
1986	Dundee United	H	Scottish League Premier Division	1–1
1998	Dundee United	H	Scottish League Premier Division	1–1

MARCH 16TH

1895	Leith Athletic	H	Scottish League	4–0
1907	Third Lanark	A	Scottish League	1–2
1910	Third Lanark	H	Scottish League	2–0
1912	Partick Thistle	A	Scottish League	1–1
1918	St Mirren	H	Scottish League	1–0
1925	St Mirren	Ibrox	Scottish Cup quarter-final 2nd replay	1–0
1927	Airdrie	H	Scottish League	2–1
1929	Aberdeen	H	Scottish League	2–2
	Chic Geatons made his debut for the club.			
1935	Dunfermline Athletic	A	Scottish League	3–1
1940	Third Lanark	A	League Western Division	2–4
1946	Queen's Park	H		
	Southern League Cup ('A' Division – Section D)			2–0
1959	Stirling Albion	A	Scottish Cup quarter-final	3–1
1960	Ayr United	A	Scottish League	1–1
1963	Queen of the South	A	Scottish League	5–2
1968	Falkirk	A	Scottish League	3–0
1969	Harry Hood was signed from Clyde.			
1974	Ayr United	H	Scottish League	4–0
1977	Motherwell	H	Scottish League Premier Division	2–2
1985	Hibernian	H	Scottish League Premier Division	0–1
1993	Hibernian	H	Scottish League Premier Division	2–1
1997	Rangers	H	Scottish League Premier Division	0–1

MARCH 17TH

1894	Leith Athletic	A	Scottish League	0–5
1900	Third Lanark	A	Inter City League	4–4
1908	Hibernian	H	Scottish League	4–0
1917	Airdrie	A	Scottish League	2–1
1923	Dundee	H	Scottish League	2–1
1926	Dundee	A	Scottish League	2–1
	Willie Maloy scored his only goal for the club on his debut.			
1928	Hearts	H	Scottish League	2–1
1934	Hibernian	A	Scottish League	2–1
1937	Motherwell	H	Scottish Cup quarter-final	4–4
1945	Clyde	H	Southern League Cup (Section B)	1–1
1951	St Mirren	H	Scottish League	2–1

1954	Airdrie	A	Scottish League	6–0
1956	Dundee	H	Scottish League	1–0
1957	Ayr Utd	H	Scottish League	4–0
1962	Airdrie	A	Scottish League	0–1
1973	Aberdeen	H	Scottish Cup quarter-final	0–0
1976	Sachsenring Zwickau	A	Cup-Winners' Cup quarter-final 2nd leg	0–1
1979	Motherwell	H	Scottish League Premier Division	2–1

Packy Bonner made his debut in goal.

1984	Motherwell	A	Scottish Cup quarter-final	6–0
1990	Dunfermline Athletic	A	Scottish Cup quarter-final	0–0
1991	Rangers	H	Scottish Cup quarter-final	2–0
1992	Motherwell	H	Scottish League Premier Division	4–1
1996	Rangers	A	Scottish League Premier Division	1–1

MARCH 18TH

| 1893 | Dumbarton | H | Scottish League | 5–1 |
| 1899 | Third Lanark | A | Glasgow League | 3–2 |

1905 Jimmy McMenemy, Peter Somers and Jimmy Quinn made their international debuts in Scotland's 4–0 victory over Ireland in Glasgow, Quinn scoring one of the goals.

1911	St Mirren	A	Scottish League	1–1
1916	St Mirren	A	Scottish League	5–0
1922	Falkirk	H	Scottish League	1–1
1931	Hearts	A	Scottish League	1–1
1933	Hearts	Hampden Park		
			Scottish Cup semi-final	0–0
1939	Falkirk	H	Scottish League	1–2

1942 Patrick McAuley joined the club for the second time in his career.

| 1944 | Partick Thistle | A | Southern League Cup (Section B) | 1–0 |
| 1950 | St Mirren | A | Scottish League | 1–0 |

Willie Fernie made his debut.

1953	Airdrie	H	Scottish League	0–1
1959	St Mirren	A	Scottish League	0–1
1961	Partick Thistle	A	Scottish League	2–1
1967	Dunfermline Athletic	H	Scottish League	3–2
1970	Fiorentina	A	European Cup quarter-final 2nd leg	0–1
1972	Hearts	H	Scottish Cup	1–1
1978	Rangers	Hampden Park		
			League Cup final	1–2

Celtic created a world record by appearing in 14 successive League Cup finals. No other club registered under FIFA guidelines has ever achieved this feat.

| 1981 | Partick Thistle | H | Scottish League Premier Division | 4–1 |
| 1989 | Hearts | H | Scottish Cup quarter-final | 2–1 |

MARCH 19TH

| 1892 | Clyde | H | Scottish League | 0–0 |
| 1898 | Third Lanark | H | Glasgow League | 4–2 |

1903	Jimmy 'Dun' Hay signed for the club.			
1904	Third Lanark	H	Scottish Cup semi-final	2–1
1921	Hearts	H	Scottish League	3–2
1929	Motherwell	H	Scottish League	2–0
1932	St Mirren	A	Scottish League	2–1

1932 Malky MacDonald signed pro forms for the club. Hugh O'Donnell also signed pro forms with Celtic to join his brother Frank in the professional ranks of the club.

1938	Third Lanark	H	Scottish League	1–1
1949	Partick Thistle	H	Scottish League	3–0
1955	Motherwell	H	Scottish League	1–0
1958	Hibernian	H	Scottish League	4–0
1960	Dunfermline Athletic	A	Scottish League	2–3
1963	Raith Rovers	H	Scottish League	4–1
1966	Hamilton Academical	A	Scottish League	7–1
1975	Partick Thistle	H	Glasgow Cup semi-final	1–0
1977	Rangers	A	Scottish League Premier Division	2–2
1980	Real Madrid	A	European Cup quarter-final 2nd leg	0–3
1983	Dundee	A	Scottish League Premier Division	1–2
1994	Hibernian	A	Scottish League Premier Division	0–0

MARCH 20TH

1890 Some two years previously William McGregor, a Scot serving on the committee of Aston Villa, had written to the secretaries of 12 leading English clubs of the day and requested a meeting that had led to the formation of the Football League. The success of the competition had brought admiring and envious glances from north of the border, and so Peter Fairley, secretary of the Renton club, had written to the representatives of 12 leading Scottish clubs requesting a meeting at 7.30pm at Holton's Commercial Hotel in Glassford Street in Glasgow. The clubs who attended were Abercorn, Cambuslang, Celtic, Cowlairs, Dumbarton, Heart of Midlothian, Rangers (who were represented by John Mellish, president, and match secretary William Wilton), Renton, St Bernards, St Mirren, Third Lanark and Vale of Leven. This list, of course, is notable for the absence of Queen's Park, undoubtedly the strongest club of the day but one which was sure the League would lead to professionalism (which it did) and the demise of the weaker clubs (which it also did). The principles of the League were agreed at the meeting, although St Bernards were not admitted to the League and this left 11 clubs to compete in the first season, due to commence on 16th August 1890. Celtic's J.H. McLaughlin was appointed League secretary and it was also agreed that League matches were to take preference over all other games with the exception of Scottish Cup ties (a similar ruling had been introduced into the English Football League constitution).

1897	Clyde	A	Glasgow League	8–0
1909	Clyde	H	Scottish Cup semi-final	0–0
1926	Aberdeen	N	Scottish Cup semi-final	2–1
1937	St Mirren	A	Scottish League	2–1
1943	Hibernian	A	Southern League Cup (Section D)	1–2

1948	Motherwell	A	Scottish League	3–0
1954	Partick Thistle	A	Scottish League	3–1
1961	Raith Rovers	H	Scottish League	1–1
1965	Dundee	A	Scottish League	3–3
1966	David Hay signed pro forms.			
1967	Falkirk	H	Scottish Cup semi-final replay	5–0
1971	Kilmarnock	A	Scottish League	4–1
1974	FC Basel	H	European Cup quarter-final 2nd leg	4–2
1976	Dundee	A	Scottish League Premier Division	1–0
1982	Airdrie	H	Scottish League Premier Division	2–0
1984	Dundee	A	Scottish League Premier Division	2–3
1985	Hearts	H	Scottish League Premier Division	3–2
1988	Rangers	A	Scottish League Premier Division	2–1
1993	Rangers	H	Scottish League Premier Division	2–1

Celtic brought an end to Rangers' 44 match unbeaten run with a 2–1 win at Parkhead, Collins and Payton scoring the goals.

MARCH 21ST

1891	Rangers	H	Scottish League	2–2
1896	Rangers	H	Glasgow League	3–2
1903	Dundee	A	Scottish League	0–2
1908	Aberdeen	A	Scottish Cup semi-final	1–0
1925	Rangers	Hampden Park		
			Scottish Cup semi-final	5–0

Such was the interest generated in the Scottish Cup semi-final clash between Rangers and Celtic that only Hampden Park was deemed large enough to accommodate all of the fans who wished to attend, with 101,714 cramming into the ground. It was the first time a football match had attracted a six-figure crowd in Scotland. McGrory and McLean scored two each with Thompson getting the other in a victory that left Rangers humiliated.

1931	Cowdenbeath	H	Scottish League	6–0
1936	Dundee	A	Scottish League	2–0
1942	Queen's Park	H	Southern League Cup (Section Two)	6–2
1950	Sean Fallon was signed from Glenavon.			
1953	East Fife	A	Scottish League	1–4
1959	Partick Thistle	H	Scottish League	2–0
1960	Motherwell	A	Scottish League	2–1
1964	Kilmarnock	A	Scottish League	0–4
1966	Partick Thistle	A	Scottish League	2–2
1970	Ayr United	H	Scottish League	3–0
1973	Aberdeen	A	Scottish Cup quarter-final replay	1–0
1981	Airdrie	A	Scottish League Premier Division	2–1
1987	Clydebank	H	Scottish League Premier Division	3–0
1992	Rangers	A	Scottish League Premier Division	2–0
1995	Kilmarnock	A	Scottish League	1–0

MARCH 22ND

Year	Opponent		Competition	Score
1902	St Mirren	A	Scottish Cup semi-final	3–2
1913	Falkirk	H	Scottish League	1–2
1924	Raith Rovers	A	Scottish League	0–1
1930	Cowdenbeath	A	Scottish League	2–1
1933	Hearts	Hampden Park		
			Scottish Cup semi-final replay	2–1
1941	Airdrie	H	Southern League Cup	3–1
1947	Partick Thistle	H	Scottish League	2–0
1952	East Fife	H	Scottish League	2–1
1958	Airdrie	H	Scottish League	4–2

Sean Fallon played his last game for the club after persistent knee trouble forced him to retire. He had made over 250 appearances for the club.

1965	Hibernian	H	Scottish League	2–4
1969	Morton	Hampden Park		
			Scottish Cup semi-final	4–1
1972	Ujpesti Dozsa	H	European Cup quarter-final 2nd leg	1–1
1975	Airdrie	A	Scottish League	0–1
1978	Motherwell	A	Scottish League Premier Division	1–2
1986	Rangers	A	Scottish League Premier Division	4–4

1989 Frank McAvennie was sold back to West Ham United for £1.25 million just 18 months after joining.

1997	Dunfermline Athletic	A	Scottish League Premier Division	2–2

MARCH 23RD

1895	Rangers	A	Scottish League	1–1
1901	St Mirren	A	Scottish Cup semi-final	1–0
1907	Dundee	H	Scottish League	0–0
1912	Aberdeen	A	Scottish League	2–3
1918	Third Lanark	H	Scottish League	1–3

Ex-Celtic player Davie McLean scored all 3 goals for Third Lanark.

1929	Kilmarnock	Ibrox	Scottish Cup semi-final	0–1

1932 George Patterson signed professional forms.

1935	Ayr United	A	Scottish League	0–1

1938 Bertie Auld was born in Maryhill.

1940	Dumbarton	H	League – Western Division	4–0
1946	Clyde	A	Southern League Cup	2–6
			('A' Division – Section D)	
1957	Kilmarnock	Hampden Park		
			Scottish Cup semi-final	1–1
1963	Dundee	H	Scottish League	4–1

1966 Joseph Baillie tragically drowned in the River Kelvin.

1968	Raith Rovers	H	Scottish League	5–0
1974	Partick Thistle	A	Scottish League	0–2
1983	Rangers	H	Scottish League Premier Division	0–0
1985	Morton	A	Scottish League Premier Division	7–2

1996	Motherwell	A	Scottish League Premier Division	0–0

MARCH 24TH

1900	Queen's Park	A	Inter City League	3–1
1913	Raith Rovers	H	Scottish League	4–1
1914	Hearts	H	Scottish League	0–0
1917	Aberdeen	A	Scottish League	0–0
1923	Morton	H	Scottish League	3–1
1925	Morton	H	Scottish League	2–1
1926	St Johnstone	H	Scottish League	4–1
1928	Queen's Park	Ibrox	Scottish Cup semi-final	2–1
1934	Ayr United	H	Scottish League	0–3
1937	Motherwell	A	Scottish Cup quarter-final replay	2–1
1945	Falkirk	A	Southern League Cup (Section B)	1–0
1951	East Fife	A	Scottish League	0–3
1956	Clyde	Hampden Park	Scottish Cup semi-final	2–1
1962	Aberdeen	H	Scottish League	2–0
1969	Hibernian	H	Scottish League	1–1
1970	Aberdeen	H	Scottish League	1–2
1971	Ajax Amsterdam	H	European Cup quarter-final 2nd leg	1–0
1973	Hearts	A	Scottish League	2–0
1990	Dunfermline Athletic	A	Scottish League Premier Division	0–0
1990	Dunfermline Athletic	H	Scottish Cup quarter-final replay	3–0
1991	Rangers	H	Scottish League Premier Division	3–0

1994   Wayne Biggins was sold to Stoke City for £125,000. He had failed to score in the 10 games he played for the club.

MARCH 25TH

1893	Renton	A	Scottish League	2–0
1905	Rangers	H	Scottish Cup semi-final	0–2
1911	Hibernian	H	Scottish League	2–0
1922	Hearts	A	Scottish League	2–1
1931	Dundee	H	Scottish League	2–2
1933	Cowdenbeath	A	Scottish League	5–1
1940	Queen's Park	A	League – Western Division	4–1
1944	Hamilton Academical	A	Southern League Cup (Section B)	3–0
1950	East Fife	H	Scottish League	4–1
1959	Aberdeen	H	Scottish League	4–0
1961	Dunfermline Athletic	H	Scottish League	2–1
1964	Clyde	H	Glasgow Cup final	2–0

1966   Anton Rogan was born in Belfast.

1967	Hearts	A	Scottish League	3–0
1968	St Johnstone	A	Scottish League	6–1

1972   Phil O'Donnell was born in Bellshill.

1972	Falkirk	A	Scottish League	1–0

1978	Rangers	H	Scottish League Premier Division	2–0
1984	Rangers	Hampden Park		
			League Cup final	2–3
1986	Manchester United	H	Friendly	1–0
1989	Dundee United	H	Scottish League Premier Division	1–0

MARCH 26TH

1904	Motherwell	A	Scottish League	2–1
1905	Peter Wilson was born in Beith.			
1921	Kilmarnock	A	Scottish League	2–3
1927	Falkirk	Ibrox	Scottish Cup semi-final	1–0
1929	Clyde	A	Scottish League	1–0
1938	Ayr United	H	Scottish League	1–1
1949	St Mirren	H	Scottish League	2–1
1951	Partick Thistle	Hampden Park		
			Glasgow Cup final replay	2–3
1955	Airdrie	Hampden Park		
			Scottish Cup semi-final	2–2
1960	Stirling Albion	H	Scottish League	1–1
1962	St Mirren	A	Scottish League	5–0
1966	Dunfermline Athletic	Ibrox	Scottish Cup semi-final	2–0
1977	Dundee United	H	Scottish League Premier Division	2–0
1983	St Mirren	H	Scottish League Premier Division	1–1
1988	Dundee United	H	Scottish League Premier Division	0–0
1994	Motherwell	H	Scottish League Premier Division	0–1

MARCH 27TH

1897	Third Lanark	A	Glasgow League	1–0
1909	Clyde	H	Scottish Cup semi-final replay	2–0
1915	Raith Rovers	H	Scottish League	3–0
1920	Falkirk	A	Scottish League	2–1
1926	Motherwell	A	Scottish League	1–2
1937	Partick Thistle	H	Scottish Cup quarter-final replay	1–1
1938	Charlie Shaw died aged 52 of pneumonia in New York.			
1943	Rangers	H	Southern League Cup (Section D)	0–2
1948	Morton	Ibrox	Scottish Cup semi-final	0–1
1951	Ronnie Glavin was born in Glasgow.			
1954	Motherwell	Hampden Park		
			Scottish Cup semi-final	2–2
1957	Kilmarnock	Hampden Park		
			Scottish Cup semi-final replay	1–3
1963	Kilmarnock	A	Scottish League	0–6
	Jimmy Johnstone made his debut.			
1965	Motherwell	Hampden Park		
			Scottish Cup semi-final	2–2
1967	Partick Thistle	A	Scottish League	4–1

1971	Falkirk	H	Scottish League	4–0
1972	Hearts	A	Scottish Cup quarter-final	1–0
1976	Motherwell	H	Scottish League Premier Division	4–0
1982	Aberdeen	H	Scottish League Premier Division	0–1
1993	Dundee United	A	Scottish League Premier Division	3–2

MARCH 28TH

1896	Third Lanark	A	Glasgow League	4–1
1903	Queen's Park	H	Inter City League	2–1
1908	Dundee	A	Scottish League	0–2
1914	Third Lanark	A	Scottish Cup semi-final	2–0
1921	Partick Thistle	A	Scottish League	1–0
1925	Raith Rovers	H	Scottish League	2–0
1928	Cowdenbeath	H	Scottish League	2–0
1932	St Mirren	H	Scottish League	1–0
1936	Dundee	A	Scottish League	2–0
1942	Hibernian	A	Southern League Cup (Section Two)	0–1
1953	Hibernian	H	Scottish League	1–3
1956	St Mirren	Hampden Park		
			Scottish League	2–0
1959	Hibernian	H	Scottish League	3–0
1960	Third Lanark	H	Scottish League	4–0
1964	Motherwell	A	Scottish League	4–0
1970	Hearts	A	Scottish League	0–0
1979	Morton	H	Scottish League Premier Division	3–0
1981	Aberdeen	H	Scottish League Premier Division	1–1
1987	Hamilton Academical	A	Scottish League Premier Division	3–2
1992	Dundee United	H	Scottish League Premier Division	3–1

MARCH 29TH

1902	Third Lanark	A	Inter City League	3–1
1908	Peter Scarff was born.			
1909	Partick Thistle	A	Scottish League	1–0
1910	Clyde	H	Scottish League	2–1
1913	Kilmarnock	H	Scottish League	4–1
1919	St Mirren	A	Victory Cup	0–1
1924	Airdrie	A	Scottish League	0–2
1930	St Johnstone	H	Scottish League	6–2
1937	Falkirk	H	Scottish League	1–0
1941	Motherwell	A	Southern League Cup	2–4
1947	Kilmarnock	A	Scottish League	2–1
1948	Third Lanark	A	Scottish League	1–5
1952	Aberdeen	H	Scottish League	2–0
1954	Stirling Albion	H	Scottish League	4–0
1958	Dundee	A	Scottish League	3–5
1966	Kilmarnock	A	Scottish League	2–0

1969	St Mirren	A	Scottish League	3–0

Harry Hood scored on his debut.

1975	Hearts	H	Scottish League	4–1
1978	Partick Thistle	A	Scottish League Premier Division	4–0
1980	Hibernian	H	Scottish League Premier Division	4–0
1986	Clydebank	A	Scottish League Premier Division	5–0

1995 Paul McStay won his 72nd and last cap for Scotland in the 0–0 draw with Russia in Moscow, thus becoming the most capped player whilst at the club.

MARCH 30TH

1895	Leith Athletic	A	Scottish League	6–5

1899 John Gilchrist was born in Glasgow.

1901 Barney Battles won the first of his 3 international caps for Scotland in the 2–2 draw with England at Crystal Palace. Johnny Campbell scored one of Scotland's goals.

1907	Hibernian	H	Scottish Cup semi-final	0–0
1912	Hearts	Ibrox	Scottish Cup semi-final	3–0
1918	Kilmarnock	A	Scottish League	3–1
1926	Aberdeen	H	Scottish League	4–1
1927	Hearts	A	Scottish League	0–3
1929	Third Lanark	A	Scottish League	3–1
1940	Motherwell	A	League Western Division	0–2
1946	Third Lanark	H	Southern League Cup ('A' Division – Section D)	1–1
1955	East Fife	A	Scottish Cup semi-final	4–3
1957	Hearts	A	Scottish League	1–3
1963	St Mirren	A	Scottish Cup quarter-final	1–0
1968	Dundee United	A	Scottish League	5–0
1971	Partick Thistle	A	Glasgow Cup	4–3
1974	Dumbarton	H	Scottish League	3–3
1977	Hibernian	A	Scottish League Premier Division	1–1

1983 Charlie Nicholas scored the equaliser in the 2–2 draw with Switzerland at Hampden Park on his international debut.

1988	Aberdeen	A	Scottish League Premier Division	1–0
1991	Motherwell	H	Scottish League Premier Division	1–2
1994	Raith Rovers	H	Scottish League Premier Division	2–1

MARCH 31ST

1900	Rangers	A	Inter City League	2–1
1902	Hearts	H	Inter City League	2–3
1917	St Mirren	H	Scottish League	3–0
1923	Hibernian	Hampden Park	Scottish Cup final	1–0

Joe Cassidy scored the winning goal which seemed appropriate as it was his 11th of the competition.

1928	Bo'ness	H	Scottish League	4–1

1934	Third Lanark	A	Scottish League	1–1
1945	Partick Thistle	H	Southern League Cup (Section B)	1–2
1951	Raith Rovers	Hampden Park		
			Scottish Cup semi-final	3–2
1956	Airdrie	H	Scottish League	3–1
1962	St Mirren	Hampden Park		
			Scottish Cup semi-final	1–3
1965	Motherwell	Hampden Park		
			Scottish Cup semi-final replay	3–0
1973	Falkirk	H	Scottish League	4–0
1979	Hibernian	A	Scottish League Premier Division	1–2
1982	Dundee United	A	Scottish League Premier Division	2–0
1984	Aberdeen	H	Scottish League Premier Division	1–0
1992	Rangers	Hampden Park		
			Scottish Cup semi-final	0–1

APRIL 1ST

1893   Johnny Campbell won the first of his 12 international caps in the 2–5 defeat away to England.

1895   Jimmy McStay was born in Netherburn.

1907	Queen's Park	H	Scottish League	2–1
1911	Hearts	A	Scottish League	1–1
1914	Third Lanark	A	Scottish League	3–1
1916	Morton	H	Scottish League	0–0
1922	Queen's Park	A	Scottish League	3–1
1925	Falkirk	H	Scottish League	6–1
1929	Partick Thistle	H	Scottish League	1–0

1933   Jimmy McGrory scored both goals as Scotland beat England 2–1 at Hampden Park. Peter Wilson played his 4th and last game for Scotland.

1939	Arbroath	H	Scottish League	2–0
1944	Falkirk	H	Southern League Cup (Section B)	3–0
1961	Airdrie	Hampden Park		
			Scottish Cup semi-final	4–0
1964	Dundee	H	Scottish League	2–1
1967	Clyde	Hampden Park		
			Scottish Cup semi-final	0–0
1969	St Johnstone	A	Scottish League	3–2
1970	Leeds United	A	European Cup semi-final 1st leg	1–0

A goal after 40 seconds from Connelly gave Celtic the vital away goal. They had to hold on for only another 90 minutes!

1972	Partick Thistle	H	Scottish League	3–1
1978	Aberdeen	H	Scottish League Premier Division	2–2
1981	Hearts	H	Scottish League Premier Division	6–0
1989	Rangers	H	Scottish League Premier Division	1–2
1990	Rangers	A	Scottish League Premier Division	0–3
1995	Motherwell	H	Scottish League	1–1

Both sets of fans observed a minute's silence in respect of former Scottish international Davie Cooper who had died suddenly earlier in the week.

| 1996 | Aberdeen | H | Scottish League Premier Division | 5–0 |

APRIL 2ND

1892	Vale of Leven	A	Scottish League	2–2
1904	Hearts	A	Scottish League	1–2
1921	Dumbarton	H	Scottish League	1–1
1923	Partick Thistle	A	Scottish League	2–0
1927	Dunfermline Athletic	H	Scottish League	2–1
1932	Morton	H	Scottish League	6–3
1934	Clyde	H	Scottish League	2–1
1938	Falkirk	A	Scottish League	0–3
1945	Third Lanark	H	Glasgow Charity Cup	5–0
1945	Queen's Park	H	League – Southern Division	3–0
1949	Motherwell	A	Scottish League	1–0
1955	Hibernian	H	Scottish League	1–2

1958 Willie Maley died aged 90 in Glasgow.

1960	Rangers		Hampden Park	
			Scottish Cup semi-final	1–1
1963	Partick Thistle	A	Scottish League	5–1

1966 Tommy Gemmell made the first of his 18 appearances for Scotland in the 3–4 defeat by England at Hampden.

1975	Dundee		Hampden Park	
			Scottish Cup semi-final	1–0
1977	Hearts	A	Scottish League Premier Division	3–0
1980	Rangers	H	Scottish League Premier Division	1–0
1983	Motherwell	H	Scottish League Premier Division	3–0

Willie McStay came on as sub for his debut. His younger brother Paul was already in the middle of the park.

1984	Rangers	H	Scottish League Premier Division	3–0
1986	Dundee	H	Scottish League Premier Division	2–1
1988	Hibernian	A	Scottish League Premier Division	2–0
1994	Dundee United	A	Scottish League Premier Division	3–1

APRIL 3RD

| 1893 | Rangers | A | Friendly | 1–3 |

1897 Willie Maley appointed secretary–manager a position he was to hold for over 40 years.

| 1899 | Third Lanark | H | Glasgow League | 2–1 |
| 1909 | St Mirren | A | Scottish League | 1–0 |

Peter Johnstone made his debut.

1915	Airdrie	H	Scottish League	3–0
1920	St Mirren	A	Scottish League	2–0
1926	Kilmarnock	H	Scottish League	0–0
1933	St Mirren	H	Scottish League	0–0

1937	Clyde	Ibrox	Scottish Cup semi-final	2–0
1940	Hamilton Academical	A	League – Western Division	0–5
1943	St Mirren	A	Southern League Cup (Section D)	1–5
1943	John Hughes was born in Coatbridge.			
1948	Hibernian	H	Scottish League	2–4
	Dan Lavery scored on his debut.			
1965	Third Lanark	H	Scottish League	1–0
1971	Airdrie	Hampden Park		
			Scottish Cup semi-final	3–3
1973	Motherwell	H	Scottish League	2–0
1974	Dundee	Hampden Park		
			Scottish Cup semi-final	1–0
1976	St Johnstone	H	Scottish League Premier Division	1–0
1982	Morton	A	Scottish League Premier Division	1–1
1985	Dumbarton	A	Scottish League Premier Division	2–0
1991	Motherwell	Hampden Park		
			Scottish Cup semi-final	0–0
1993	Motherwell	A	Scottish League Premier Division	0–2

APRIL 4TH

1891	St Mirren	A	Scottish League	0–1
1903	St Mirren	A	Inter City League	0–0
1904	Hibernian	H	Inter City League	0–0
1908	Morton	H	Scottish League	2–0
1931	Ayr United	H	Scottish League	4–1
1936	Johnny Crum made his debut for Scotland at Wembley in the 1–1 draw with England.			
1942	Hamilton Academical	A	Southern League Cup (Section Two)	2–1
1953	Dundee	A	Scottish League	0–4
1955	Airdrie	Hampden Park		
			Scottish Cup semi-final replay	2–0
1959	St Mirren	Hampden Park		
			Scottish Cup semi-final	0–4
	Sammy Wilson played his last game for the club. In just 70 games he scored 46 goals.			
1962	Partick Thistle	A	Scottish League	2–1
1964	St Johnstone	A	Scottish League	1–1
1970	Motherwell	H	Scottish League	6–1
1979	Motherwell	A	Scottish League Premier Division	4–3
1987	Rangers	H	Scottish League Premier Division	3–1
1992	Falkirk	A	Scottish League Premier Division	3–0

APRIL 5TH

1913	St Mirren	H	Scottish League	2–1
1915	Queen's Park	A	Scottish League	3–0
1920	Partick Thistle	A	Scottish League	2–1
1924	Ayr United	H	Scottish League	3–0
1926	Partick Thistle	A	Scottish League	0–0

1930	Partick Thistle	H	Scottish League	2–0
1939	Motherwell	A	Scottish League	3–2
1941	Partick Thistle	A	Southern League Cup	1–0
1954	Motherwell	Hampden Park		
			Scottish Cup semi-final replay	3–1
1958	Aberdeen	A	Scottish League	1–0
1961	St Johnstone	H	Scottish League	1–1
1966	St Mirren	A	Scottish League	3–0
1969	Hibernian	Hampden Park		
			League Cup final	6–2

Bobby Lennox scored a hat-trick to claim the club's 6th League Cup trophy at their 7th attempt. The total of 41 goals scored in the season's competition is a club record.

1972	Internazionale	A	European Cup semi-final 1st leg	0–0
1975	Morton	H	Scottish League Premier Division	1–1
1978	Hibernian	H	Scottish League Premier Division	2–1
1980	Aberdeen	H	Scottish League Premier Division	1–2
1981	Partick Thistle	A	Scottish League Premier Division	1–0
1986	St Mirren	A	Scottish League Premier Division	2–1
1988	St Mirren	H	Scottish League Premier Division	2–0
1997	Raith Rovers	A	Scottish League Premier Division	1–1
1998	Rangers	Hampden Park		
			Scottish Cup semi-final	1–2

APRIL 6TH

1901	Hearts	Ibrox	Scottish Cup final	3–4
1907	Hibernian	A	Scottish Cup semi-final replay	0–0
1910	Morton	H	Scottish League	3–0
1912	Clyde	Ibrox	Scottish Cup final	2–0
1918	Hibernian	A	Scottish League	2–0
1927	Falkirk	A	Scottish League	1–4
1927	Neil Mochan was born in Larbert.			
1929	St Johnstone	A	Scottish League	1–1
1931	Clyde	A	Scottish League	2–0
1937	Third Lanark	A	Scottish League	2–4
1940	Rangers	H	League – Western Division	1–2
1942	Partick Thistle	A	League – Southern Division	3–1
1959	Raith Rovers	A	Scottish League	1–3
1960	Rangers	Hampden Park		
			Scottish Cup semi-final replay	1–4
1963	Hibernian	H	Scottish League	2–0
1967	Clyde	Hampden Park		
			Scottish Cup semi-final replay	2–0
1968	Hearts	A	Scottish League	2–0
1974	Arbroath	H	Scottish League	1–0
1977	Dundee	Hampden Park		
			Scottish Cup semi-final	2–0

1983	Dundee United	H	Scottish League Premier Division	2–0
1985	Hearts	A	Scottish League Premier Division	2–0
1991	Aberdeen	A	Scottish League Premier Division	0–1
1993	Airdrie	H	Scottish League Premier Division	4–0
1994	Dundee	H	Scottish League Premier Division	1–1

APRIL 7TH

1906 Donald McLeod made his international debut for Scotland in the 2–1 victory over England at Hampden in front of over 100,000 fans, a record attendance at the time in Britain.

1917	Dumbarton	A	Scottish League	3–1
1923	Hearts	H	Scottish League	2–1
1928	Motherwell	A	Scottish League	1–3
1934	Airdrie	A	Scottish League	4–2

Frank Murphy scored twice on his debut.

1945	Partick Thistle	H	League – Southern Division	3–0
1951	Hearts	A	Scottish League	1–1
1954	St Mirren	A	Scottish League	3–1
1958	Queen's Park	H	Scottish League	5–1
1962	Hibernian	A	Scottish League	1–1
1965	Hibernian	A	Scottish League	4–0
1970	Dundee	A	Scottish League	2–1
1971	Airdrie	Hampden Park	Scottish Cup semi-final replay	2–0
1973	Dundee	Hampden Park	Scottish Cup semi-final	0–0
1979	Partick Thistle	H	Scottish League Premier Division	2–0
1984	St Johnstone	A	Scottish League Premier Division	0–0
1990	St Mirren	H	Scottish League Premier Division	0–3
1995	Hibernian	Ibrox	Scottish Cup semi-final	0–0
1996	Rangers	Hampden Park	Scottish Cup semi-final	1–2

APRIL 8TH

1911	Hamilton Academical	Ibrox	Scottish Cup final	0–0
1914	Kilmarnock	A	Scottish League	1–0
1916	Falkirk	A	Scottish League	2–0
1922	Dundee	H	Scottish League	4–0
1939	Hibernian	A	Scottish League	0–1
1944	Partick Thistle	H	Southern League Cup (Section B)	6–0

Jackie Gallacher scored 5 goals.

1959	Motherwell	A	Scottish League	0–2
1961	Dundee	A	Scottish League	1–0
1963	Third Lanark	Hampden Park	Glasgow Cup final	1–2
1967	Motherwell	A	Scottish League	2–0
1972	Kilmarnock	A	Scottish League	3–1

1978	Clydebank	A	Scottish League Premier Division	2–3
1980	Dundee United	A	Scottish League Premier Division	0–3
1989	Hamilton Academical	A	Scottish League Premier Division	0–2
1992	St Mirren	A	Scottish League Premier Division	1–1
1998	Kilmarnock	A	Scottish League Premier Division	2–1

APRIL 9TH

| 1892 | Queen's Park | Ibrox | Scottish Cup final | 5–1 |

Celtic's first major honour in their history in their 2nd appearance in the Scottish Cup final. 2 goals each by Campbell and McMahon plus an own-goal ensured victory that sparked wild celebrations in the East End of Glasgow.

1898	Clyde	H	Glasgow League	3–0
1910	Aberdeen	H	Scottish League	2–0
1917	Third Lanark	H	Scottish League	2–0
1921	Raith Rovers	A	Scottish League	0–2
1927	Dundee United	A	Scottish League	3–3
1928	Airdrie	A	Scottish League	1–3
1932	Airdrie	A	Scottish League	1–1

Chic Napier made his international debut for Scotland in the 0–3 defeat by England at Wembley.

1938	Motherwell	H	Scottish League	4–1
1940	Clyde	H	League Western Division	4–1
1954	Tom McAdam was born in Glasgow.			
1955	Dundee	A	Scottish League	1–0
1958	Clyde	H	Scottish League	6–2
1962	Rangers	H	Scottish League	1–1
1966	St Mirren	H	Scottish League	5–0
1969	Falkirk	H	Scottish League	5–2
1977	Kilmarnock	H	Scottish League Premier Division	1–0
1983	Hibernian	A	Scottish League Premier Division	3–0
1988	Hearts	Hampden Park		
			Scottish Cup semi-final	2–1
1991	Motherwell	Hampden Park		
			Scottish Cup semi-final replay	2–4
1994	Hearts	H	Scottish League Premier Division	2–2

APRIL 10TH

1909	Rangers	Hampden Park		
			Scottish Cup final	2–2
1915	Aberdeen	H	Scottish League	1–0
1920	Aberdeen	H	Scottish League	5–0
1923	St Mirren	A	Scottish League	0–1
1926	St Mirren	Hampden Park		
			Scottish Cup final	0–2
1933	Clyde	H	Scottish League	2–1
1937	Dunfermline Athletic	A	Scottish League	4–3

1939	Queen's Park	A	Scottish League	2–1
1943	Rangers	H	League – Southern Division	2–2
1944	Queen's Park	A	League – Southern Division	4–1
1948	Third Lanark	H	Scottish League	1–3
1950	Partick Thistle	A	Scottish League	0–1
1956	Aberdeen	H	Scottish League	1–1
1957	Partick Thistle	A	Scottish League	1–3
1961	Dundee United	A	Scottish League	1–1
1968	Aberdeen	A	Scottish League	1–0
1971	Dundee United	H	Scottish League	1–1
1974	Atletico Madrid	H	European Cup semi-final 1st leg	0–0

Another night of soccer violence by the opposition as the Spaniards came to kick and stop Celtic playing. 3 were sent off and most of the others booked in a game which ended with a free for all on the pitch among the players. Atletico were later fined £14,000 and had 6 players banned for the 2nd leg, which once again Celtic contemplated not playing but in the end had to.

1976	Dundee United	A	Scottish League Premier Division	2–3
1982	Rangers	H	Scottish League Premier Division	2–1
1984	Motherwell	H	Scottish League Premier Division	4–2

Owen Archdeacon scored on his debut after coming on as substitute for Tommy Burns.

1993	St Johnstone	A	Scottish League Premier Division	1–1
1996	Kilmarnock	H	Scottish League Premier Division	1–1

APRIL 11TH

1891	Dumbarton	H	Scottish League	1–0
1896	Rangers	A	Glasgow League	2–2
1898	Rangers	H	Scottish League	0–0
1903	Hibernian	A	Inter City League	1–2
1908	Queen's Park	H	Scottish League	2–0
1914	Hibernian	Ibrox	Scottish Cup final	0–0
1925	Dundee	Hampden Park		
			Scottish Cup final	2–1
1931	Motherwell	Hampden Park		
			Scottish Cup final	2–2
1934	St Mirren	H	Scottish League	3–0
1936	Arbroath	A	Scottish League	2–0
1949	Dundee	A	Scottish League	2–3
1951	Airdrie	H	Scottish League	0–1
1953	St Mirren	H	Scottish League	3–2
1959	Stirling Albion	A	Scottish League	1–0

1959 Dunky MacKay made his first of 14 appearances for Scotland in the 0–1 defeat by England at Wembley. Bobby Evans captained the side that day.

1969	Rangers	H	Glasgow Cup	3–4
1970	Aberdeen	Hampden Park		
			Scottish Cup final	1–3

1973	Dundee	Hampden Park		
			Scottish Cup semi-final replay	3–0
1979	Dundee United	A	Scottish League Premier Division	1–2
1981	Dundee United	Hampden Park		
			Scottish Cup semi-final	0–0
1987	Hibernian	A	Scottish League Premier Division	4–1
1992	St Johnstone	H	Scottish League Premier Division	3–2
1995	Hibernian	Ibrox	Scottish Cup semi-final replay	3–1

APRIL 12TH

1909	Third Lanark	A	Scottish League	1–1
1919	Clydebank	A	Scottish League	2–0
1924	St Mirren	H	Scottish League	0–1

Andy McAtee made his last appearance for the club. After 14 years of terrorising defences, he had played over 430 games and scored 72 goals. He won 4 Championship medals and 4 Scottish Cup winners' medals.

1930	St Mirren	A	Scottish League	0–0
1941	Clyde	H	League – Southern Division	1–1
1947	Hibernian	A	Scottish League	0–2
1952	Third Lanark	A	Scottish League	3–3
1958	Partick Thistle	A	Scottish League	1–0
1960	Partick Thistle	H	Scottish League	2–4
1967	Dukla Prague	H	European Cup semi-final 1st leg	3–1
1971	Motherwell	H	Scottish League	3–0
1972	Kilmarnock	Hampden Park		
			Scottish Cup semi-final	3–1
1975	Dunfermline Athletic	A	Scottish League	3–1
1978	Hibernian	A	Scottish League Premier Division	1–1
1980	Hibernian	Hampden Park		
			Scottish Cup semi-final	5–0
1986	Aberdeen	A	Scottish League Premier Division	1–0

1988 The court case against Frank McAvennie of Celtic and Chris Woods, Terry Butcher and Graham Roberts of Rangers was held at the Glasgow Sheriff Court, the case arising from incidents during the Rangers and Celtic match the previous October. All four were charged with 'behaviour likely to cause a breach of the peace', with the evidence on the first day comprising the watching of video evidence of the game provided by the police.

1989	Motherwell	A	Scottish League Premier Division	2–2
1997	Falkirk	Hampden Park		
			Scottish Cup semi-final	1–1
1998	Rangers	A	Scottish League Premier Division	0–2

APRIL 13TH

1903	Rangers	A	Inter City League	2–2
1907	Hibernian	H	Scottish Cup semi-final 2nd replay	3–0
1912	Kilmarnock	H	Scottish League	2–0

1914	Queen's Park	Ibrox	Scottish Cup final replay	5–0
1918	Motherwell	H	Scottish League	1–1
1929	Hibernian	H	Scottish League	1–4
1935	Airdrie	H	Scottish League	2–0
1936	Clyde	H	Scottish League	2–1
1940	Queen's Park	H	League – Western Division	4–4

1946 Jimmy Delaney scored the winning goal for Scotland in the 1–0 victory over England at Hampden.

1956	Kilmarnock	A	Scottish League	0–0
1957	Dunfermline Athletic	A	Scottish League	1–0
1963	Raith Rovers	Ibrox	Scottish Cup semi-final	5–2

1963 Mo Johnstone was born in Glasgow.

1968	Dundee	H	Scottish League	5–2
1974	Dundee United	A	Scottish League	2–0
1977	Motherwell	A	Scottish League Premier Division	0–3
1985	Motherwell	Hampden Park	Scottish Cup semi-final	1–1
1991	Dundee United	A	Scottish League Premier Division	1–2

APRIL 14TH

1900	Queen's Park	Ibrox	Scottish Cup final	4–3

1901 Patrick Connolly was born in Hamilton.

1917	Hibernian	A	Scottish League	1–0
1920	Albion Rovers	A	Scottish League	5–0
1926	Morton	H	Scottish League	3–0
1928	Rangers	Hampden Park	Scottish Cup final	0–4
1934	Hamilton Academical	A	Scottish League	1–1
1953	Aberdeen	H	Scottish League	1–3
1954	Falkirk	A	Scottish League	3–0
1965	Falkirk	A	Scottish League	2–6
1966	Liverpool	H	Cup-Winners' Cup semi-final 1st leg	1–0
1973	St Johnstone	A	Scottish League	3–1
1979	St Mirren	A	Scottish League Premier Division	1–0
1982	Airdrie	A	Scottish League Premier Division	5–1
1984	St Mirren	Hampden Park	Scottish Cup semi-final	2–1

The verdicts in the breach of the peace case against four players involved in the Rangers and Celtic match the previous October were delivered. Frank McAvennie was found not guilty. The case against Graham Roberts was found not proven, but both Chris Woods and Terry Butcher were found guilty and fined £250 each. Both Woods and Butcher took their case to the Court of Appeal and subsequently lost.

1990	Clydebank	Hampden Park	Scottish Cup semi-final	2–0
1996	Hibernian	A	Scottish League Premier Division	2–1

APRIL 15TH

1911 Hamilton Academical   Ibrox   Scottish Cup final replay   2–0
This was the 7th Cup final victory out of 13 appearances and the 2–0 margin also meant that the Cup was won without conceding a goal in the competition.

1916 Raith Rovers   H   Scottish League   6–0
Due to fixture congestion the Raith game was played in the afternoon and the Motherwell game played in the evening. 10 players played in both games.

1916 Motherwell   A   Scottish League   3–1

1922 Albion Rovers   A   Scottish League   2–0

1925 Kilmarnock   A   Scottish League   1–2

1930 Hamilton Academical   H   Scottish League   3–0

1931 Motherwell   Hampden Park
   Scottish Cup final replay   4–2

1933 Motherwell   Ibrox   Scottish Cup final   1–0

1944 Queen's Park   A   Glasgow Charity Cup   4–1

1946 Rangers   N   Friendly   1–2

1950 Clyde   A   Scottish League   2–2
Sean Fallon made his debut.

1961 Billy McNeill made his international debut for Scotland in the disastrous 3–9 defeat by England at Wembley.

1964 MTK-VM   H   Cup-Winners' Cup semi-final 1st leg   3–0

1967 At the age of 36 Ronnie Simpson won the first of his 5 caps for Scotland in the 3–2 victory over England at Wembley. Bobby Lennox scored one of the goals.

1970 Leeds United   H (Hampden Park)
   European Cup semi-final 2nd leg   2–1
The match, watched by a crowd of 136,505, a European Cup record, saw Celtic come back after conceding an early goal by Scot Billy Bremner. Hughes and Murdoch scored, the winner coming shortly after Leeds' goalkeeper had been carried off and replaced.

1972 East Fife   A   Scottish League   3–0

1975 Bobby Hogg died aged 61 in Paisley.

1978 Hibernian   H   Scottish League Premier Division   1–4

1981 Dundee United   Hampden Park
   Scottish Cup semi-final replay   2–3

1995 Aberdeen   A   Scottish League   0–2

1997 Manchester United   A   Brian McClair testimonial   2–1

APRIL 16TH

1892 Cambuslang   H   Scottish League   3–1

1893 Patsy Gallagher was born in Co Donegal.

1900 Rangers   H   Inter City League   2–1

1904 Rangers   Hampden Park
   Scottish Cup final   3–2
A Jimmy Quinn hat-trick sealed Celtic's 4th Scottish Cup final victory at their 9th attempt. It took another 68 years before another player – Dixie Deans of Celtic – was to score a hat-trick in the Cup final.

1914 Hibernian   Ibrox   Scottish Cup final replay   4–1

After overcoming Hibs at the 2nd attempt, 2 goals apiece from McColl and Browning helped Celtic to the League and Cup double. This feat would not be matched for another 40 years.

1927	East Fife		Hampden Park	
			Scottish Cup final	3–1
1937	Arbroath	H	Scottish League	5–1
1938	Dundee	A	Scottish League	3–2
1949	Third Lanark	H	Scottish League	1–2
1951	Partick Thistle	H	Scottish League	0–3
1955	Aberdeen	H	Scottish League	2–1
1958	Queen of the South	A	Scottish League	3–4
1960	Dundee	A	Scottish League	0–2
1966	Hibernian	A	Scottish League	0–0
1977	Hibernian	A	Scottish League Premier Division	1–0
1980	Kilmarnock	H	Scottish League Premier Division	2–0
1983	Aberdeen		Hampden Park	
			Scottish Cup semi-final	0–1
1988	Hearts	A	Scottish League Premier Division	1–2
1989	Hibernian		Hampden Park	
			Scottish Cup semi-final	3–1
1994	Kilmarnock	A	Scottish League Premier Division	0–2

APRIL 17TH

1897	Queen's Park	A	Glasgow League	0–2
1909	Rangers		Hampden Park	
			Scottish Cup final replay	1–1

At the end of normal time with the scores level thanks to Jimmy Quinn's 7th goal in as many games in the competition, the players, after waiting a while, started to leave the field, realising extra time was not going to be played. Fans then invaded the pitch demanding to know what was happening. Things got out of hand and the now famous 'Hampden Riot' was in full swing. Later on that night after a meeting between Celtic, Rangers and the SFA, it was decided that the Cup be withheld for a year and no 2nd replay should take place to decide the winners. As a result of this the chance of winning a hat-trick of Scottish Cups was lost.

1911	Third Lanark	A	Scottish League	1–1
1915	Third Lanark	A	Scottish League	4–0
1920	Motherwell	A	Scottish League	0–0

John McFarlane made his debut for the club.

1922	Partick Thistle	H	Scottish League	3–0
1926	Hamilton Academical	A	Scottish League	3–1
1929	Queen's Park	H (played away)		
			Scottish League	1–2
1935	Falkirk	H	Scottish League	7–3

Frank O'Donnell scored on his last appearance for the club. Not one of the most popular players with the fans on the terraces, nevertheless he scored 58 goals in his 83 games for Celtic.

| 1940 | Queen of the South | A | League – Western Division | 3–1 |
| 1948 | Dundee | A | Scottish League | 3–2 |

Whilst his career at the club was only brief, Jock Weir's hat-trick will be remembered as it helped the club avoid relegation.

1954	Hibernian	A	Scottish League	3–0
1957	St Mirren	H	Scottish League	2–3
1965	Partick Thistle	H	Scottish League	1–2
1968	Clyde	Hampden Park		
			Glasgow Cup final	8–0
1971	Aberdeen	A	Scottish League	1–1
1974	East Fife	A	Scottish League	6–1
1976	Aberdeen	H	Scottish League Premier Division	1–1
1978	Clydebank	H	Scottish League Premier Division	5–2
1982	Dundee	H	Scottish League Premier Division	4–2
1985	Motherwell	Hampden Park		
			Scottish Cup semi-final replay	3–0
1990	Hibernian	A	Scottish Cup semi-final	0–1
1993	Hibernian	A	Scottish League Premier Division	1–3

APRIL 18TH

1892	Leith Athletic	A	Scottish League	1–2
1896	Third Lanark	H	Glasgow League	1–2
1903	Third Lanark	A	Inter City League	0–3
1908	St Mirren	Hampden Park		
			Scottish Cup final	5–1

Victory ensured the club's 2nd consecutive League and Cup 'Double'.

| 1914 | Hibernian | Ibrox | Scottish Cup final replay | 3–0 |
| 1925 | Queen's Park | H | Scottish League | 1–1 |

Alec McNair played his last game for the club shortly before retiring from the game. He spent a staggering 21 years at Celtic, making over 600 appearances in all. He won 11 Championship medals and 6 Scottish Cup winners' medals as well as 15 caps for Scotland.

1927	Rangers	H	Scottish League	0–1
1928	St Johnstone	H	Scottish League	3–0
1931	Airdrie	H	Scottish League	3–1
1933	Airdrie	H	Scottish League	2–1
1934	Clyde	A	Scottish League	1–1
1936	Ayr United	H	Scottish League	6–0

Jimmy McGrory scored another hat-trick, with the last goal being his 50th League goal of the season, a club record.

1938	Dundee	H	Scottish League	3–0
1949	Clyde	H	Scottish League	2–1
1953	East Fife	H	Scottish League	1–1
1959	Hearts	H	Scottish League	2–1
1960	Airdrie	A	Scottish League	5–2
1964	Hearts	H	Scottish League	1–1

| 1970 | St Mirren | A | Scottish League | 3–2 |

1970 David Hay made his international debut for Scotland in the 1–0 victory over Northern Ireland in Belfast.

1973	Dumbarton	H	Scottish League	5–0
1979	Hearts	A	Scottish League Premier Division	3–0
1981	Rangers	A	Scottish League Premier Division	1–0
1984	St Mirren	A	Scottish League Premier Division	4–2
1987	Dundee United	H	Scottish League Premier Division	1–1
1992	Airdrie	A	Scottish League Premier Division	0–0
1998	Motherwell	H	Scottish League Premier Division	4–1

APRIL 19TH

1902	Queen's Park	A	Inter City League	3–1
1909	Hearts	A	Scottish League	2–1
1919	Falkirk	H	Scottish League	4–0
1920	Hibernian	A	Scottish League	2–1
1930	Kilmarnock	H	Scottish League	4–0
1941	Hearts	Easter Road	Southern League Cup semi-final	0–2
1966	Liverpool	A	Cup-Winners' Cup semi-final 2nd leg	0–2
1967	Aberdeen	H	Scottish League	0–0
1969	Airdrie	H	Scottish League	2–2
1972	Internazionale	H	European Cup semi-final 2nd leg	0–0

After 210 minutes of trying, both teams failed to produce a goal, which meant penalty kicks would have to decide who played Ajax in the final. Craig, Johnstone, McClusky and Murdoch all scored but substitute Dixie Deans missed the all-important kick that could have taken the club into its 3rd European Cup final.

| 1975 | Dundee | H | Scottish League | 1–2 |

Tommy Burns made his debut.

1980	Dundee	A	Scottish League Premier Division	1–5
1986	Hibernian	H	Scottish League Premier Division	2–0
1995	Hearts	H	Scottish League	0–1

APRIL 20TH

1898	Rangers	H	Glasgow League	3–2
1903	Hearts	A	Inter City League	0–3
1907	Hearts	Hampden Park	Scottish Cup	3–0
1908	Hearts	H	Scottish League	6–0
1912	Raith Rovers	H	Scottish League	1–1
1918	Queen's Park	H	War Cup Fund	2–1
1921	Clydebank	H	Scottish League	1–1
1927	Motherwell	H	Scottish League	3–2
1929	Falkirk	H (Played Away)	Scottish League	3–0
1940	Airdrie	H	League – Western Division	4–2

1946	St Johnstone	A	Victory Cup	8–2

Jackie Gallacher scored 4 goals and Tommy Kiernan scored a hat-trick.

1957	Airdrie	H	Scottish League	3–0
1963	Third Lanark	H	Scottish League	2–1
1968	Morton	H	Scottish League	2–1

1971 Sir Robert Kelly became President of the club and Desmond White took over as Chairman.

1974	Aberdeen	H	Scottish League	2–0
1977	Aberdeen	H	Scottish League Premier Division	4–1
1983	Dundee United	H	Scottish League Premier Division	2–3
1985	St Mirren	H	Scottish League Premier Division	3–0
1991	Dunfermline Athletic	H	Scottish League Premier Division	5–1
1993	Falkirk	H	Scottish League Premier Division	1–0
1994	Elgin City	A	Centenary	1–2
1996	Falkirk	H	Scottish League Premier Division	4–0
1997	Aberdeen	H	Scottish League Premier Division	3–0

APRIL 21ST

1894 Willie McStay was born in Netherburn.

1900	Hearts	A	Inter City League	2–3
1902	Hearts	A	Inter City League	2–4
1906	Hearts	H	Scottish League	1–0
1909	Hamilton Academical	H	Scottish League	1–1
1913	Hearts	A	Scottish League	0–0
1917	Kilmarnock	H	Scottish League	0–2

This was Celtic's first defeat in 62 matches in which they won 49, stretching back to 13th November 1915.

1919	Airdrie	H	Scottish League	3–0
1923	Motherwell	A	Scottish League	0–0
1928	Partick Thistle	A	Scottish League	3–3
1930	Clyde	H	Scottish League	0–2
1934	Dundee	H	Scottish League	3–2

Peter Wilson played his last game for the club. In 12 years at the club he made nearly 400 appearances scoring 15 times. He won 1 Championship medal and 4 Scottish Cup winners' medals.

1951	Motherwell		Hampden Park	
			Scottish Cup final	1–0

Jimmy McPhail scored the winning goal that brought the Scottish Cup back to Parkhead for the first time in 14 years.

1956	Hearts		Hampden Park	
			Scottish Cup final	1–3
1958	Motherwell	H	Scottish League	2–2
1962	Raith Rovers	H	Scottish League	0–1
1969	Kilmarnock	A	Scottish League	2–2
1973	Arbroath	H	Scottish League	4–0
1976	Hibernian	A	Scottish League Premier Division	0–2

1979	Aberdeen	H	Scottish League Premier Division	1–1
1982	Dundee United	H	Scottish League Premier Division	3–1
1984	Rangers	A	Scottish League Premier Division	0–1

Peter Grant made his debut.

| 1990 | Dundee | H | Scottish League Premier Division | 1–1 |

APRIL 22ND

1891	Rangers	H	Scottish League	3–0
1893	Third Lanark	A	Scottish League	6–0
1899	Rangers	Hampden Park		
			Scottish Cup final	0–2
1909	Morton	H	Scottish League	5–1
1916	Hearts	H	Scottish League	0–0
1920	St Mirren	H	Scottish League	2–2
1931	Dundee	A	Scottish League	0–0
1933	Dundee	A	Scottish League	0–3
1939	St Johnstone	H	Scottish League	1–1
1949	Queen's Park	H	Glasgow Charity Cup	0–0
1957	Aberdeen	A	Scottish League	1–0
1961	Dunfermline Athletic	Hampden Park		
			Scottish Cup final	0–0
1972	Motherwell	H	Scottish League	5–2
1978	Partick Thistle	H	Scottish League Premier Division	5–2
1981	Dundee United	A	Scottish League Premier Division	3–2
1989	Dundee	H	Scottish League Premier Division	2–1

APRIL 23RD

1892	Dumbarton	A	Scottish League	0–1
1898	Queen's Park	H	Glasgow League	3–4
1904	Kilmarnock	H	Scottish League	6–1
1910	Falkirk	A	Scottish League	0–2
1921	Hibernian	H	Scottish League	3–0
1927	St Johnstone	A	Scottish League	0–1
1928	Raith Rovers	H	Scottish League	0–3
1932	Kilmarnock	H	Scottish League	4–1
1934	Hamilton Academical	H	Scottish League	5–1

Alec Thomson played his 450th and last game for the club. In a career that lasted 12 years at Parkhead, he scored 98 goals and won a Championship medal and 3 Scottish Cup winners' medals.

1938	St Mirren	A	Scottish League	3–1
1940	Albion Rovers	H	League – Western Division	3–1
1955	Clyde	Hampden Park		
			Scottish Cup final	1–1
1956	Partick Thistle	Hampden Park		
			Scottish League	0–2

Jim Kennedy made his debut.

1962	Motherwell	A	Scottish League	4–0
1966	Rangers		Hampden Park	
			Scottish Cup final	0–0

Celtic were ultimately to win the first of their nine League titles in a row, despite being dogged by Rangers for much of the second half of the campaign. A tense and close match ensued, witnessed by a crowd of 126,599 at Hampden Park and the two sides would have to try again four days later.

1977	Partick Thistle	A	Scottish League Premier Division	1–1
1980	Aberdeen	H	Scottish League Premier Division	1–3
1983	Aberdeen	A	Scottish League Premier Division	0–1
1988	Dundee	H	Scottish League Premier Division	3–0
1994	Dundee	A	Scottish League Premier Division	2–0
1997	Falkirk		Hampden Park	
			Scottish Cup semi-final replay	0–1

APRIL 24TH

1907	Partick Thistle	A	Scottish League	2–0
1909	Airdrie	H	Scottish League	0–0

1911 John Browning was signed from Vale of Leven.

1914	Hamilton Academical	A	Scottish League	2–1
1915	Motherwell	A	Scottish League	1–1
1916	Third Lanark	H	Scottish League	4–1
1920	Ayr United	H	Scottish League	4–0
1926	Dundee United	H	Scottish League	6–2

1928 Tommy Docherty was born in Glasgow.

1937	Aberdeen		Hampden Park	
			Scottish Cup final	2–1

Goals by Johnny Crum and Willie Buchan secured Celtic's 15th Scottish Cup final victory in front of 146,433 spectators, a record crowd for a Scottish Cup final – and in fact for any club game in Europe – which still stands today.

1954	Aberdeen		Hampden Park	
			Scottish Cup final	2–1
1965	Dunfermline Athletic		Hampden Park	
			Scottish Cup final	3–2

Bertie Auld scored 2 of the goals in Celtic's 30th Scottish Cup final appearance, giving them their 18th victory.

1974	Atletico Madrid	A	European Cup semi-final 2nd leg	0–2
1976	Ayr United	H	Scottish League Premier Division	1–2
1982	Partick Thistle	A	Scottish League Premier Division	3–0
1984	Dundee	H	Scottish League Premier Division	3–0

APRIL 25TH

1868 Willie Maley was born in Newry.

1891	Third Lanark	H	Scottish League	1–1
1896	Queen's Park	H	Glasgow League	0–3
1898	Third Lanark	A	Glasgow League	2–2

1903	Partick Thistle	A	Inter City League	0–3
1908	Rangers	A	Scottish League	1–0
1910	Hibernian	H	Scottish League	0–0
1914	Partick Thistle	H	Scottish League	1–1
1923	Ayr United	A	Scottish League	1–0
1925	St Mirren	A	Scottish League	1–2
1931	Leith Athletic	A	Scottish League	3–0
1936	Partick Thistle	A	Scottish League	3–1
1942	Third Lanark	H	Glasgow Charity Cup	2–0
1951	Motherwell	H	Scottish League	3–1
1956	Hibernian	H	Scottish League	0–3

1956 Willie McGonagle was given a free transfer by the club after 10 years' service, before joining Hamilton a few weeks later. He had made 325 appearances for the club, scoring 8 times.

| 1967 | Dukla Prague | A | European Cup semi-final 2nd leg | 0–0 |
| 1972 | Dundee United | H | Scottish League | 3–0 |

Victory virtually ensured Celtic's 7th consecutive Championship, creating a new Scottish record.

| 1979 | St Mirren | H | Scottish League Premier Division | 2–1 |
| 1981 | Kilmarnock | H | Scottish League Premier Division | 1–1 |

1983 Charlie Nicholas was named Scotland's Player of the Year.

1987	St Mirren	A	Scottish League Premier Division	3–1
1992	Dunfermline Athletic	H	Scottish League Premier Division	2–0
1998	Hibernian	H	Scottish League Premier Division	0–0

APRIL 26TH

| 1899 | Partick Thistle | H | Glasgow League | 3–0 |

1904 Jimmy McGrory was born in Garngad.

1909	Motherwell	H	Scottish League	4–0
1911	Hamilton Academical	H	Scottish League	3–0
1913	Hamilton Academical	A	Scottish League	1–0
1920	Dundee	H	Scottish League	1–1

The match was abandoned after continuous crowd invasions, but the League ruled the result should stand.

1924	Hibernian	H	Scottish League	1–1
1941	Partick Thistle	A	League – Southern Division	2–3
1947	Falkirk	H	Scottish League	0–0
1954	Hamilton Academical	H	Scottish League	1–0

Victory ensured Celtic claimed their 20th Championship win 2 days after winning the Cup claiming their 4th League and Cup 'Double'.

| 1957 | Kilmarnock | A | Scottish League | 0–0 |
| 1961 | Dunfermline Athletic | Hampden Park | Scottish Cup final replay | 0–2 |

Willie O'Neill made his debut.

| 1969 | Rangers | Hampden Park | Scottish Cup final | 4–0 |

Celtic won the treble in 1969, obviously including the Scottish Cup, the final of which attracted 132,870, the biggest crowd since 1956. Lennox, Chalmers, McNeill and Connolly scored the all-important goals. This game also saw Alex Ferguson, later to become one of the most successful managers of the modern era on both sides of the border, make his last appearance for Rangers, for he was deemed by the manager to be responsible for Celtic's first goal and was subsequently sold.

1975	St Johnstone	A	Scottish League	1–2
1976	Rangers	H	Scottish League Premier Division	0–0
1978	Clydebank	A	Scottish League Premier Division	1–1
1980	Partick Thistle	H	Scottish League Premier Division	2–1

1983 Charlie Nicholas was voted Scotland's Player of the Year.

| 1986 | Dundee | H | Scottish League Premier Division | 2–0 |

APRIL 27TH

| 1895 | Clyde | A | Scottish League | 2–0 |
| 1898 | Clyde | A | Glasgow League | 1–3 |

1899 Adam McLean was born in Greenock.

| 1907 | St Mirren | H | Scottish League | 1–1 |

Jimmy Weir made his debut for the club.

1908	Falkirk	A	Scottish League	1–1
1918	Clydebank	H	War Cup Fund	2–0
1929	Kilmarnock	A	Scottish League	3–2

Willie McStay played his last game for the club. In over 17 years' service he made nearly 450 appearances, scoring 39 times. He won 4 Championship medals and 3 Scottish cup winners' medals as well as 13 caps for Scotland. He was succeeded as captain by his younger brother Jimmy.

| 1935 | St Mirren | H | Scottish League | 2–1 |
| 1940 | Ayr United | A | League – Western Division | 0–1 |

John Morrison made his last appearance for the club after 12 years' service. He played over 200 games before and during the war winning 2 Championship medals and 1 Scottish Cup winners' medal.

1955	Clyde	Hampden Park		
			Scottish Cup final replay	0–1
1957	Hibernian	H	Scottish League	2–1
1963	Dunfermline Athletic	A	Scottish League	1–1
1966	Rangers	Hampden Park		
			Scottish Cup final	0–1

Celtic had beaten Rangers in the League Cup final the previous October by 2–1. This defeat prevented Celtic from winning the cup double for the first time since 1954.

1971	St Mirren	A	Scottish League	2–2
1974	Falkirk	A	Scottish League	1–1
1985	Aberdeen	A	Scottish League Premier Division	1–1
1991	Hearts	A	Scottish League Premier Division	1–0
1994	St Johnstone	H	Scottish League Premier Division	1–1
1996	Partick Thistle	A	Scottish League Premier Division	4–2

APRIL 28TH

1902	Hibernian	Ibrox	Scottish Cup final	0–1
1909	Queen's Park	A	Scottish League	5–0

Jimmy Quinn scored his 2nd hat-trick in 3 days as Celtic played their 6th game in 9 days.

1913	Rangers	Kingsmill Park		
			Friendly	0–0
1917	Clyde	A	Scottish League	5–0
1919	Hearts	A	Scottish League	3–2
1920	Airdrie	H	Scottish League	1–0
1923	Airdrie	H	Scottish League	1–1
1931	Queen's Park	H	Scottish League	1–1
1934	St Mirren	A	Scottish League	2–1
1951	Clyde	H	Scottish League	1–0
1953	Clyde	H	Glasgow Charity Cup	4–0
1956	Queen of the South	H	Scottish League	1–3
1965	Dunfermline Athletic	A	Scottish League	1–5
1969	Morton	H	Scottish League	2–4
1973	Hibernian	A	Scottish League	3–0
1979	Dundee United	H	Scottish League Premier Division	2–1
1982	Dunfermline Athletic	A	League Cup	7–1
1984	Hibernian	H	Scottish League Premier Division	3–2

Paul McGugan made his senior debut for the club. He had previously scored in the Glasgow Cup final of 1982.

| 1990 | Motherwell | A | Scottish Cup quarter-final | 1–1 |

APRIL 29TH

1891	Cowlairs	A	Scottish League	5–0
1893	Rangers	H	Scottish League	3–0
1899	Partick Thistle	A	Glasgow League	3–1
1909	Hibernian	A	Scottish League	0–1
1911	Aberdeen	H	Scottish League	0–0
1914	Raith Rovers	H	Scottish League	2–1

When Charlie Shaw conceded Raith's goal it was only the 14th of the season that he had let in in 38 League games – a club record and a Scottish League record that still stands today.

| 1916 | Partick Thistle | H | Scottish League | 5–0 |

A Gallagher hat-trick sealed Celtic's 3rd consecutive Championship and 13th overall.

1922	Morton	A	Scottish League	1–1
1939	St Mirren	A	Scottish League	1–2
1944	Rangers	Hampden Park		
			Southern League Cup (Section B)	2–4
1950	Clyde	H	Glasgow Charity Cup	1–0
1957	Queen of the South	H	Scottish League	0–0
1961	Motherwell	A	Scottish League	2–2
1963	Hearts	A	Scottish League	3–4
1964	Mtk-Vm	A	Cup-Winners' Cup semi-final 2nd leg	0–4

| 1967 | Aberdeen | Hampden Park | | |
| | | Scottish Cup final | | 2–0 |

1968 Kenny Dalglish signed pro forms.

1969 Harry Hood was given a free transfer by the club after 7 years. The formidable striker played 317 games and scored 123 goals.

1971	Ayr United	H	Scottish League	2–0
1972	Hearts	A	Scottish League	1–4
1974	Aberdeen	A	Scottish League	0–0

The draw meant that unless a mathematical miracle happened in the last 2 games Celtic were Champions for the 9th consecutive time, a record that may never be beaten (although it was equalled by Rangers in 1996–97).

| 1978 | St Mirren | A | Scottish League Premier Division | 1–3 |
| 1981 | Partick Thistle | A | Glasgow Cup final | 0–1 |

1985 Mark Reid was sold to Charlton. The elegant left-back had made 178 appearances for the club scoring 12 goals.

| 1989 | Aberdeen | A | Scottish League Premier Division | 0–0 |
| 1995 | Falkirk | A | Scottish League | 2–1 |

APRIL 30TH

1892	Abercorn	H	Scottish League	3–1
1898	Rangers	A	Glasgow League	3–4
1902	Sunderland	H	British League Cup	5–1
1904	Rangers	H	Inter City League	2–0

1904 Willie McGonagle was born in Hamilton.

| 1907 | Hearts | Hampden Park | | |
| | | Scottish Cup final | | 3–0 |

Willie Orr became the first player to score in a Scottish Cup final from the penalty spot and 2 goals by Peter Somers helped Celtic to their first League and Cup 'Double'. This was the first time this was achieved by any club in Scotland.

1908	St Mirren	A	Scottish League	2–2
1909	Hamilton Academical	A	Scottish League	2–1
1910	Dundee	A	Scottish League	0–0

The draw sealed Celtic's 10th Championship and their 6th consecutive title, a record not to be equalled until the club achieved the feat again in 1972. In the record achievement they had lost only 23 games out of 192, scoring 444 goals and conceding only 153.

1921	Airdrie	A	Scottish League	3–2
1927	Partick Thistle	H	Scottish League	2–1
1932	Partick Thistle	A	Scottish League	2–0

Malky MacDonald started his Celtic career with both goals on his debut.

| 1937 | Motherwell | A | Scottish League | 0–8 |

This result is a record defeat for the club.

1938	Hibernian	H	Scottish League	3–0
1947	Queen's Park	A	Glasgow Charity Cup	0–0
1951	Hibernian	A	Scottish League	1–3

Jimmy Walsh made his debut.

1955	Hearts	A	Scottish League	3–0
1956	Falkirk	H	Scottish League	1–0
1958	Third Lanark	H	Scottish League	4–1

Frank Haffey made his debut.

1960	St Mirren	H	Scottish League	3–3
1965	Rangers	H	Glasgow Cup	2–1
1966	Morton	A	Scottish League	2–0
1968	Dunfermline Athletic	A	Scottish League	2–1

George Connolly made his senior debut after coming on as substitute. The victory meant the club had won 3 consecutive Championships and their points total of 63 was a post-war record.

1974	Morton	H	Scottish League	1–1
1977	Ayr United	H	Scottish League Premier Division	2–0
1980	Dundee	A	Scottish League Premier Division	2–0
1983	Kilmarnock	A	Scottish League Premier Division	5–0
1986	Motherwell	A	Scottish League Premier Division	2–0
1988	Motherwell	A	Scottish League Premier Division	1–0

MAY 1ST

1897	Rangers	H	Glasgow League	1–1

1897 Willie Orr signed for the club from Preston North End.

1903 'Sunny' Jim Young signed for the club.

1912	Partick Thistle	A	Glasgow Charity Cup	0–0
1915	Queen's Park	H	Glasgow Charity Cup	2–1
1920	Hearts	H	Scottish League	3–0
1923	Clyde	Firhill Park		
			Glasgow Charity Cup	1–1
1926	Partick Thistle	A	Glasgow Charity Cup	2–1
1943	Queen's Park	H	Glasgow Charity Cup	3–0

1950 Danny McGrain was born in Finnieston.

1954	Rangers	Hampden Park		
			Glasgow Charity Cup final	0–1
1957	Rangers	A	Glasgow Charity Cup	0–1

Michael Haughey played his last game for the club. He had made over 230 appearances and scored just under 50 goals. Bertie Auld made his first senior appearance for the club.

1961	Queen's Park	H	Glasgow Charity Cup semi-final	3–3

1968 Ian Young was given a free transfer by the club after 7 years' service. The stylish right-back made over 160 appearances.

1971	Clyde	H	Scottish League	6–1

14 years to the day since he made his debut, Bertie Auld made his final appearance for the club. Even a hat-trick by Bobby Lennox couldn't take away his moment as he was carried round the pitch by the rest of the team at the final whistle. He played nearly 280 games and scored 85 goals. He won 5 Championship medals, 3 Cup and 4 League Cup medals.

1972	Dundee	A	Scottish League	1–1
1976	Ayr United	A	Scottish League Premier Division	5–3

1982	Hibernian	H	Scottish League Premier Division	6–0
1985	Rangers	H	Scottish League Premier Division	1–1
1993	Aberdeen	H	Scottish League Premier Division	1–0

MAY 2ND

1891	Rangers	A	Scottish League	2–1
1892	Dumbarton	Ibrox	Glasgow Charity Cup semi-final	3–1
1893	St Mirren	H	Scottish League	4–1
1901	Rangers	Exhibition Ground		
			Glasgow Charity Cup semi-final	0–0
1903	Dundee	H	Inter City League	2–2

Jimmy Campbell played his last game for Celtic. In his two spells with the club he made over 200 appearances scoring 109 times.

| 1904 | Alec McNair joined the club almost 1 year after he had his initial trial. |

| 1908 | Partick Thistle | H | Glasgow Charity Cup | 3–2 |
| 1910 | Third Lanark | A | Glasgow Charity Cup | 0–1 |

| 1913 | Charlie Shaw was signed from Queen's Park Rangers. |

1922	Partick Thistle	A	Glasgow Charity Cup	3–3
1925	Partick Thistle	H	Glasgow Charity Cup	1–2
1931	Rangers	Hampden Park		
			Glasgow Charity Cup	2–2
1933	Clyde	H	Glasgow Charity Cup	3–1
1934	Clyde	H	Glasgow Charity Cup	2–1
1939	Clyde	H	Glasgow Charity Cup	2–3
1942	Rangers	Hampden Park		
			Southern League Cup	0–2
			(Section Two) semi-final	
1949	Third Lanark	Hampden Park		
			Glasgow Charity Cup semi-final	2–0
1951	Rangers	N	Glasgow Charity Cup	1–2
1953	Third Lanark	H	Glasgow Charity Cup semi-final	1–1
1959	Rangers	A	Glasgow Charity Cup semi-final	1–1
1961	Hearts	H	Scottish League	1–3
1969	Dundee	A	Scottish League	2–1

Danny McGrain was named Scotland's Player of the Year.

1979	Hibernian	H	Scottish League Premier Division	3–1
1981	St Mirren	A	Scottish League Premier Division	1–3
1987	Falkirk	H	Scottish League Premier Division	1–2

Brian McClair scored from the penalty spot in what was to be his last goal for the club in his penultimate match. It was his 10th goal in 7 matches and typified the high goalscoring ratio he achieved.

1990	Aberdeen	H	Scottish League Premier Division	1–3
1992	Hibernian	H	Scottish League Premier Division	1–2
1995	Partick Thistle	H	Scottish League	1–3

MAY 3RD

1897	Queen's Park	H	Glasgow League	0–4
1901	Rangers		Exhibition Ground	
			Glasgow Charity Cup semi-final replay	1–0
1913	Clyde	H	Glasgow Charity Cup	1–0
1930	Queen's Park	A	Glasgow Charity Cup	4–1
1932	Partick Thistle	A	Glasgow Charity Cup	2–1
1947	Motherwell	H	Scottish League	3–2
1950	Third Lanark		Hampden Park	
			Glasgow Charity Cup	1–0
1952	Clyde	H	Glasgow Charity Cup	0–0

John Higgins made his debut.

1957	Sammy Wilson joined the club after being given a free transfer by St Mirren.			
1958	Partick Thistle	H	Glasgow Charity Cup	1–0
1965	Clyde	H	Glasgow Cup semi-final	3–0
1967	Dundee United	H	Scottish League	2–3
1975	Airdrie		Hampden Park	
			Scottish Cup final	3–1

Billy McNeill's last task as captain and player was to lift the Scottish Cup for the 7th time in a career that had spanned 18 years. In those glorious years he had made a club record 790 first-class appearances. As well as the Cup wins he also led the team to 9 Championship wins and 6 Scottish League Cup wins as well as having the greatest honour of skippering the team to glory on the famous night in Lisbon in the European Cup final victory. One of the greatest players ever to wear the green and white was later to return for two spells as manager.

1976	Hearts	A	Scottish League Premier Division	0–1
1980	St Mirren	A	Scottish League Premier Division	0–0
1982	St Mirren	H	Scottish League Premier Division	0–0
1986	St Mirren	A	Scottish League Premier Division	5–0
1998	Dunfermline	A	Scottish League Premier Division	1–1

MAY 4TH

1889	Renton	N	Glasgow Charity Cup	2–5
1895	Dundee	H	Scottish League	2–1
1907	Port Glasgow Athletic	A	Scottish League	1–1
1912	Queen's Park		Cathkin Park	
			Glasgow Charity Cup semi-final	2–1
1918	Morton		Hampden Park	
			War Cup Fund	1–0
1929	Queen's Park	A	Glasgow Charity Cup	6–5
1938	Queen's Park	A	Glasgow Charity Cup	3–1
1940	St Mirren	A	League – Western Division	1–2
1946	Queen of the South	H	Victory Cup	3–0
1948	Third Lanark	H	Glasgow Charity Cup semi-final	1–0
1962	Third Lanark		Hampden Park	
			Glasgow Cup final	1–1

Ian Young made his debut in place of Dunky Mackay who was injured playing for Scotland a couple of days earlier.

| 1963 | Rangers | | Hampden Park | |
| | | | Scottish Cup final | 1–1 |

This was the first time since 1928 that both Rangers and Celtic had battled through to the final of the Scottish FA Cup, a fact that was sufficient to draw a huge crowd of 129,643 to Hampden Park. The first clash was hardly a classic, the wind saw to that; but the undoubted man of the match was Celtic's goalkeeper Frank Haffey, who saved all but one of the shots that Rangers had. Haffey hadn't frozen on the day of a big occasion; two years previously he had had a nightmare match against England and let in nine.

1966	Dunfermline Athletic	H	Scottish League	2–1
1974	Dundee United		Hampden Park	
			Scottish Cup final	3–0
1985	Dundee	H	Scottish League Premier Division	0–1
1996	Raith Rovers	H	Scottish League Premier Division	4–1
1997	Hibernian	A	Scottish League Premier Division	3–1

MAY 5TH

1891	Vale of Leven	H	Scottish League	9–1
1892	Renton	A	Scottish League	4–0
1894	Third Lanark		Hampden Park	
			Glasgow Charity Cup semi-final	3–3
1900	Third Lanark	H	Inter City League	1–1
1906	Rangers		Hampden Park	
			Glasgow Charity Cup final	3–5
1908	Rangers	A	R. Robertson Benefit Match	0–0
1915	Partick Thistle	H	Glasgow Charity Cup semi-final	1–1
1923	Rangers	H	Glasgow Charity Cup semi-final	0–1
1928	Rangers	H	Glasgow Charity Cup semi-final	0–2

Tommy McInally played his final game for the club. In two spells with the club he played over 200 games scoring a very respectable 127 goals. He won 2 Championship medals in 1922 and 1926 and a Scottish Cup winners' medal in 1927.

| 1934 | Third Lanark | | Hampden Park | |
| | | | Glasgow Charity Cup semi-final | 4–1 |

Frank O'Donnell's hat-trick was overshadowed by what was to be the last appearance of Jimmy McStay. In 14 years at the club he had made over 470 appearances. He was later to manage the club during the war.

1936	Partick Thistle	H	Glasgow Charity Cup semi-final	1–0
1945	Partick Thistle	A	Glasgow Charity Cup semi-final	1–1
1947	Third Lanark	H	Glasgow Charity Cup semi-final	1–1
1948	Matt Lynch was given a free transfer by the club after 13 years. He had made over 200 appearances before and during the war, and scored 30 goals.

1956	Clyde	H	Glasgow Charity Cup	4–1
1967	Ronnie Simpson was voted Scotland's Player of the Year.
1973	Rangers		Hampden Park	
			Scottish Cup final	2–3

Celtic were denied back-to-back doubles in one of the more entertaining clashes between the two great rivals. It was the last time the crowd topped 100,000 – 122,714 filling Hampden Park with their passion and colours. The game was also witnessed by royalty for the first time, with Princess Alexandra presenting the cup at the end of the game.

1979	Rangers	A	Scottish League Premier Division	0–1
1984	Hearts	A	Scottish League Premier Division	1–1
1991	St Mirren	H	Scottish League Premier Division	1–0

MAY 6TH

1893	Clyde	A	Scottish League	2–1
1899	Rangers	H	Glasgow League	4–1
1905	Rangers	Hampden Park		
			Scottish League Championship play-off.	2–1

Both Celtic and Rangers finished the season with a total of 41 points. No method of deciding the Championship was in force at the time (i.e. goal difference or average), so a play-off was held to decide the outcome. Celtic won their 5th Championship.

1907	Rangers	H	St Mary's (Lanark) Convalescent Home	
			Benefit Match	1–2
1911	Third Lanark	H	Glasgow Charity Cup semi-final	5–2
1913	Third Lanark	A	Glasgow Charity Cup	2–1

Charlie Shaw made his debut in goal.

1916	Rangers	H	Glasgow Charity Cup semi-final	3–0
1922	Rangers	Hampden Park		
			Glasgow Charity Cup semi-final	0–0

Joe Dodds played his last game for the club. Possibly the finest left-back Celtic has ever had, he made just over 370 appearances for the club and scored 30 goals.

1924	Queen's Park	A	Glasgow Charity Cup semi-final	2–0
1930	Clyde	H	Glasgow Charity Cup semi-final	1–0
1933	Queen's Park	A	Glasgow Charity Cup semi-final	2–3
1935	Queen's Park	H	Glasgow Charity Cup	1–4
1950	Rangers	Hampden Park		
			Glasgow Charity Cup final	3–2
1963	Clyde	H	Scottish League	2–0
1967	Rangers	A	Scottish League	2–2

One of the closest title races of many a year took Celtic to Ibrox in the very last game of the season two points ahead of Rangers. Celtic needed only a point to lift the title, Rangers a sizeable win to clinch it on goal average. It was enough to bring 78,000 to Ibrox, and it ended in pure joy for the travelling Celtic fans, getting the draw they needed to move one step closer to the clean sweep of League, League Cup, Scottish FA Cup and the European Champions' Cup. Two goals by Jimmy Johnstone ensured Celtic's 22nd Championship victory.

| 1970 | Feyenoord | Milan | European Cup final | 1–2 |

After winning the League and League Cup and losing the Scottish Cup final to Aberdeen, the 2nd most important game in the club's history proved too much as they were outplayed by better opposition on the day, despite forcing the game to go to extra time. They held on until just 4 minutes from the end before conceding the 2nd goal.

| 1971 | Clyde | A | Glasgow Cup | 1–2 |

Steve Chalmers made his final appearance for the club. Whilst he will be remembered as the man who scored the winning goal of the European Cup in 1967, he played over 400 times for the club scoring a very impressive 228 goals (241 in all comps). John Clark also made his final appearance for the club after 318 outings. The club had seen the last of two great servants on the same day. As Chalmers and Clark finished their careers at the club, another one began as Pat McCluskey made his debut.

| 1972 | Hibernian | Hampden Park | | |
| | | | Scottish Cup final | 6–1 |

A Dixie Deans hat-trick and 2 goals from Macari helped Celtic to a record victory in Cup final and to their 4th consecutive Cup win and a tally of 22 Scottish Cup final wins. Jim Craig played his last game for the club after 7 years' service. He had made 231 appearances.

| 1974 | Morton | A | Scottish League | 0–0 |

The club had already won the Championship for a record-breaking 9th successive time and for the 29th time in their history. In this period they had the remarkable record of playing 306 games, winning 235, losing only 26 and drawing on 45 occasions. They had scored 868 goals, letting in 258 and gaining 515 points. David Hay made his last appearance for the club before his summer transfer to Chelsea. He played over 230 games for the club, winning 5 Championship medals, 2 Scottish Cup winners' medals and a League Cup winners' medal as well as winning 27 caps for Scotland whilst at the club. Also making his last appearance was Evan Williams, the goalkeeper who had been brought in to replace Ronnie Simpson 5 years earlier. Whilst he was no Simpson he served the club well, playing nearly 150 games. He won 4 Championship medals and 2 Scottish Cup winners' medals.

| 1989 | Hibernian | H | Scottish League Premier Division | 1–0 |

MAY 7TH

1892	Rangers	A	Scottish League	1–1
1898	Rangers	Cathkin Park		
			Glasgow Charity Cup	0–2
1900	Hearts	H	Inter City League	5–0
1906	Third Lanark	H	Scottish League	0–1
1921	Partick Thistle	H	Glasgow Charity Cup semi-final	2–0
1927	Rangers	H	Glasgow Charity Cup	1–4
1932	Third Lanark	H	Glasgow Charity Cup	1–2
1938	Partick Thistle	H	Glasgow Charity Cup semi-final	3–2
1949	Partick Thistle	Hampden Park		
			Glasgow Charity Cup final	1–2
1955	Rangers	H	Glasgow Charity Cup	0–1
1958	Rangers	A	Glasgow Charity Cup	1–1
1960	Clyde	H	Glasgow Charity Cup	3–3
1966	Motherwell	A	Scottish League	1–0

| 1970 | Ronnie Simpson retired from first-class football through injury. In his 6 years at the club he made 188 appearances for the club with nearly half of them being shut-outs. |

| 1977 | Rangers | | Hampden Park | |
| | | | Scottish Cup final | 1–0 |

Andy Lynch scored what was to be the winner in the 18th minute after Dalglish had refused to take the spot kick. Alfie Conn had returned to Glasgow from his sojourn in England but had signed for Celtic! Here he won a winners' medal in the final against Rangers, having previously collected a winners' medal in 1973 for Rangers against Celtic. This is unique in the modern game. After the match Celtic manager Jock Stein and player Kenny Dalglish had been conducting interviews with the media, explaining their success on the day which took rather longer than expected to complete. They rushed out of Hampden Park and jumped onto the first coach they saw, carrying the Scottish Cup with them. Quite who was more surprised, Stein and Dalglish, or the Rangers team whose coach it was, has never been revealed!

1979	Partick Thistle	A	Scottish League Premier Division	2–1
1983	Morton	H	Scottish League Premier Division	2–0
1987	Rangers	H	Glasgow Cup final	0–1
1988	Dunfermline Athletic	H	Scottish League Premier Division	1–0
1995	Rangers	H	Scottish League	3–0
1997	Kilmarnock	H	Scottish League Premier Division	0–0

MAY 8TH

1907	Hibernian	A	Scottish League	1–0
1909	Clyde	H	Glasgow Charity Cup semi-final	2–1
1915	Rangers	A	Glasgow Charity Cup final	3–2
1920	Rangers	A	Glasgow Charity Cup semi-final	2–1
1926	Third Lanark	H	Glasgow Charity Cup semi-final	2–0
1929	Clyde	N	Glasgow Charity Cup semi-final	3–1
1937	Clyde	H	Glasgow Charity Cup semi-final	3–1
1948	Rangers		Hampden Park	
			Glasgow Charity Cup final	0–2

1953 Neil Mochan was signed from Middlesbrough for £8,000.

1956 Davie Provan was born in Gourock.

1965 John Hughes won the first of his 8 caps for Scotland in the 0–0 draw with Spain at Hampden.

1971	Rangers		Hampden Park	
			Scottish Cup final	1–1
1979	Clyde	H	Glasgow Cup semi-final	3–2
1982	Dundee United	A	Scottish League Premier Division	0–3
1993	Partick Thistle	A	Scottish League Premier Division	1–0

MAY 9TH

| 1893 | Leith Athletic | H | Scottish League | 3–1 |

2 goals by James Davidson helped the club to their first Championship trophy.

1894	Third Lanark		Hampden Park	
			Glasgow Charity Cup semi-final replay	2–0
1896	Rangers		Hampden Park	
			Glasgow Charity Cup semi-final	6–1

1900	Queen's Park		Cathkin Park	
			Glasgow Charity Cup semi-final	6–1
1901	Third Lanark		Exhibition Ground	
			Glasgow Charity Cup final	0–0
1902	Rangers	H	Inter City League	2–0
1904	Queen's Park		Cathkin Park	
			Glasgow Charity Cup semi-final	2–1
1908	Clyde	H	Glasgow Charity Cup semi-final	2–0
1914	Queen's Park	A	Glasgow Charity Cup semi-final	3–0
1936	Rangers		Hampden Park	
			Glasgow Charity Cup final	4–2
1945	Queen's Park		Hampden Park	
			Victory In Europe Challenge Match	1–1
1953	Queen's Park	A	Glasgow Charity Cup final	3–1

Neil Mochan scored 2 goals on his debut.

1956	Third Lanark	H	Glasgow Charity Cup	0–0
1959	Clyde		Hampden Park	
			Glasgow Charity Cup final	5–0
1960	Rangers	A	Glasgow Charity Cup	1–1
1961	Clyde		Hampden Park	
			Glasgow Charity Cup final	1–1
1986	Rangers	A	Glasgow Cup final	2–3
1986	Anton Rogan signed for the club.			
1987	Hearts	A	Scottish League Premier Division	0–1

Brian McClair played his last game for the club after 4 successful years at the club. In 199 games he had scored 120 goals (99 in the league).

| 1998 | St Johnstone | H | Scottish League Premier Division | 2–0 |

Henrik Larsson's goal helped the team to the victory that ensured that Celtic won their first Championship for 10 years. More importantly it stopped Rangers winning 10 in a row and breaking Celtic's own achievement of 9 in a row. Wim Jansen in his first season as head coach masterminded the campaign superbly, but indicated that due to differences with Jock Brown he was considering resigning and would announce his decision soon. The news was a huge disappointment to the fans who cheered him vociferously on the team's lap of honour.

MAY 10TH

1899	Queen's Park	A	Glasgow League	5–1
1911	Rangers		Hampden Park	
			Glasgow Charity Cup final	1–2

Willie Nichol scored on his debut.

| 1913 | Rangers | H | Glasgow Charity Cup final | 3–2 |

Johnny McMaster made his debut.

1914	Bobby Hogg was born in Larkhall.			
1919	Ayr United	H	Scottish League	2–0
1924	Rangers		Hampden Park	
			Glasgow Charity Cup final	2–1

Joe Cassidy made his final appearance for the club. Leading goalscorer for three consecutive seasons in the early 1920s, he played over 200 games and scored 104 times.

| 1930 | Rangers | | Hampden Park | |
| | | | Glasgow Charity Cup final | 2–2 |

Paddy Connolly made what was to be his final appearance for the club, even though it was to be quite a while before he left Celtic due to wranglings over a new contract. The flying right-winger made just under 300 appearances for the club. He scored 46 goals and created many more for the likes of McGrory and Scarff.

| 1975 | Rangers | | Hampden Park | |
| | | | Glasgow Cup final | 2–2 |

Jim Brogan skippered the team in his final game for the club. He made over 330 appearances, scoring 9 times. He won 7 Championships and 4 Cup winners' medals.

| 1977 | Motherwell | A | Scottish League Premier Division | 2–2 |

Celtic completed their 30th Championship win and their 10th League and Cup 'Double'.

| 1980 | Rangers | | Hampden Park | |
| | | | Scottish Cup final | 1–0 |

George McCluskey deflected a Danny McGrain shot into the net in the first period of extra time to bring Celtic their 26th Cup final victory which was a record at the time. Unfortunately the game will also be remembered for the ugly crowd scenes that followed the final whistle with thousands of fans fighting on the pitch in one of the worst riots seen for many a year; over 200 people were arrested. Both Celtic and Rangers were subsequently fined £20,000 each, even though it was generally accepted that the police strategy for the match had gone wrong; assuming that because there had been no trouble inside the ground, the bulk of the police had been moved to patrol the immediate vicinity outside just before the final whistle blew, with the result that those left inside the ground were inadequate to prevent the pitch invasion.

| 1995 | Hibernian | A | Scottish League | 1–1 |
| 1997 | Dundee United | H | Scottish League Premier Division | 3–0 |

MAY 11TH

| 1897 | Rangers | | Hampden Park | |
| | | | Glasgow Charity Cup final | 1–4 |

John Reynolds scored his only goal for the club on his debut. He was to make just 3 more appearances.

1907	Hearts	A	Scottish League	3–3
1912	Clyde		Hampden Park	
			Glasgow Charity Cup final	0–0
1929	Rangers	A	Glasgow Charity Cup final	2–4
1932	St Mirren	Saltcoats	St Vincent De Paul Cup	4–3
1953	Arsenal		Hampden Park	
			Coronation Cup	1–0

Only a super display by Arsenal goalkeeper Swindin prevented the margin of victory being greater by at least another 5 goals in a super display against the English Champions.

1960	Eric Smith was sold to Leeds United for £11,000. In his 7 years at the club he played 130 games and scored 20 goals.			
1962	Third Lanark	Celtic Park		
			Glasgow Cup final replay	3–2
1963	Dundee United	A	Scottish League	0–3
1965	Queen's Park	A	Glasgow Cup final	5–0
1976	Manchester United	H	Friendly	4–0
1979	St Mirren	A	Scottish League Premier Division	2–0
1985	Dumbarton	H	Scottish League Premier Division	2–0
1991	St Johnstone	A	Scottish League Premier Division	3–2

MAY 12TH

1891	Abercorn	H	Scottish League	2–0
1894	Queen's Park	Ibrox	Glasgow Charity Cup final	2–1
1900	Rangers	Hampden Park		
			Glasgow Charity Cup final	1–5
1914	Third Lanark	Hampden Park		
			Glasgow Charity Cup final	6–0
1917	Rangers	A	Glasgow Charity Cup semi-final	2–0
1925	Tommy McInally rejoined the club after a 3-year spell with Third Lanark.			
1934	Rangers	Hampden Park		
			Glasgow Charity Cup final	0–1
1971	Rangers	Hampden Park		
			Scottish Cup final replay	2–1

2 goals inside a minute by Lou Macari and Harry Hood gave the club its 21st Scottish Cup final success.

1973	Danny McGrain won the 1st of his 62 caps for Scotland in the 2–0 win over Wales in Cardiff.			
1984	Dundee United	H	Scottish League Premier Division	1–1

1987 Just one day short of completing 20 years' service with the club Danny McGrain MBE was given a free transfer by the club. The world-class right-back made over 600 appearances and won 5 Championship medals, 4 Scottish Cup winners' medals and a League Cup winners' medal.

1990	Aberdeen	Hampden Park		
			Scottish Cup final	0–0

For the first time in its history the Scottish FA Cup was decided by a penalty shoot-out. Aberdeen won 9–8.

1991	Republic of Ireland	H	Friendly	3–2
1998	Sporting Lisbon	A	Friendly	1–2

Wim Jansen carried out his threat and left the club after just one season in charge. It was to be a further 10 weeks before a replacement was found.

MAY 13TH

1899	Rangers	A	Glasgow League	1–1
1907	Jimmy Weir signed pro forms with the club.			
1908	Joe Dodds signed from his local team Carluke Milton Rovers.			

1916	Partick Thistle		Hampden Park		
			Glasgow Charity Cup final	2–0
1920	Jimmy McMenemy won his 12th and last cap for Scotland 15 years after he made his debut against the same team, Ireland, in Glasgow.			
1938	Bobby Carroll was born.			
1942	Rangers		Hampden Park		
			Glasgow Charity Cup	1–2
1944	Clyde	H	Glasgow Charity Cup	1–4
1946	Rangers	H	Glasgow Charity Cup semi-final	1–3
1963	Motherwell	H	Scottish League	6–0
1965	Jock Stein took over as part-time manager of Scotland.			
1967	Shortly after his 17th birthday Danny McGrain signed pro forms with the club.			
1982	Rangers	A	Glasgow Cup final	2–1
	Paul McGugan scored in his first appearance for the club.			
1989	St Mirren	A	Scottish League Premier Division	1–0
1995	Dundee United	A	Scottish League	1–0

Phil O'Donnell scored the goal that relegated Dundee United for the first time in 35 years. A brief appearance as substitute marked the end of Charlie Nicholas's career as a Celtic player. Three separate spells at the club by this mercurial player produced over 140 goals in nearly 250 appearances.

MAY 14TH

1883	Davy Adams was born in Oathlaw.			
1892	Leith Athletic	H	Scottish League	2–0
1895	Queen's Park	A	Glasgow Charity Cup semi-final	1–0
1904	Rangers		Hampden Park		
			Glasgow Charity Cup final	2–5
1907	Queen's Park		Cathkin Park		
			Glasgow Charity Cup semi-final	6–2
1921	Rangers		Hampden Park		
			Glasgow Charity Cup final	2–0
1938	Rangers		Hampden Park		
			Glasgow Charity Cup final	2–0
1947	Rangers	A	Glasgow Charity Cup final	0–1
1960	For the friendly against Sparta Rotterdam at Celtic Park (score unknown), Celtic wore numbers for the first time in their history. They were on the shorts.			
1961	Pat Crerand was sent off for Scotland in the 0–4 defeat by Czechoslovakia in Bratislava.			
1978	Packy Bonner was signed by Jock Stein, his last acquisition for the club.			
1979	Hearts	H	Scottish League Premier Division	1–0
1983	Rangers	A	Scottish League Premier Division	4–2
1985	Queen's Park	H	Glasgow Cup semi-final	2–3
1988	Dundee United		Hampden Park		
			Scottish Cup final	2–1

MAY 15TH

| 1890 | Willie Cringan was born. | | | |

1907	Motherwell	H	Scottish League	1–1
1909	Rangers	H	Glasgow Charity Cup final	2–4
1920	Queen's Park	A	Glasgow Charity Cup final	1–0
1926	Queen's Park	Ibrox	Glasgow Charity Cup final	2–1
1937	Queen's Park	A	Glasgow Charity Cup final	4–3
1943	Clyde	H	Glasgow Charity Cup semi-final	3–1
1963	Rangers	Hampden Park		
			Scottish Cup final replay	0–3
1967	Kilmarnock	H	Scottish League	2–0

The final match of the domestic season saw Celtic claim their first 'Treble' of the League, Scottish Cup and League Cup.

1982	St Mirren	H	Scottish League Premier Division	3–0

1987 Gerry Creaney signed pro forms. Mark McNally also signed pro forms shortly after his 16th birthday.

1993	Dundee	H	Scottish League Premier Division	2–0
1994	Manchester United	A	Mark Hughes testimonial	3–1

MAY 16TH

1896	Queen's Park	Ibrox	Glasgow Charity Cup final	2–1
1903	Hibernian	Cathkin Park		
			Glasgow Charity Cup semi-final	0–0

'Sunny Jim' Young made his debut.

1953	Manchester United	Hampden Park		
			Coronation Cup semi-final	2–1
1979	Rangers	A	Glasgow Cup final	1–3

MAY 17TH

1905	Queen's Park	Cathkin Park		
			Glasgow Charity Cup semi-final	3–0

1966 Jock Stein was voted Britain's Manager of the Year.

1992 Gordon Marshall kept a clean sheet on his international debut as Scotland beat the USA 1–0 in Mile High Stadium, Denver.

1994 Gary Gillespie given a free transfer to ease the wage bill. He made just over 80 appearances for the club. Dariusz Wdowczyk was also given a free transfer and he was to join Mark McGee at Reading. The left-back had played nearly 150 games for the club.

MAY 18TH

1893	Third Lanark	A	Scottish League	2–5

1905 Jimmy McMenemy made his international debut against Ireland in the 3–0 victory in Glasgow.

1907	Rangers	Cathkin Park		
			Glasgow Charity Cup final	0–1
1918	Third Lanark	Hampden Park		
			Glasgow Charity Cup semi-final	2–1
1940	Third Lanark	H	Glasgow Charity Cup	3–2

| 1946 | Raith Rovers | A | Victory Cup | 2–0 |

1961 Bertie Peacock left the club after 12 years to take over as player-manager at his home town club Coleraine. He had made nearly 500 appearances for the club, scoring over 50 goals. He won 1 Championship medal and 1 Scottish Cup winners' medal as well as 2 Scottish League Cup winners' medals. He later went on to manage Coleraine and became Northern Ireland manager in 1962.

| 1985 | Dundee United | | Hampden Park | |
| | | | Scottish Cup final | 2–1 |

1991 Paul Elliott was named Scottish Players Player of the Year.

| 1997 | Republic Of Ireland XI | A | Pat Bonner testimonial | 2–3 |

MAY 19TH

| 1902 | Hearts | H | Glasgow Charity Cup | 3–1 |

Davie Hamilton scored on his debut.

| 1917 | Queen's Park | A | Glasgow Charity Cup final | 1–0 |
| 1957 | Spurs | New York | Friendly | 3–4 |

1981 Tommy Burns made his international debut for Scotland in the 2–0 victory over Northern Ireland at Hampden.

| 1984 | Aberdeen | | Hampden Park | |
| | | | Scottish Cup final | 1–2 |

MAY 20TH

| 1899 | Queen's Park | | Cathkin Park | |
| | | | Glasgow Charity Cup semi-final | 4–0 |

1942 Willie Miller signed for the club.

| 1953 | Hibernian | | Hampden Park | |
| | | | Coronation Cup final | 2–0 |

1954 Scotland's World Cup squad was announced and Evans, Fernie and Mochan were included.

1960 After 16 years' fantastic service Bobby Evans left the club for Chelsea for a reputed £12,500. He made over 550 senior appearances for the club, winning a Championship medal, and 2 Scottish Cup and 2 League Cup winners' medals as well as being remembered for being the hero of the Coronation Cup win. He is also the 3rd most capped Celt behind McGrain and McStay.

1987 David Hay made his last signing when he bought Mick McCarthy from Manchester City for £450,000.

| 1989 | Rangers | | Hampden Park | |
| | | | Scottish Cup final | 1–0 |

MAY 21ST

| 1903 | Hibernian | A | Glasgow Charity Cup semi-final replay | 5–0 |

1921 Joe Dodds rejoined the club for a second time from Cowdenbeath.

1938 Frank Murphy scored on his international debut in Scotland's 3–1 victory over Holland in Amsterdam.

| 1941 | Queen's Park | A | Glasgow Charity Cup | 5–2 |
| 1945 | Rangers | N | Glasgow Charity Cup final | 1–2 |

1966	Spurs	Toronto	Friendly	1–0
1970	Eintracht Frankfurt	Randalls Island		
			USA Tour	1–3
1979	Rangers	H	Scottish League Premier Division	4–2

MAY 22ND

| 1940 | Rangers | A | Glasgow Charity Cup | 1–5 |

There was not much charity in evidence during the match with Celtic, with one man from each side being sent off and after the game five players being suspended for one month, to commence at the start of the following season!

| 1943 | Third Lanark | N | Glasgow Charity Cup final | 3–0 |

1991 Four years after his second appointment as manager Billy McNeill is dismissed as manager.

| 1994 | Hearts | Ontario | Hamilton Cup | 1–1 |

MAY 23RD

1891	Third Lanark	Ibrox	Glasgow Charity Cup	8–1
1901	Third Lanark	Exhibition Ground		
			Glasgow Charity Cup final replay	0–3
1903	St Mirren	Ibrox	Glasgow Charity Cup final	5–2

1981 Packy Bonner made his international debut as Republic of Ireland lost 0–3 to Poland in Bydgoszcz.

| 1993 | Jersey Scottish | A | Friendly | 4–0 |

MAY 24TH

1892	Third Lanark	A	Scottish League	3–1
1894	Rangers	H	Friendly	1–1
1919	Queen's Park	A	Glasgow Charity Cup	1–3
1941	Partick Thistle	H	Glasgow Charity Cup semi-final	1–2

1960 'Packy' Bonner was born in Clochglas, Co Donegal.

1972 Lou Macari made his international debut for Scotland in the 1–0 victory over Wales at Hampden.

MAY 25TH

1895	Rangers	Cathkin Park		
			Glasgow Charity Cup final	4–0
1918	Partick Thistle	Hampden Park		
			Glasgow Charity Cup final	2–0
1922	Slavia Prague	A	Friendly	2–3
1938	Sunderland	Ibrox	Empire Exhibition Trophy	0–0

1954 Willie Fernie made his international debut for Scotland in the 2–1 victory over Finland in Helsinki.

| 1967 | Internazionale | Lisbon | European Cup final | 2–1 |

Celtic completed the greatest season in their illustrious history, after winning all 3 domestic trophies and the Glasgow Cup, by becoming the first British team to win the European Cup. Despite going a goal down, Tommy Gemmell and Steve Chalmers, who got the winner with 5 minutes to go, secured the trophy and the greatest night in the club's history.

1992   Jock Morrison died aged 83.

MAY 26TH

1938	Sunderland	Ibrox	Empire Exhibition Trophy replay	3–1
1945	Albion Rovers	A	Summer Cup	1–1

1993   Paul Byrne was signed from Bangor for £70,000.

1996	Republic Of Ireland	A	Mick McCarthy testimonial	0–3

MAY 27TH

1899	Rangers	Hampden Park		
			Glasgow Charity Cup final	2–0
1902	Third Lanark	A	Glasgow Charity Cup semi-final	5–0
1905	Partick Thistle	Ibrox	Glasgow Charity Cup final	2–0

1959   Bertie Auld won the first of his 3 international caps for Scotland in the 2–1 win over Holland in Amsterdam.

1969   John Mallen died aged 42 in Glasgow.

1989   Peter Grant made his international debut coming on as a substitute in Scotland's 0–2 defeat by England at Hampden.

1993   Simon Donnelly signed pro forms after spending a short time on the ground staff at Parkhead.

1995   Airdrie   Hampden Park

                        Scottish Cup final   1–0

After a 6-year barren spell Celtic won the Scottish Cup thanks to a goal by Dutchman Pierre Van Hooijdonk. Rudi Vata became the first Albanian to play in a Scottish Cup final.

MAY 28TH

1888   Rangers Swifts   H   Friendly (Inaugural Match)   5–2

This was the first ever game to be played in the club's illustrious history. It was witnessed by nearly 2000 people and the was first of many Old Firm derby matches. Rangers appeared to field an under-strength team for the game. The Celtic line-up on this historic occasion was Dolan, Pearson, McLaughlin, Willie Maley, Kelly, Murray, McCallum, Tom Maley, Madden, Dunbar, Gorevin. Reports suggest that Tom Maley scored three of the goals, although there is no confirmation of the third goal, with Kelly scoring one and Neil McCallum having the honour of scoring Celtic's first ever goal, after 10 minutes. After the match both teams and officials retired to the nearby St Mary's Hall to enjoy supper and a concert and toast their opponents' health. Indeed, relations between the two sides in these early days were extremely good, with little indication of what would happen in the future.

1949   Bertie Peacock was signed from Glentoran.

1978   Ironically, 90 years to the day since the club's first ever game, Jock Stein resigned from the manager's job after leading Celtic to their most successful period – one that is unlikely ever to be matched again. He won 10 Championships, including the 9 in a row of 1965–66 to 1973–74, 8 Scottish Cups and 6 League Cups and of course the

European Cup, bringing the total to 25 trophies at an average of 2 per season.

Sean 'Iron Man' Fallon also left the club. After a distinguished playing career for Celtic, Sean spent over 14 years in various capacities at the club from first-team coach, manager, assistant manger, acting manager, chief scout (he was responsible for finding great talent like Gemmell, Hay, Dalglish and Bonner to name just a few).

1987 After being asked to resign and subsequently refusing, David Hay officially became the first Celtic manager to be sacked. Billy McNeill was appointed as manager for the second time in 9 years. At the press conference he just said: 'I always knew I would return!'

MAY 29TH

1943	Motherwell	A	Summer Cup	2–2

1978 Billy McNeill returned to the club as manager in succession to Jock Stein. John Clark was appointed assistant manager at Celtic after spending the previous 5 months in the same position at Aberdeen.

1990 Martin Hayes was signed from Arsenal for £625,000.

1994	Aberdeen	Ontario	Hamilton Cup	1–0

MAY 30TH

1891	Third Lanark	H	Glasgow Charity Cup	6–1
1908	Queen's Park	A	Glasgow Charity Cup final	3–0
1942	Partick Thistle	H	Summer Cup	2–1
1950	Lazio	A	Friendly	0–0

Pat McAuley played his last game for the club after 10 years' service. He played in over 220 matches during and after the war, scoring 27 goals.

1989	Liverpool	H	Friendly	0–4

MAY 31ST

1902	Hibernian	Hampden Park		
			Glasgow Charity Cup final	2–6
1931	Fall River	USA Tour		
			Friendly	0–1

1998 Craig Brown named his World Cup squad of 22 and 7 Celtic players were included: Tosh McKinlay, Craig Burley, Paul Lambert, Darren Jackson, Simon Donnelly, Tommy Boyd and Jonathan Gould, who came in to replace Andy Goram who decided not to go to France for personal reasons.

JUNE 1ST

1892	Rangers	H	Glasgow Charity Cup final	2–0

The very first cup final meeting between Rangers and Celtic attracted a crowd of 8,000 to Celtic Park to see the two sides who were already beginning to take over from Queen's Park as Scotland's biggest clubs. Up until this point, therefore, Celtic had won every cup tie they had played against Rangers, to continue a depressing run for the men from Ibrox.

1946	Rangers	Hampden Park		
			Victory Cup semi-final	0–0

The clash between the two traditional rivals of Scottish football attracted a crowd of 90,000 to Hampden Park for the semi-final of the Victory Cup, although there were no goals to cheer as both sides cancelled each other out.

| 1957 | Tottenham Hotspur | Vancouver | Friendly | 3–6 |

1958 Bobby Collins scored both goals as Scotland beat Poland in Warsaw.

| 1966 | Tottenham Hotspur | San Fransisco | Friendly | 2–1 |

JUNE 2ND

| 1945 | Albion Rovers | H | Summer Cup | 4–2 |

JUNE 3RD

1878 Peter Somers was born in Avondale.

| 1938 | Hearts | Ibrox | Empire Exhibition Trophy semi-final | 1–0 |

1976 Sean Fallon was given the job as Head of Youth Development.

JUNE 4TH

| 1906 | Southampton | Budapest Friendly | 1–0 |

1933 Alec Byrne was born in Greenock.

1949 Lou Macari was born in Edinburgh.

1977 Kenny Dalglish scored the winning goal as Scotland beat England 2–1 at Wembley, clinching the Home International Championship for the 2nd year running. Danny McGrain also played.

JUNE 5TH

1900 William Loney signed pro forms.

| 1943 | Motherwell | H | Summer Cup | 3–2 |

1944 Jim Brogan was born.

| 1946 | Rangers | Hampden Park | Victory Cup semi-final | 0–2 |

1965 Joe McBride was signed from Motherwell for £22,000.

1975 Roy Aitken signed pro forms.

1979 Ronny Glavin was sold to Barnsley. The attacking midfielder played just under 150 games for the club, scoring a respectable 48 goals.

1994 Packy Bonner became the most capped player for the Republic of Ireland when he won his 73rd cap in the 3–1 defeat by the Czech Republic at Lansdowne Road.

JUNE 6TH

1902 Jimmy McMenemy signed pro forms with the club.

| 1942 | Partick Thistle | A | Summer Cup | 2–0 |

1991 Lex Baillie sold to St Mirren for £90,000 after making 33 appearances for Celtic in just over 9 years.

JUNE 7TH

| 1941 | Hibernian | H | Summer Cup | 2–5 |

1975   Jock Stein turned down the offer to take over the job as permanent manager of the Scotland national team.

1980   Paul McStay scored 2 goals as Scotland schoolboys beat England 5–4 at Wembley.

JUNE 8TH

| 1941 | Hibernian | H | Summer Cup | 2–5 |
| 1957 | Spurs | Toronto | Friendly | 1–3 |

1994   Former player, chief scout and coach John Higgins died aged 61.

JUNE 9TH

| 1957 | Spurs | Montreal | Friendly | 2–0 |

The fourth and final meeting with Celtic on the tour of North America saw Celtic win for the only time. A crowd of 8,500 saw 2 goals from Neil Mochan in the second half give Celtic some compensation for their previous efforts.

1975   Jimmy Johnstone was sensationally given a free transfer by the club after 14 years at the club. 'Jinky' had made over 500 appearances for Celtic, scoring 130 goals. He had won 9 Championship medals and 5 Scottish Cup and 5 League Cup winners' medals along with a European Cup winners' medal. Surprisingly, he won only 23 caps for Scotland.

JUNE 10TH

1891	Dumbarton	Ibrox	Glasgow Charity Cup	0–3
1921	Jimmy McGrory signed pro forms with the club.			
1938	Everton	Ibrox	Empire Exhibition Trophy final	1–0

1993   Ex-player and crowd favourite Tom McAdam rejoined the club and took up a position on the coaching staff.

1998   Scotland unluckily lost to Brazil in the opening game of the World Cup 1–2. Darren Jackson became the first player in the tournament to get booked and the unfortunate Tommy Boyd was the last player to touch the ball for the Brazilian decider even though he could do nothing about it. Ex-Celtic player John Collins scored Scotland's goal from the penalty spot.

JUNE 11TH

1865   John Madden was born in Dumbarton.

1958   Bobby Collins scored one of Scotland's goals in the 2–3 defeat by Paraguay in the World Cup match in Norrkoping, Sweden, Bobby Evans and Willie Fernie also played in the game. Bertie Peacock played in Northern Ireland's 1–3 defeat by Argentina in the World Cup match in Halmstad.

JUNE 12TH

1935   Chic Napier was sold to Derby County for a fee of around £5000. He had made over 200 appearances scoring 90 goals in his 7 years at the club. Contract negotiations forced him to hand in a transfer request which prematurely ended his time at the Club. He won 2 Scottish Cup winners' medals in 1931 and 1933.

1943	Rangers	N	Summer Cup	0–4
1966	Atlas (Mexico)	Los Angeles		
			Friendly	1–0

CLOCKWISE FROM TOP LEFT: Jimmy
McGrory; Bertie Auld; Willie McStay;
Tommy Gemmell

A selection of Celtic shields and badges

ABOVE: Alec McNair
RIGHT: A Celtic shield

ABOVE: Programme from the 1972 Scottish Cup final between Celtic and Hibernian, which Celtic won 6–1

RIGHT: Programme from the 1973 League Cup semi-final between Celtic and Rangers, which Celtic won 3–1

ABOVE: The Celtic team which won the
European Cup in Lisbon in 1967

LEFT: Jimmy McGrory was the greatest
goalscorer in the history of Scottish
football. He scored over 550 goals during
his career

Danny McGrain, one of the best left-backs the world
has ever seen

Roy Aitken, who played a major midfield role for Celtic
in the 1980s

TOP: David Hay was a key player in Jock Stein's teams of the early 1970s. Hay became Celtic's manager during the 1980s

RIGHT: Pat Bonner was a record-breaking goalkeeper for Celtic and the Republic of Ireland

1971   John Clark was sold to Morton.

1985   Frank McGarvey was sold to St Mirren for the lowly sum of £70,000. He had made 245 appearances for the club, scoring 113 goals. He also won 5 Scottish caps in his 5 years at Parkhead. He won back to back Championship medals in 1981 and 1982 as well as Scottish Cup winners' medals in 1980 and 1985 where he scored the winning goal.

1991   Eric Smith died aged 66 in Dubai.

1998   Marc Rieper scored the only goal in Denmark's 1–0 victory over Saudi Arabia in the opening game of their World Cup group.

JUNE 13TH

1942   Motherwell   H   Summer Cup   1–2
Frank Murphy played his last game for the club after 13 years' service. He played in nearly 250 first-class games, scoring over 70 goals and winning 2 Championship medals and 1 Scottish Cup winners' medal.

1994   Andy Walker rejoined the club after a two-year spell at Bolton. A tribunal fixed the fee at £550,000 a few weeks later after Bolton had asked for over £2.2 million.

JUNE 14TH

1901   Alec Thomson was born.

1941   Hibernian   A   Summer Cup   1–0

1994   Lou Macari sacked as manager for alleged lack of responsibility in his duties after barely 8 months in the job.

JUNE 15TH

1977   Kenny Dalglish and Danny McGrain played in Scotland's 4–2 victory over Chile in Santiago.

1989   Mike Galloway was signed from Hearts for £500,000.

JUNE 16TH

1934   Alex Thomson joined Dunfermline Athletic on a free transfer.

1987   Murdo MacLeod was sold to Borussia Dortmund after 9 years at the club. He played just 9 short of 400 games for the club, scoring 81 goals. He won 4 Championship medals, 2 Scottish Cup winners' medals and 1 League Cup winners' medal.

1998   Craig Burley scored the equaliser for Scotland in the 1–1 draw with Norway to keep the nation's hopes alive of qualifying for round 2 of the World Cup.

JUNE 17TH

1902   Rangers   Cathkin Park
                              British League Cup final   3–2
Immediately following the Ibrox disaster of April 1902, donations had flooded into the club from all around Britain (and beyond) for the benefit of the dependants of those who were killed. Rangers decided to organise a charity competition between the champions and runners-up of both Scotland and England and donated the Glasgow International Exhibition Cup, won the previous September, as the trophy on offer. With Rangers and Celtic representing Scotland and Everton and Sunderland England,

the competition was inevitably billed as the British League Cup. Rangers overcame Everton after a replay to take their place in the final, whilst Celtic saw off Sunderland to take theirs. The final itself was delayed owing to the coronation of King Edward VII, but on June 17th Celtic and Rangers came out at Cathkin Park to be greeted by a crowd of 16,000. The final went to extra time before Jimmy Quinn completed his hat-trick for Celtic and thus won the cup for where the trophy can still be found in the trophy room at Parkhead.

1953   Patsy Gallagher died in Scotstoun aged 63.

1976   John 'Dixie' Deans was sold to Luton Town. He made 184 appearances for the club scoring an incredible 124 goals in that time to have one of the highest goal per game ratios in the history of the club.

JUNE 18TH

1895   Tully Craig born in Falkirk. After an unsuccessful trial with Everton he joined Celtic in June 1919 and spent three years at Celtic Park without being given much of a run in the side. After a brief spell on loan with Clyde he joined Alloa in 1922, apparently being released by Celtic because they thought he was too slight to survive in the top division. He joined Rangers in 1923.

1967   Willie Fernie was appointed coach.

1987   Charlie Nicholas signed pro forms for the club a few months before his 18th birthday.

JUNE 19TH

1965   George Connelly was signed on full pro forms.

1943   Rangers   A   Summer Cup   1–4

JUNE 20TH

1873   Willie Orr was born.

1920   After 18 years' service Jimmy McMenemy was granted a free transfer. 'Napoleon' as he was nicknamed had made well over 500 appearances for the club, scoring 168 goals. He guided the club to an amazing 11 Championship wins and 6 Scottish Cup wins, which could have been more had the competition been held during the war, as well as winning 12 Scottish caps.

1929   John McFarlane left the club for Middlesbrough. The artistic left-half played just over 300 games for the club, scoring 13 goals. He helped the club to 2 Championships and 3 Scottish Cup wins.

1942   Motherwell   A   Summer Cup   1–2
        Johnny Crum scored in his last game for the club. Altogether he played over 270 games and scored 111 goals.

1970   Chic Geatons died at Lochgelly (his birthplace), aged 63.

1983   Brian McClair was signed from Motherwell for £75,000.

JUNE 21ST

1925   Andrew Young was born in Fife.

1985   Chairman Desmond White died whilst on a family holiday aged 73.

JUNE 22ND

1982 Danny McGrain came on as sub for Scotland in the World Cup game in Malaga which ended 2–2. It was his 62nd and last appearance for his country.

1983 Charlie Nicholas was sold to Arsenal for £650,000. He turned down a move to Anfield, where he had been much sought after, in favour of the bright lights of London.

JUNE 23RD

1940 Willie Wallace was born.

1945 Hibernian   Tynecastle
                         Summer Cup semi-final   0–2

1965 Jimmy McMenemy died aged 85.

1998 Craig Burley was sent off for Scotland in the 3–0 defeat by Morocco in the final game of the World Cup group in St Etienne. The result meant that Scotland failed to qualify for the 2nd round.

JUNE 24TH

1994 Packy Bonner won his 75th cap as Ireland lost 2–1 to Mexico in Orlando in the last match of their World Cup group. The game will be remembered for the argument Jack Charlton had trying to make a substitution, later being fined and banned.

JUNE 25TH

1966 Steve Chalmers scored Scotland's goal against the mighty Brazil at Hampden Park in the 1–1 draw. At the end of the game he managed to swap shirts with Pele. John Clark also played in the match.

JUNE 26TH

1901 Alex Crawford joined the club from Clyde.

1905 R.G. Campbell signed from Queen's Park.

JUNE 27TH

1946 David Cattanach was born in Falkirk.

JUNE 28TH

1961 Ian Young signed for the club.

1983 Dominic Sullivan was given a free transfer. He had played 113 games for the club and scored 15 goals.

1998 Marc Rieper played for Denmark in their 2nd round 4–1 victory over Nigeria in the World Cup. He also received a yellow card.

JUNE 29TH

1973 Adam McLean died aged 74.

JUNE 30TH

1983 Billy McNeill left Parkhead to take over as manager of Manchester City.

JULY 1ST

1952   Frank Meechan signed for the club.

1987   After nearly 3 years at the club. Mo Johnstone was sold to French club Nantes for £373,500. He made 127 appearances and scored 71 goals. Brian McClair was sold to Manchester United for £850,000 (fee decided by tribunal later in the month). He had made just one short of the 200 mark, scoring 120 goals. Andy Walker arrived from Motherwell as McClair's replacement. Davie Provan decided to retire as a player through illness. He was later diagnosed as having ME, but took over the U-18 team as coach at Parkhead. He made just over 300 appearances for the club, scoring on 42 occasions. He won 4 Championship medals, 2 Scottish Cup winners' medals and 1 League Cup winners' medal.

JULY 2ND

1888   Andy McAtee was born in Cumberland.

1987   Willie Stark was signed from Aberdeen.

JULY 3RD

1974   David Hay was sold to Chelsea for £225,000.

1989   Paul Elliott was signed from Italian club Pisa.

JULY 4TH

1983   David Hay was appointed manager following Billy McNeill's departure.

1994   Packy Bonner made a very uncharacteristic mistake for the second goal for the Republic against Holland in Orlando, which proved to be his last World Cup game.

JULY 5TH

1983   John Clark was dismissed as assistant manager after 5 years in the job.

1997   FC Beatrix   A   Dutch Tour   21–0

JULY 6TH

1888   Peter Johnstone was born in Fife.

1969   John Crum died in Hyndland aged 57.

1990   Charlie Nicholas rejoined the club from Aberdeen.

JULY 7TH

1956   John Divers signed pro forms.

1981   Roddie Macdonald was sold to Hearts for £55,000. He played over 250 games for the club and scored an impressive total of 35 goals as centre-half. In his 9 years' service, he helped the club to 3 Championship wins and a Scottish Cup win.

1992   Stuart Gray signed professional terms with the club.

JULY 8TH

1878   Jimmy Quinn was born in Croy.

1987   Chris Morris was signed from Sheffield Wednesday for £100,000.

1991   Paul Elliott was sold to Chelsea for £1.4 million after just two years at Parkhead. After just being voted Scotland's Players' Player of the Year, the popular Londoner wanted to return home after spending nearly 6 years away. He made 66 appearances for the club.

| 1997 | SV Veere | A | Dutch Tour | 8–0 |

JULY 9TH

| 1997 | FC Groningen | A | Dutch Tour | 0–3 |

JULY 10TH

1989 Mark McGhee was sold to Newcastle United. He made 113 appearances but scored only 34 goals in his brief 4 years with the club.

1991 Brian O'Neil rejoined the club after a brief spell in New Zealand.

JULY 11TH

1924 Charlie Tully was born in Belfast.

1931 Jerry Sollis, possibly the only Jewish player to play for the club, signed pro forms.

JULY 12TH

1907 Bertie Thomson was born in Johnstone.

1994 One day after resigning as Kilmarnock player-manager, Tommy Burns was appointed as the new Celtic manager following the departure of Lou Macari. Ex-player Willie Stark was named as Burns' assistant manager.

JULY 13TH

1993 Steve Fullerton was sold to Bolton for £300,000. The stylish midfielder had made just under 100 appearances for the club, scoring 6 goals.

JULY 14TH

1887 Joe Dodds was born in Carluke.

1937 Dunky Mackay was born in Springburn.

| 1951 | Hearts | H | St Mungo Cup | 2–1 |

1975 Peter Latchford was signed from West Brom.

1989 Jackie Dziekanowski was signed from Polish club Legia Warsaw.

JULY 15TH

1956 Andy McAtee died in Condorrat aged 68.

1958 Former Celtic centre-half Alec Boden was appointed coach. In 1967 he was working as scout and coach for the youths, and recommended that Celtic keep tabs on a fine young player named Kenny Dalglish.

| 1997 | Derry City | A | Irish International Club Tournament | 2–3 |

JULY 16TH

1907 Chic Geatons was born in Lochgelly.

1927 Bobby Evans was born in Glasgow.

| 1997 | PSV Eindhoven | A | Irish International Club Tournament | 2–2 |

JULY 17TH

1964   Paul McGugan was born in Glasgow.

1992   League of Ireland Select   A   Bord Gais Tournament   5–0

1998   After nearly ten weeks of searching for a replacement for Wim Jansen, the club announced that Dr Jozef Venglos would take control of the team. However, he could not officially start because a work permit had still to be obtained. It had been widely tipped that Gerard Houllier would be taking over but instead the Frenchman surprisingly joined the staff at Liverpool.

Venglos, who was working as a technical director to Slovan Bratislava, was no stranger to British football. He managed Aston Villa in season 1990–91 and guided them to 17th place. Let's hope he has more success at Parkhead.

JULY 18TH

1997   St Patrick's Athletic   A   Friendly   1–1

1998   Kilmarnock   A   Friendly   2–1

JULY 19TH

1916   Willie McStay re-signed for the club after a loan period at Ayr United.

1951   Clyde   Firhill Park
                                St Mungo Cup   4–4

1989   Rheydter   A   German Tour   0–0

1991   Tony Cascarino was signed from Aston Villa for £1.1 million as one of Liam Brady's first signings for the club.

1992   Man City   A   Bord Gais Tournament   3–1

1994   Packy Bonner was re-signed by Tommy Burns.

JULY 20TH

1951   Clyde   Firhill Park
                                St Mungo Cup   4–1

1987   Alan McInally was sold to Aston Villa. He scored 22 goals in 85 appearances for the club.

1994   Carl Muggleton was sold to Stoke City for £200,000, he made just 13 appearances. Tommy Burns re-signed Charlie Nicholas a week after taking over as manager, for Charlie's 3rd period at the club.

1991   Shelbourne   A   Irish Tour   3–0

1995   VFB Lubeck   A   German Tour   2–1

JULY 21ST

1966   Lou Macari signed pro forms.

1989   Kickers Offenbach   A   German Tour   0–0

1992   Cork City   A   Irish Tour   2–0

JULY 22ND

1974   George McCluskey signed pro forms.

1989   Borussia   A   German Tour   1–4
           Monchengladbach

JULY 23RD

1944	Bobby Evans signed pro forms.			
1945	After 5 years in the job Jimmy McStay was dismissed as manger.			
1949	Joe Cassidy died aged 53.			
1991	Cork City	A	Irish Tour	0–2
1992	University College Dublin	A	Irish Tour	1–0
1995	Kickers Emden	A	German Tour	0–2
1996	Reuni Borculi	A	Dutch Tour	16–0
1997	Cable Tel	A	UEFA QP 1st round 1st leg	3–0

JULY 24TH

1945	Jimmy McGrory named manager.			
1989	Hohenlinberg	A	German Tour	2–4
1993	Atalanta	A	Gianni Brera Tournament	0–3
1996	SV Gouda	A	Dutch Tour	8–0

JULY 25TH

1903	Dan Mcarthur joined Clyde. Possibly Celtic's bravest goalkeeper left after 11 years' service during which he played 120 times, a figure that would have been far higher if not for his injuries.			
1995	Wilhelmshaven	A	German Tour	1–2

JULY 26TH

1914	John Mulrooney sadly died aged just 28. The former Celtic goalkeeper had made 51 appearances for the club before the war.			
1948	Tommy Docherty signed for the club just 14 days after being demobbed from Palestine.			
1957	Michael Jackson decided against joining Manchester United and instead signed for his hometown club.			
1983	George McCluskey was sold to Leeds United for £161,000 (the fee fixed by tribunal). He made just over 200 appearances for the club, scoring 78 goals.			
1991	Dundalk	A	Irish Tour	0–0
1992	Middlesbrough	A	Tony Mowbray testimonial	1–1
1993	Napoli	A	Gianni Brera Tournament	1–3
1994	Cork City	A	Friendly	3–2
1995	St Pauli	A	German Tour	0–0
1996	SV Veere	A	Dutch Tour	9–1
1997	Parma	H	Friendly	1–1

JULY 27TH

1911	Jimmy 'Dun' Hay was sold to Newcastle United for £1,250. Hay had made over 250 appearances and scored 17 goals in his 8 years at the club.			
1971	Charlie Tully died shortly after his 47th birthday in his hometown, Belfast.			
1974	Airdrie	A	Dryborough Cup	4–2
1980	Ayr United	H	Dryborough Cup	0–1

1982   Peter Grant signed pro forms.
1996   SC Halsteren   A   Dutch Tour   3–0

JULY 28TH

1951   Raith Rovers   Hampden Park
                                            St Mungo Cup   3–1
1973   Dunfermline Athletic   H   Dryborough Cup   6–1
        Stephen Murray made his debut.
1991   Shamrock Rovers   A   Irish Tour   2–0
1993   Joe Miller was sold back to Aberdeen to help finance the deal to bring Pat McGinlay
        to the club from Hibs. The right-winger had made nearly 200 appearances in his 6
        years at the club, scoring over 30 goals.
1995   Andreas Thom signed from Bayer Leverkusen for a club record fee of £2.2 million.

JULY 29TH

1934   Eric Smith was born in Glasgow
1940   Patrick McAuley joined the club for the first time.
1972   Dumbarton   H   Dryborough Cup   2–1
1994   Flamengo   Ireland   Friendly   1–1
1995   Birmingham City   A   Friendly   0–1
1996   SC Berkum   A   Dutch Tour   8–1
1997   Cable Tel   H   UEFA QP 1st round 2nd leg   5–0

JULY 30TH

1946   John 'Dixie' Deans was born in Linwood.
1979   Clydebank   H   Dryborough Cup   5–0
1989   Buckie Thistle   A   Highland Tour   3–0
1991   Arsenal   A   Paul Davis testimonial   2–2
1993   Pat McGinlay was signed from Hibernian for a fee of £525,000.

JULY 31ST

1922   Sean Fallon was born in Sligo.
1961   Billy Price was signed for £1000 from Falkirk to cover for the suspended Pat Crerand.
1971   Dumbarton   H   Dryborough Cup   5–2
1973   Dundee   H   Dryborough Cup semi-final   4–0
1974   Dundee   A   Dryborough Cup semi-final   2–1
1993   Sheff Wed   H   Friendly   1–1
1996   Arsenal   H   Friendly   2–1

AUGUST 1ST

1888   Abercorn   Exhibition Ground
                                            Exhibition Cup   1–1
1950   Willie Miller joined Clyde. One of the bravest goalkeepers in the history of the club,
        he had made 123 appearances in the 8 years at the club. He won 6 Scotland Caps.
1951   Aberdeen   Hampden Park
                                            St Mungo Cup final   3–2

1979	Dundee United	H	Dryborough Cup semi-final	3–2
1987	Arsenal	H	Friendly	1–5
1989	Inverness Caley	A	Highland Tour	3–0
1992	Hearts	A	Scottish League Premier Division	1–0
1995	Everton	A	Neville Southall testimonial	2–2

John Collins scored 2 goals in front of a 21,000 crowd, who ensured a good pay day for the popular Welsh goalkeeper.

AUGUST 2ND

| 1966 | Rangers | A | Glasgow Cup | 4–0 |

Bobby Lennox scored a hat-trick in front of 76,000 people. Celtic were to go on and win the remaining games in the competition all by the same 4–0 scoreline.

1972	Aberdeen	H	Dryborough Cup semi-final	3–2
1973	Penarol	H	Friendly	3–1
1975	Derby County	H	Friendly	1–0
1986	Aston Villa	H	Friendly	1–0
1994	Flamengo	H	Friendly	2–2

AUGUST 3RD

1968	Leeds United	H	Friendly	1–2
1974	Kilmarnock	H	Scottish League	5–0
1975	Rangers	Hampden Park	Dryborough Cup final	2–2

A crowd of 57,558 poured into Hampden Park for this Dryborough Cup final clash between Celtic and Rangers. The two rivals fought out a battling 2–2 draw, which Celtic won 4–2 on penalties.

1978	Clyde	H	Anglo Scottish Cup 1st round 1st leg	2–1
1993	Manchester United	A	25th anniversary of European Cup win	0–1
1996	Sporting Lisbon	H	Opening of East Stand	2–2
1997	Hibernian	A	Scottish League Premier Division	1–2

AUGUST 4TH

1970	Manchester City	H	Friendly	0–0
1971	St Johnstone	Firhill Park	Dryborough Cup semi-final	4–2
1973	Hibernian	Hampden Park	Dryborough Cup final	0–1
1975	Clyde	A	Glasgow Cup semi-final	2–1
1979	Rangers	Hampden Park	Dryborough Cup final	1–3
1980	Manchester United	H	Danny McGrain testimonial	0–0

Over 45,000 fans turned out for the testimonial of one of the club's greatest servants.

1984	Arsenal	H	Friendly	3–2
1990	Kickers Emden	A	German/ Dutch Tour	2–2
1991	Tottenham Hotspur	H	Friendly	1–0

1963	Hoops beat the Whites 8–0 in a public practice match			
1967	Tottenham Hotspur	N	Friendly	3–3
1969	Leeds United	H	Friendly	1–1
1972	Hibernian	Hampden Park		
			Dryborough Cup final	3–5
1972	Roddie Macdonald signed pro forms for the club.			
1978	Clyde	A	Anglo Scottish Cup 1st round 2nd leg	6–1
1989	Dynamo Moscow	H	Friendly	2–2
1990	TSV Verden	A	German/ Dutch Tour	3–1
1991	Dundee	A	Friendly	1–1
1992	Aberdeen	A	Scottish League Premier Division	1–1
1995	Newcastle	H	Opening of North Stand	1–1

AUGUST 6TH

1889	Rangers	A	Rangers & Clydesdale Harriers	12–0
			Sports Cup final	
1966	Manchester United	H	Friendly	4–1
1973	Sunderland	H	Friendly	1–2
1994	Clyde	A	Friendly	1–0
1996	Kosice	A	UEFA Cup qualifying 1st leg	0–0
1997	Roma	H	Friendly	1–0

AUGUST 7TH

1965	Sunderland	A	Friendly	5–0
1971	Aberdeen	A	Dryborough Cup final	1–2
1972	Tottenham Hotspur	H	Friendly	1–0
1976	Penarol	H	Friendly	3–0
1984	Nottingham Forest	H	Friendly	0–0
1988	Cruzeiro	H	Friendly	4–2
1993	Motherwell	A	Scottish League Premier Division	2–2

AUGUST 8TH

1931	Leith Athletic	A	Scottish League	3–0
1936	St Johnstone	H	Scottish League	3–2
1942	Dumbarton	H	League – Southern Division	2–3
1953	Aberdeen	H	League Cup	0–1
1959	Raith Rovers	A	League Cup	1–2
1964	Partick Thistle	H	League Cup	0–0
1970	Hearts	A	League Cup	2–1
1975	'Shuggie' Johannes Edvaldson was signed from Danish team Holbeck.			
1978	Arsenal	H	Friendly	0–3
1979	China	H	Friendly	6–1
1981	St Mirren	H	League Cup	1–3
1987	Morton	A	Scottish League Premier Division	4–0

Chris Morris, Andy Walker and Billy Stark made their debuts in this match. Walker scored twice and Stark once.

1990	Herford Amateur Select	A	German/ Dutch Tour	3–1
1992	Motherwell	H	Scottish League Premier Division	1–1
1994	Blackburn Rovers	H	Friendly	1–0

AUGUST 9TH

1867	Dan McArthur was born.			
1924	Joe Cassidy was sold to Bolton Wanderers for £4,500.			
1930	Kilmarnock	H	Scottish League	3–1
1941	Hearts	A	League – Southern Division	0–3
1947	Rangers	A	League Cup	0–2
1952	St Mirren	A	League Cup	1–0

John MaCdonald scored on his debut for the club.

| 1958 | Clyde | A | League Cup | 4–0 |

Duncan MacKay made his debut for the club.

1969	Airdrie	H	League Cup	6–1
1975	Aberdeen	H	League Cup	1–0
1980	Morton	H	Scottish League Premier Division	2–1
1983	Partick Thistle	A	Glasgow Cup semi-final	2–0
1986	Dundee	H	Scottish League Premier Division	1–0
1987	Liverpool	H	Friendly	0–1
1997	Berwick Rangers	A	League Cup 2nd round	7–0

AUGUST 10TH

1891 Dan Doyle was signed for Celtic from Everton. He had already been nominated as the Toffeemen's captain for the forthcoming season but had decided to take up the offer of playing in the green and white shirt.

| 1895 | Dundee | A | Scottish League | 2–1 |

Barney Battles made his debut.

| 1929 | Hearts | H | Scottish League | 2–1 |
| 1935 | Aberdeen | A | Scottish League | 1–3 |

Willie Lyon made his debut.

1940	Hamilton Academical	H	League – Southern Division	2–2
1946	Morton	H	Scottish League	1–2
1957	Airdrie	H	League Cup	3–2
1963	Rangers	H	League Cup	0–3
1968	Rangers	A	League Cup	2–0
1969	Rangers	Hampden Park		
			Glasgow Cup final	3–1
1974	Motherwell	H	League Cup	2–1
1976	Rangers	H	Glasgow Cup final	3–1

This was the final of the 1969–70 season held over to the start of the following season. Over 58,000 were at Hampden Park to see Celtic win 3–1.

1977 Kenny Dalglish was sold to Liverpool for £440,000, a British transfer record at the time. A winner of 4 Championships, 4 Scottish Cup and a League Cup Winners medal, Dalglish made over 320 appearances for the club, scoring 170 goals. In his time at Liverpool he was to win a further 11 medals, making him one of football's greatest achievers. He went on to make his mark as a manager, winning more trophies on the way.

1985	Hearts	A	Scottish League Premier Division	1–1
1990	TSV Ottersburg	A	German/ Dutch Tour	6–0
1991	Dundee United	A	Scottish League Premier Division	4–3
1993	Stirling Albion	A	League Cup	2–0
1995	Liverpool	H	Homecoming Match	0–0
1996	Aberdeen	A	Scottish League Premier Division	2–2

AUGUST 11TH

1888	Rangers	H	Friendly	1–9
1894	Dundee	A	Scottish League	1–1
1928	Dundee	A	Scottish League	1–0
1934	Kilmarnock	H	Scottish League	4–1
1945	Morton	A	League – 'A' Division	1–1
1951	Third Lanark	H	League Cup	1–1
1956	Aberdeen	A	League Cup	2–1

Billy McPhail made his debut.

1962	Hearts	H	League Cup	3–1

Bobby Murdoch scored on his debut.

1973	Arbroath	H	League Cup	2–1
1979	Morton	H	Scottish League Premier Division	3–2
1984	Hibernian	A	Scottish League Premier Division	0–0

Alan McInally came on as sub to make his debut.

AUGUST 12TH

1893	Third Lanark	H	Scottish League	5–0
1933	Queen of the South	A	Scottish League	2–3
1939	Aberdeen	A	Scottish League	1–3
1944	Hearts	H	League – Southern Division	4–1
1950	East Fife	H	League Cup	2–0
1953	East Fife	A	League Cup	1–1
1959	Partick Thistle	H	League Cup	1–2
1961	Partick Thistle	A	League Cup	3–2
1964	Hearts	A	League Cup	3–0
1967	Dundee United	H	League Cup	1–0
1970	Clyde	H	League Cup	5–3
1972	Stirling Albion	A	League Cup	3–0
1974	Liverpool	H	Friendly	1–1
1978	Morton	A	Scottish League Premier Division	2–1
1981	St Johnstone	A	League Cup	0–2
1982	Graeme Sinclair was bought from Dumbarton for £65,000 as a replacement for Danny McGrain.			
1987	Hearts	H	Scottish League Premier Division	1–0
1989	Hearts	A	Scottish League Premier Division	3–1

Mike Galloway made his debut for the club.

1990	Volendam	A	German/ Dutch Tour	1–1
1992	Stirling Albion	A	League Cup	3–0

1992   Derek Whyte was sold to Middlesbrough. The centre-half made over 270 appearances for the club in 7 years.

1997	Tirol	A	UEFA QP 2nd round 1st leg	1–2

AUGUST 13TH

1925   Alec Boden was born in Hardgate. On his 18th birthday 1943 he signed professional forms with the Club.

1927	Hibernian	H	Scottish League	3–0
1932	Aberdeen	H	Scottish League	3–0
1938	Kilmarnock	H	Scottish League	9–1
1947	Airdrie	A	Scottish League	2–3
1949	Rangers	H	League Cup	3–2

Bobby Collins and Michael Haughney made their debuts with Haughney scoring one of the goals.

1952	Partick Thistle	H	League Cup	2–5
1955	Queen of the South	H	League Cup	4–2
1958	Airdrie	H	League Cup	3–3
1960	Third Lanark	H	League Cup	2–0

John Hughes scored on his debut for the club.

1966	Hearts	A	League Cup	2–0
1969	Rangers	A	League Cup	1–2
1975	Hearts	A	League Cup	0–2
1977	Dundee United	H	Scottish League Premier Division	0–0
1983	Rangers	Hampden Park		
			Glasgow Cup final	0–1
1986	Motherwell	A	Scottish League Premier Division	4–0
1988	Hearts	H	Scottish League Premier Division	1–0
1991	Dunfermline Athletic	A	Scottish League Premier Division	3–1
1994	Falkirk	A	Scottish League	1–1

AUGUST 14TH

1926	Kilmarnock	A	Scottish League	3–2
1937	Queen of the South	A	Scottish League	2–2
1943	Clyde	A	League – Southern Division	2–1
1946	Clyde	A	Scottish League	2–2
1948	Morton	H	Scottish League	0–0

Charlie Tully made his debut.

1954	Falkirk	H	League Cup	3–0
1957	East Fife	A	League Cup	4–1

Sammy Wilson made his debut.

1963	Kilmarnock	A	League Cup	0–0
1965	Dundee United	A	League Cup	1–2
1968	Morton	H	League Cup	4–1
1971	Rangers	H (played at Ibrox)		

				2–0
			League Cup	2–0
1974	Ayr United	A	League Cup	2–3
1976	Dundee United	A	League Cup	1–0
1978	Liverpool	H	Friendly	2–3
1979	Queen's Park	A	Glasgow Cup	3–1

Charlie Nicholas scored on his first senior appearance for the club.

| 1982 | Dunfermline Athletic | H | League Cup | 6–0 |

1992 Liam Brady paid West Ham £1.5 million for Stuart Slater, a club record at the time. Also arriving were Albanian Rudi Vata, who cost £200,000 from Dinamo Tirana, and Andy Payton, who arrived in a swap deal with Chris Morris from Middlesbrough. Morris had played over 200 games for the club in his 5 years there and was a big success for Jack Charlton and the Republic of Ireland.

| 1993 | Hibernian | H | Scottish League Premier Division | 1–1 |
| 1996 | Clyde | A | League Cup | 3–1 |

AUGUST 15TH

1891	Hearts	A	Scottish League	1–3
1896	Hibernian	A	Scottish League	1–3
1900	Partick Thistle	H	Scottish League	3–3
1903	Partick Thistle	H	Scottish League	2–1

Davie Russell made his debut for the club.

Jimmy Hay made his debut.

1907	Hamilton Academical	H	Scottish League	3–0
1908	Morton	A	Scottish League	5–0
1911	Airdrie	H	Scottish League	3–0
1914	Hearts	A	Scottish League	0–2
1921	Raith Rovers	H	Scottish League	4–0
1925	Hibernian	H	Scottish League	5–0
1931	Dundee United	H	Scottish League	3–2
1936	Clyde	A	Scottish League	1–1
1942	Queen's Park	A	League – Southern Division	2–2
1951	Airdrie	A	League Cup	1–1
1953	Airdrie	A	League Cup	1–2
1956	Rangers	H	League Cup	2–1
1959	Airdrie	A	League Cup	2–4
1960	Rangers	H	Glasgow Cup	4–2
1962	Dundee	H	League Cup	0–1
1964	Kilmarnock	H	League Cup	4–1
1970	Dundee United	H	League Cup	2–2
1973	Falkirk	A	League Cup	2–0
1977	Chelsea	H	Friendly	2–2
1981	Hibernian	H	League Cup	4–1
1987	Motherwell	H	Scottish League Premier Division	4–0
1989	Dumbarton	A	League Cup	3–0

1990 Richard Beattie died at the age of 54 in Old Kilpatrick.
1991 Gary Gillespie was signed from Liverpool for £925,000

| 1992 | Dundee United | H | Scottish League Premier Division | 2–0 |

AUGUST 16TH

| 1902 | Hibernian | A | Scottish League | 1–1 |
| 1906 | Rangers | A | Finlay Speedie Benefit Match | 2–4 |

A crowd of 6,000 turned out for the game in honour of Finlay Speedie, who scored twice. Midway through the game Celtic goalkeeper David Adams lacerated his hand on a rough nail at Ibrox and, with the new season just two days away and with Celtic having no adequate cover, Rangers offered them the use of reserve goalkeeper Tom Sinclair! In his six League appearances for Celtic, he kept clean sheets in all of them (his six shut-outs from his debut remained the record for the club until 1994 when Carl Muggleton equalled it); the only goals he conceded were in a benefit match and the Glasgow Cup final, but as Celtic won the latter 3–2 it hardly mattered. When Adams was fit again Sinclair returned to Ibrox, complete with a winners' medal attained whilst representing Celtic. His taste of first-team football at Celtic Park meant he was unhappy to remain a reserve at Ibrox and by March 1907 he had signed for Newcastle and helped them win the League! Nothing he did in his career thereafter ever matched the drama of 1906–07.

| 1913 | Ayr United | H | Scottish League | 5–1 |
| 1919 | Clydebank | H | Scottish League | 3–1 |

Tommy McInally made his debut for the club and scored all 3 goals.

1922	Rangers	H	Willie McStay Benefit Match	3–1
1923	Rangers	H	Adam McLean Benefit Match	2–1
1924	Dundee	A	Scottish League	0–0
1927	Kilmarnock	H	Scottish League	6–1
1930	Falkirk	A	Scottish League	2–3
1932	Third Lanark	H	Scottish League	4–2
1941	Albion Rovers	H	League – Southern Division	4–2
1945	Queen's Park	A	League – 'A' Division	0–2
1947	Dundee	H	League Cup	1–1
1950	Third Lanark	A	League Cup	2–1
1952	Hibernian	H	League Cup	1–0
1958	St Mirren	H	League Cup	3–0
1961	St Johnstone	H	League Cup	0–1
1967	Rangers	A	League Cup	1–1
1969	Raith Rovers	H	League Cup	5–0
1972	East Fife	H	League Cup	1–1
1975	Dumbarton	H	League Cup	3–1
1978	Dundee	H	League Cup	3–1
1980	Kilmarnock	A	Scottish League Premier Division	3–0
1983	Tottenham Hotspur	H	Friendly	1–1
1986	Clydebank	A	Scottish League Premier Division	1–0
1990	Bohemains Dublin	A	Centenary	2–0
1994	Ayr United	A	League Cup	1–0
1997	Dunfermline	H	Scottish League Premier Division	1–2

1896	Clyde	A	Scottish League	7–2
1901	Dundee	H	Scottish League	1–1
1907	Motherwell	H	Scottish League	3–0
1909	Hamilton Academical	H	Scottish League	3–1
1910	Airdrie	H	Scottish League	3–0
1912	Falkirk	A	Scottish League	0–0
1918	Hibernian	A	Scottish League	3–0
1929	Morton	A	Scottish League	2–1
1935	Hamilton Academical	H	Scottish League	1–0
1938	Third Lanark	A	Glasgow Cup	1–1
1940	Morton	A	League – Southern Division	0–2

1944 Bobby Murdoch was born in Bothwell.

1946	Aberdeen	A	Scottish League	2–6
1949	Aberdeen	A	League Cup	5–4
1955	Queen of the South	A	League Cup	2–0
1957	Hibernian	A	League Cup	1–3
1959	Rangers	H	Glasgow Cup	1–2
1960	Partick Thistle	A	League Cup	1–1
1963	Queen of the South	H	League Cup	1–1
1966	Clyde	H	League Cup	6–0
1968	Partick Thistle	H	League Cup	4–0
1974	Dundee United	H	League Cup	1–0
1985	Motherwell	H	Scottish League Premier Division	2–1
1988	Ayr United	H	League Cup	4–1
1991	Falkirk	H	Scottish League Premier Division	4–1

Gary Gillespie scored on his debut. Brian O'Neil also made his debut.

1996	Raith Rovers	H	Scottish League Premier Division	4–1

AUGUST 18TH

1894	St Bernards	H	Scottish League	5–2
1895	Clyde	H	Scottish League	3–0
1900	Morton	A	Scottish League	3–2
1906	Motherwell	A	Scottish League	6–0
1909	Rangers	H	Jimmy Quinn Benefit Match	8–4
1913	Rangers	H	Alec McNair Benefit Match	0–2
1914	Rangers	A	Herbert Lock Benefit Match	6–4
1917	Ayr United	H	Scottish League	4–0
1919	Dumbarton	H	Scottish League	3–1

John Gilchrist made his debut.

1920	Hamilton Academical	A	Scottish League	2–1
1923	Falkirk	H	Scottish League	2–1
1928	Airdrie	H	Scottish League	4–1
1934	Hearts	A	Scottish League	0–0

Jimmy Delaney made his debut.

1937	Hamilton Academical	A	Scottish League	2–1
1945	Clyde	H	League – 'A' Division	2–2

1948	Aberdeen	A	Scottish League	0–1
1951	Morton	H	League Cup	2–0
1953	Queen's Park	H	Glasgow Cup	o–o
1954	Dundee	A	League Cup	1–3
1956	East Fife	H	League Cup	2–1
1958	Third Lanark	H	Glasgow Cup	2–4
1962	Dundee United	H	League Cup	4–0
1965	Motherwell	H	League Cup	1–0
1971	Morton	A	League Cup	1–0
1973	Rangers	A	League Cup	2–1
1976	Dumbarton	H	League Cup	3–0
1979	Rangers	A	Scottish League Premier Division	2–2
1982	Alloa	A	League Cup	5–0
1984	Dundee United	H	Scottish League Premier Division	1–1

AUGUST 19TH

1889	Third Lanark	N	Glasgow Charity Cup	0–2
1893	Dundee	A	Scottish League	4–1
1899	Clyde	H	Scottish League	3–2
1905	Motherwell	H	Scottish League	3–1
1907	Rangers	H	William Loney Benefit Match	3–2
1911	Falkirk	H	Scottish League	3–1
1912	Rangers	A	R.G. Campbell Benefit Match	1–2

Robert Gordon Campbell was unique in the rivalry between Celtic and Rangers. He played for both clubs and also served Rangers as a director. He'd begun his career with Queen's Park in 1904 and transferred to Celtic in June 1905, going on to make 11 appearances for the club. He might well have remained with Celtic but for an injury crisis at Ibrox in 1906 which prompted a raid on the transfer market, with Celtic happy to let him go for £350 and Rangers reciprocating the following season when Celtic were hit by a lack of goalkeepers! Campbell remained at Ibrox until 1914 when he joined Kilmarnock, later playing for Ayr United before his retirement in 1917.

| 1916 | St Mirren | A | Scottish League | 5–1 |

Willie McStay made his debut.

1922	Alloa	A	Scottish League	3–2
1924	Partick Thistle	A	Scottish League	2–2
1931	Hearts	H	Scottish League	3–0
1933	Falkirk	H	Scottish League	2–2
1936	St Johnstone	A	Scottish League	1–2
1939	Hearts	H	Scottish League	2–0
1944	Albion Rovers	A	League – Southern Division	1–0
1947	Clyde	H	Glasgow Cup	1–1
1950	Raith Rovers	H	League Cup	2–1
1952	Queen's Park	H	Glasgow Cup	0–0
1957	Rangers	A	Glasgow Cup	0–2
1959	Kilmarnock	H	Scottish League	2–0

1961	Hibernian	A	League Cup	2–2

Billy Price made his debut.

1964	Motherwell	A	Scottish League	3–1
1967	Aberdeen	H	League Cup	3–1
1970	Clyde	A	League Cup	2–0
1972	Arbroath	A	League Cup	5–0
1978	Hearts	H	Scottish League Premier Division	4–0
1981	St Johnstone	H	League Cup	4–1
1987	Forfar Athletic	H	League Cup	3–1
1989	Dunfermline Athletic	H	Scottish League Premier Division	1–0
1990	Everton	H	Friendly	2–2
1992	Dundee	A	League Cup	1–0
1995	Ayr United	A	League Cup	3–0

Andreas Thom scored on his debut.

1997	St Johnstone	A	League Cup 3rd round	1–0

AUGUST 20TH

1892	Renton	H	Scottish League	4–3
1898	Third Lanark	H	Scottish League	2–1

Willie McAulay scored on his only appearance for the club.

1902	Rangers	Second Hampden Park		
			Ibrox Disaster Fund Benefit Tournament	7–2
1904	Partick Thistle	A	Scottish League	5–0

Finlay McLean scored on his debut.

1910	Falkirk	A	Scottish League	1–2
1921	Hibernian	H	Scottish League	3–1
1927	Hamilton Academical	A	Scottish League	0–0
1932	Hamilton Academical	A	Scottish League	1–1
1938	Hamilton Academical	A	Scottish League	1–0
1949	St Mirren	A	League Cup	0–1
1953	Queen's Park	A	Glasgow Cup replay	1–0
1955	Falkirk	H	League Cup	5–1
1957	Billy McNeill signed pro forms with the club.			
1958	Clyde	A	Scottish League	1–2
1960	Rangers	A	League Cup	3–2
1966	St Mirren	H	League Cup	8–2
1969	Rangers	H	League Cup	1–0
1975	Hearts	H	League Cup	3–1
1980	Diosgyori	H	Cup-Winners' Cup prelim round 1st leg	6–0
1983	Hibernian	A	Scottish League Premier Division	2–0
1986	Airdrie	H	League Cup	2–0
1988	Dundee United	A	Scottish League Premier Division	0–1
1994	Dundee United	H	Scottish League	2–1
1996	Kosice	H	UEFA Cup qualifying round 2nd leg	1–0

1888	Dumbarton		Exhibition Ground	
			Exhibition Cup	3–1
1909	Falkirk	H	Scottish League	2–0
1911	Rangers	H	Jim Young Benefit Match	0–0
1915	Motherwell	H	Scottish League	3–1
1920	Albion Rovers	A	Scottish League	1–0
1926	Cowdenbeath	H	Scottish League	2–0
1937	Morton	H	Scottish League	4–0
1943	Morton	H	League – Southern Division	2–1
1946	Hearts	H	Scottish League	2–3
1948	Rangers	H	Scottish League	0–1
1954	Hearts	H	League Cup	1–2
1956	Rangers	H	Glasgow Cup	3–4
1963	Queen of the South	H	Scottish League	4–0
1965	Dundee	H	League Cup	0–2

Joe McBride made his debut.

1971	Ayr United	A	League Cup	3–0
1974	Ayr United	H	League Cup	5–2
1976	Arbroath	A	League Cup	5–0
1982	Arbroath	A	League Cup	3–0
1985	Queen of the South	A	League Cup	4–1
1991	Morton	A	League Cup	4–2
1993	Rangers	H	Scottish League Premier Division	0–0

AUGUST 22ND

1896	St Bernards	H	Scottish League	2–0
1903	St Mirren	A	Scottish League	1–0
1908	Kilmarnock	H	Scottish League	5–1
1914	Motherwell	H	Scottish League	1–0
1925	Clydebank	A	Scottish League	2–1
1931	Aberdeen	A	Scottish League	1–1
1934	Motherwell	H	Scottish League	0–1
1936	Queen of the South	H	Scottish League	5–0
1942	Hamilton Academical	H	League – Southern Division	2–2

Willie Miller made his debut in goal.

1950	Clyde	H	Glasgow Cup	3–0
1953	Aberdeen	A	League Cup	2–5
1959	Raith Rovers	H	League Cup	1–0

Charlie Gallagher made his debut.

1962	Falkirk	A	Scottish League	3–1
1964	Partick Thistle	A	League Cup	5–1
1967	Partick Thistle	h	Glasgow Cup	5–0
1970	Hearts	H	League Cup	4–2
1973	Falkirk	H	League Cup	2–1
1979	Clyde	H	Glasgow Cup semi-final	3–0
1981	St Mirren	A	League Cup	5–1

1984	Dunfermline Athletic	A	League Cup	3–2
1987	Dunfermline Athletic	A	Scottish League Premier Division	1–2
1989	Queen of the South	H	League Cup	2–0
1990	Ayr United	H	League Cup	4–0

John Collins made his debut.

1992	Rangers	A	Scottish League Premier Division	1–1
1993	Rangers	A	League Cup	0–1

AUGUST 23RD

1880	Jimmy McMenemy was born in Rutherglen.			
1890	Hearts	A	Scottish League	5–0
1902	St Mirren	H	Scottish League	2–2
1913	Motherwell	A	Scottish League	1–1
1919	Hamilton Academical	A	Scottish League	2–1
1924	Airdrie	H	Scottish League	1–1
1930	Hibernian	H	Scottish League	6–0

Hugh Smith scored on his debut.

1933	Partick Thistle	A	Scottish League	3–0
1939	Aberdeen	H	Scottish League	1–3
1941	Dumbarton	A	League – Southern Division	5–2
1947	Third Lanark	H	League Cup	3–1

Alec Boden made his debut for the club.

1952	St Mirren	H	League Cup	3–1
1955	Clyde	H	Glasgow Cup	4–0
1958	Clyde	H	League Cup	2–0

Billy McNeill made his senior debut for the club.

1961	Kilmarnock	A	Scottish League	2–3
1969	Airdrie	A	League Cup	3–0
1972	East Fife	A	League Cup	3–2
1973	Tommy Burns signed pro forms.			
1975	Dumbarton	A	League Cup	8–0
1978	Dundee	A	League Cup	3–0
1980	Rangers	H	Scottish League Premier Division	1–2
1986	Aberdeen	H	Scottish League Premier Division	1–1
1997	St Johnstone	A	Scottish League Premier Division	2–0

AUGUST 24TH

1895	Hibernian	H	Scottish League	2–4
1901	Morton	A	Scottish League	2–1
1904	Rangers	A	Neil Gibson Benefit Match	0–1
1907	Morton	A	Scottish League	3–2

Willie Kivlichan scored twice on his debut.

1910   Jimmy Weir was sold to Middlesbrough. He had played in nearly 100 games and was a part of the team that had won 4 Championships and the Scottish Cup of 1908.

1912	Hibernian	H	Scottish League	1–1
1918	Morton	H	Scottish League	1–1

1921	Airdrie	A	Scottish League	2–0
1929	Aberdeen	H	Scottish League	3–4
1932	Partick Thistle	H	Scottish League	1–2
1935	St Johnstone	A	Scottish League	3–2
1938	Kilmarnock	A	Scottish League	0–0
1940	Hearts	H	League – Southern Division	2–1
1946	Clyde	H	Glasgow Cup	0–2
1957	Airdrie	A	League Cup	2–1
1960	Kilmarnock	A	Scottish League	2–2
1963	Rangers	A	League Cup	0–3
1968	Rangers	H	League Cup	1–0
1974	Dundee United	A	League Cup	1–0
1983	Brechin City	A	League Cup	1–0

Brian McClair made his debut.

1985	Clydebank	A	Scottish League Premier Division	2–0
1988	Hamilton Academical	H	League Cup	7–2
1991	Aberdeen	A	Scottish League Premier Division	0–1
1996	Kilmarnock	A	Scottish League Premier Division	3–1

AUGUST 25TH

1894	Third Lanark	A	Scottish League	1–2
1900	Hibernian	H	Scottish League	3–1
1906	Kilmarnock	H	Scottish League	5–0

Bobby Templeton made his debut.

1917	Falkirk	A	Scottish League	3–1
1923	Clydebank	A	Scottish League	0–0
1928	Ayr United	A	Scottish League	2–0
1934	St Johnstone	H	Scottish League	0–0
1936	Third Lanark	A	Glasgow Cup	3–1
1937	Queen of the South	H	Scottish League	2–2
1951	Third Lanark	A	League Cup	1–0
1956	Aberdeen	H	League Cup	3–2
1962	Hearts	A	League Cup	2–3
1965	Dundee United	A	Scottish League	4–0
1971	Morton	H	League Cup	0–1
1973	Rangers	H	League Cup	1–3
1976	Dumbarton	A	League Cup	3–3
1979	Kilmarnock	H	Scottish League Premier Division	5–0
1982	Alloa	H	League Cup	4–1
1984	Rangers	A	Scottish League Premier Division	0–0
1990	Motherwell	A	Scottish League Premier Division	0–2
1993	Arbroath	A	League Cup	9–1

AUGUST 26TH

1893	Dumbarton	H	Scottish League	0–0
1899	Kilmarnock	A	Scottish League	2–2

1901	Rangers	H	Dan McArthur Benefit Match	1–1
1905	Kilmarnock	A	Scottish League	4–2
1908	Rangers	H	Peter Somers Benefit Match	3–1
1911	Morton	A	Scottish League	1–1
1922	Hamilton Academical	H	Scottish League	2–1
1931	Cowdenbeath	H	Scottish League	7–0
1933	Kilmarnock	A	Scottish League	3–4
1939	Cowdenbeath	A	Scottish League	2–1
1944	Third Lanark	H	League – Southern Division	1–0
1945	Rangers	A	Glasgow Cup	1–3
1950	East Fife	A	League Cup	1–1
1953	East Fife	H	League Cup	0–1
1959	Partick Thistle	A	League Cup	2–0
1961	Partick Thistle	H	League Cup	3–2
1964	Hearts	H	League Cup	6–1
1967	Dundee United	A	League Cup	1–0
1970	Dundee United	A	League Cup	2–2

Danny McGrain came on as substitute to make his debut.

1972	Stirling Albion	H	League Cup	3–0
1978	Motherwell	A	Scottish League Premier Division	5–1
1981	Hibernian	A	League Cup	4–1
1987	Dumbarton	A	League Cup	5–1
1989	Rangers	H	Scottish League Premier Division	1–1
1992	Hearts	A	League Cup	2–1
1995	Raith Rovers	A	Scottish League Premier Division	1–0
1997	Tirol	H	UEFA QP 2nd round 2nd leg	6–3

AUGUST 27TH

1892	Hearts	A	Scottish League	1–3
1898	Clyde	A	Scottish League	0–0
1904	Port Glasgow Athletic	H	Scottish League	4–1
1910	Morton	H	Scottish League	0–1
1919	Kilmarnock	A	Scottish League	1–0
1921	Raith Rovers	A	Scottish League	1–1
1927	Falkirk	H	Scottish League	3–0

Willie McGonagle made his debut.

1928 Adam McLean was sold to Sunderland after contract negotiations reached a stalemate. In 11 years at the club the left-winger (regarded by many as the club's greatest ever) made over 400 appearances and scored 138 goals, creating many more. He won 3 Championship medals and 3 Scottish Cup winners' medals.

1932	Morton	H	Scottish League	7–1
1934	Rangers	H	Jimmy McGrory Benefit Match	0–4
1938	Aberdeen	H	Scottish League	1–2
1947	Queen's Park	H	Scottish League	4–0

1948 Bobby Collins signed from Pollok.

| 1949 | Rangers | A | League Cup | 0–2 |

1952	Partick Thistle	A	League Cup	1–0
1955	Rangers	A	League Cup	4–1
1958	Airdrie	A	League Cup	2–1
1960	Third Lanark	A	League Cup	3–1
1966	Hearts	H	League Cup	3–0
1969	Raith Rovers	A	League Cup	5–2
1975	Aberdeen	A	League Cup	2–0
1977	Motherwell	H	Scottish League Premier Division	0–1
1980	Stirling Albion	A	League Cup	0–1
1983	Brechin City	H	League Cup	0–0
1988	Rangers	A	Scottish League Premier Division	1–5
1991	Raith Rovers	H	League Cup	3–1
1994	Rangers	A	Scottish League	2–0

AUGUST 28TH

1899	Rangers	H	Sandy McMahon Benefit Match	2–2
1902	Rangers	A	Jock Drummond Benefit Match	1–1
1909	Hibernian	A	Scottish League	0–1
1915	Airdrie	A	Scottish League	5–0
1916	Hibernian	H	Scottish League	3–1
1920	Aberdeen	A	Scottish League	2–1
1926	Queen's Park	A	Scottish League	6–1
1935	Third Lanark	H	Scottish League	6–0

Jimmy McGrory scored his 50th hat-trick in all competitions for the club.

1937	Kilmarnock	A	Scottish League	1–2
1940	Queen's Park	A	Glasgow Cup	5–2
1943	Partick Thistle	H	Glasgow Cup	1–3
1946	Hamilton Academical	A	Scottish League	2–2
1954	Falkirk	A	League Cup	2–2
1957	East Fife	H	League Cup	6–1

Bertie Auld scored his first goal for the club.

1963	Kilmarnock	H	League Cup	2–0
1965	Dundee United	H	League Cup	3–0
1968	Morton	A	League Cup	3–0
1971	Rangers	A	League Cup	3–0
1972	Arbroath	H	League Cup	3–3
1974	Motherwell	A	League Cup	2–2
1976	Arbroath	H	League Cup	2–1

1982 Graeme Sinclair made his debut.

1985	Brechin City	H	League Cup	7–0
1986	Dumbarton	H	League Cup	3–0
1993	Partick Thistle	A	Scottish League Premier Division	1–0

1994 Neil Mochan died aged 67 in Falkirk from leukemia.

1888	Partick Thistle		Exhibition Ground	
			Exhibition Cup semi-final	0–2
1891	Clyde	A	Scottish League	7–2
1896	Abercorn	A	Scottish League	6–0
1900	Rangers	A	David Mitchell Benefit Match	1–3
1903	Third Lanark	H	Scottish League	1–3
1908	Dundee	A	Scottish League	1–2
1914	St Mirren	A	Scottish League	3–3
1925	Hamilton Academical	H	Scottish League	2–0
1931	Hamilton Academical	H	Scottish League	6–1

Jimmy McGrory and Peter Scarff scored a hat-trick apiece.

1936	Albion Rovers	A	Scottish League	3–1
1942	Clyde	A	League – Southern Division	3–1
1951	Airdrie	H	League Cup	2–0
1953	Airdrie	H	League Cup	2–0
1956	Rangers	A	League Cup	0–0
1959	Airdrie	H	League Cup	2–2
1960	Third Lanark	A	Glasgow Cup semi-final	0–0
1962	Dundee	H	League Cup	3–0
1964	Kilmarnock	A	League Cup	0–2
1970	Morton	H	Scottish League	2–0
1973	Arbroath	A	League Cup	3–1

Centre-half Roddy MacDonald made his senior debut for the club (he had played on trial in the Dryborough Cup a few weeks earlier).

1977	Ayr United	A	Scottish League Premier Division	1–2
1979	Falkirk	A	League Cup	2–1
1981	Airdrie	H	Scottish League Premier Division	5–2
1984	Airdrie	A	League Cup	4–0
1987	Rangers	H	Scottish League Premier Division	1–0
1990	Hamilton Academical	A	League Cup	1–0
1992	Airdrie	A	Scottish League Premier Division	1–1

AUGUST 30TH

1890	Cambulsang	H	Scottish League	5–2
1902	Third Lanark	A	Scottish League	2–1

Donald McLeod made his debut.

1913	Falkirk	H	Scottish League	4–0
1919	Raith Rovers	H	Scottish League	3–0
1920	Rangers	A	Bert Manderson Benefit Match	1–2
1924	Falkirk	A	Scottish League	2–1
1930	East Fife	A	Scottish League	6–2
1932	Ayr United	H	Scottish League	4–1

Charlie McGillivary scored on his debut.

1933	Third Lanark	A	Glasgow Cup	4–1
1941	Queen's Park	H	League – Southern Division	2–0
1943	Bobby Lennox was born in Saltcoats.			

1950	Third Lanark	H	League Cup	3–1
1952	Hibernian	A	League Cup	0–3

Frank Meechan made his debut.

1958	St Mirren	A	League Cup	3–6
1961	St Johnstone	A	League Cup	0–2
1967	Rangers	H	League Cup	3–1
1969	St Johnstone	H	Scottish League	2–2
1971	Ayr United	H	League Cup	4–1
1975	Rangers	A	Scottish League Premier Division	1–2

On the opening day of the Scottish Premier League a Kenny Dalglish goal was not enough to ensure victory in front of a crowd of 69,594 which is an attendance record for a Scottish Premier League match.

1978	Dundee United	A	League Cup	3–2
1980	Stirling Albion	H	League Cup	6–1
1989	Hearts	A	League Cup quarter-final	2–2

AUGUST 31ST

1895	St Mirren	H	Scottish League	4–0
1901	Third Lanark	H	Scottish League	3–2
1907	Dundee	H	Scottish League	3–2
1911	Frank O'Donnell was born in Buckhaven			
1912	Kilmarnock	A	Scottish League	2–0
1918	Clyde	A	Scottish League	3–0
1929	Hamilton Academical	A	Scottish League	3–2
1935	Queen's Park	H	Scottish League	3–0
1938	Third Lanark	H	Glasgow Cup	8–1

John Divers scored 4 goals.

1940	Albion Rovers	A	League – Southern Division	3–1
1946	St Mirren	A	Scottish League	1–0
1949	Aberdeen	H	League Cup	1–3

Bertie Peacock made his debut.

1955	Rangers	H	League Cup	0–4
1957	Hibernian	H	League Cup	2–0
1960	Partick Thistle	H	League Cup	1–2
1963	Queen of the South	A	League Cup	3–2
1966	Clyde	A	League Cup	3–1
1968	Partick Thistle	A	League Cup	6–1
1968	Derek Whyte was born in Glasgow.			
1977	Motherwell	H	League Cup	0–0
1983	Airdrie	A	League Cup	6–1
1985	Rangers	H	Scottish League Premier Division	1–1
1986	Rangers	A	Scottish League Premier Division	0–1
1988	Dundee United	A	League Cup quarter-final	0–2
1991	Rangers	H	Scottish League Premier Division	0–2
1993	Airdrie	H	League Cup	1–0
1994	Dundee	A	League Cup	2–1

Captain Paul McStay was sent off for retaliation, the first dismissal in his distinguished career.

| 1995 | Raith Rovers | H | League Cup | 2–1 |

SEPTEMBER 1ST

1888	Shettleston	H	Scottish Cup	5–1
1900	Third Lanark	A	Scottish League	2–1
1906	Morton	A	Scottish League	2–0
1917	Clyde	H	Scottish League	3–2
1920	Morton	H	Scottish League	1–1
1923	Partick Thistle	H	Scottish League	1–2
1928	Rangers	A	Glasgow Cup	2–1
1934	Queen's Park	A	Scottish League	0–1
1945	Aberdeen	H	League – 'A' Division	1–1
1947	Rangers	H	League Cup	2–0
1948	Queen of the South	H	Scottish League	2–2
1951	Morton	A	League Cup	0–2
1953	Rangers	A	Glasgow Cup semi-final	1–1
1954	Dundee	H	League Cup	0–1
1956	East Fife	A	League Cup	1–0
1962	Dundee United	A	League Cup	0–0
1965	Motherwell	A	League Cup	3–2
1971	National	H	Friendly	3–0
1973	Dunfermline Athletic	A	Scottish League	3–2
1976	Dundee United	H	League Cup	1–1
1979	Falkirk	H	League Cup	4–1
1982	Arbroath	H	League Cup	4–1
1984	Morton	H	Scottish League Premier Division	5–0
1987	Aberdeen	A	League Cup quarter-final	0–1
1990	Aberdeen	H	Scottish League Premier Division	0–3

SEPTEMBER 2ND

1893	Rangers	A	Scottish League	0–5
1899	Third Lanark	H	Scottish League	5–2
1905	Hibernian	H	Scottish League	1–0
1911	Clyde	H	Scottish League	3–2
1916	Ayr United	A	Scottish League	1–0
1918	Clyde	H	Glasgow Cup semi-final	3–1
1922	Queen's Park	A	Glasgow Cup	3–4
1931	Third Lanark	H	Scottish League	6–1
1933	Hearts	H	Scottish League	0–0
1939	Clyde	H	Scottish League	1–0
1944	Hamilton Academical	A	League – Southern Division	2–6
1950	Raith Rovers	A	League Cup	2–2

Charlie Tully was granted a free transfer by the club after 11 years' service. He had played in over 300 games and scored nearly 50 goals, winning 1 Championship medal, 2 Scottish Cup and 2 Scottish League Cup winners' medals.

1961	Hibernian	H	League Cup	2–1
1967	Aberdeen	A	League Cup	5–1
1970	Feyenoord	H	Friendly	1–1
1972	Kilmarnock	H	Scottish League	6–2
1978	Dundee United	H	League Cup	1–0
1992	St Johnstone	H	Scottish League Premier Division	3–1

SEPTEMBER 3RD

1898	St Mirren	H	Scottish League	4–1
1904	Hearts	H	Scottish League	1–1
1910	Kilmarnock	A	Scottish League	0–1

1914 James Delaney was born in Cleland.

1921	Queen's Park	H	Glasgow Cup	2–1
1927	Raith Rovers	A	Scottish League	3–0
1932	Falkirk	A	Scottish League	1–1
1934	Queen's Park	H	Glasgow Cup	1–0
1938	Hearts	A	Scottish League	5–1
1947	Clyde	A	Glasgow Cup	2–0
1949	St Mirren	H	League Cup	4–1
1950	Queen's Park	H	Glasgow Cup semi-final	2–1
1951	Third Lanark	A	Glasgow Cup semi-final	5–2
1952	Queen's Park	A	Glasgow Cup replay	2–2
1953	Rangers	H	Glasgow Cup semi-final replay	0–4
1955	Falkirk	A	League Cup	1–1

Richard Beattie made his debut in goal.

| 1960 | Rangers | H | League Cup | 1–2 |

1960 Willie McStay died aged 66.

1964 Ronnie Simpson was signed from Hibernian, where Jock Stein was manager, for the bargain price of £2,000.

| 1966 | St Mirren | A | League Cup | 1–0 |

Willie O'Neill became Celtic's first ever substitute when he replaced the injured Jimmy Johnstone.

1969	Kilmarnock	A	Scottish League	4–2
1977	Motherwell	A	League Cup	4–2
1980	Diosgyori	A	Cup-Winners' Cup prelim round 2nd leg	1–2
1983	Rangers	H	Scottish League Premier Division	2–1
1986	Aberdeen	A	League Cup quarter-final	1–1
1988	Hamilton Academical	H	Scottish League Premier Division	2–1
1991	Airdrie	A	League Cup quarter-final	0–0

SEPTEMBER 4TH

| 1897 | Hibernian | H | Scottish League | 4–1 |

Willie Orr made his debut.

| 1905 | Rangers | H | Friendly | 1–0 |
| 1909 | Motherwell | H | Scottish League | 2–2 |

1915	Falkirk	H	Scottish League	2–1
1920	Third Lanark	H	Glasgow Cup	3–0
1922	'Sunny' Jim Young died aged 40.			
1926	Morton	H	Scottish League	3–0
1937	Hamilton Academical	H	Scottish League	4–2
1943	Dumbarton	H	League – Southern Division	1–4
1946	Third Lanark	H	Scottish League	1–4
1948	Albion Rovers	A	Scottish League	3–3
1952	Frank O'Donnell died aged 41.			
1954	Hearts	A	League Cup	2–3
1965	Dundee	A	League Cup	3–1
1971	Clyde	H	Scottish League	9–1
1976	Rangers	H	Scottish League Premier Division	2–2
1982	Dundee	H	Scottish League Premier Division	2–0
1984	Dundee United	A	League Cup quarter-final	1–2
1985	Hibernian	A	League Cup quarter-final	4–4
1993	Aberdeen	H	Scottish League Premier Division	0–1
1996	Alloa	A	League Cup	5–1

SEPTEMBER 5TH

1891	Renton	H	Scottish League	3–0
1896	Hearts	H	Scottish League	3–0
1901	Hearts	N	Glasgow Exhibition Trophy semi-final	2–1
1903	Hibernian	A	Scottish League	2–0
1908	St Mirren	H	Scottish League	0–1
1914	Morton	H	Scottish League	6–2
1925	Partick Thistle	A	Glasgow Cup	1–1
1931	Rangers	A	Scottish League	0–0

One of the saddest days in the history of the club. Goalkeeper John Thomson died in hospital after being knocked unconscious when he came out to dive at the feet of Sam English. Thomson had suffered a depressed fracture of the skull. At the age of 22 he had already amassed 188 appearances and would have surely gone on to make many more before tragedy struck in his young life. He won 2 Scottish Cup winners' medals in 1927 and 1931.

1936	Kilmarnock	H	Scottish League	2–4
1942	Rangers	A	Glasgow Cup	1–2
1953	Hamilton Academical	A	Scottish League	0–2
1959	Rangers	A	Scottish League	1–3
1961	Bobby Lennox signed pro forms.			
1964	Rangers	H	Scottish League	3–1
1967	Penarol	H	Friendly	2–1
1970	Clyde	A	Scottish League	5–0
1973	Charlie Napier died aged 63.			
1981	Aberdeen	A	Scottish League Premier Division	3–1
1987	Dundee United	A	Scottish League Premier Division	0–0
1990	Queen of the South	H	League Cup quarter-final	2–1

SEPTEMBER 6TH

1888	Cowlairs		Exhibition Ground	
			Exhibition Cup final	0–2
1890	Rangers	H	Scottish Cup	1–0
1902	Queen's Park	H	Scottish League	1–1
1913	Hibernian	A	Scottish League	2–1
1919	Rangers	H	Glasgow Cup	1–0
1921	Dumbarton	H	Scottish League	4–0
1924	Aberdeen	A	Scottish League	4–0
1927	Queen's Park	A	Glasgow Cup	4–1
1930	Aberdeen	H	Scottish League	1–0
1932	Clyde	A	Glasgow Cup	1–1
1941	Rangers	A	League – Southern Division	0–3
1952	Falkirk	H	Scottish League	5–3
1958	Rangers	H	Scottish League	2–2
1969	Dunfermline Athletic	A	Scottish League	1–2
1975	Dundee	H	Scottish League Premier Division	4–0
1977	Tom McAdam was signed from Dundee United for £60,000.			
1980	Partick Thistle	H	Scottish League Premier Division	4–1
1986	Hamilton Academical	H	Scottish League Premier Division	4–1

SEPTEMBER 7TH

1889	Queen's Park	A	Scottish Cup	0–0
	Jerry Reynolds made his debut.			
1895	Rangers	A	Scottish League	4–2
1897	Rangers	H	Friendly	1–3
1901	St Mirren	A	Scottish League	3–2
1907	Falkirk	H	Scottish League	3–2
1912	Aberdeen	H	Scottish League	2–0
1918	Ayr United	H	Scottish League	1–0
1920	Motherwell	H	Scottish League	1–0
1929	Clyde	A	Glasgow Cup	1–1
1935	Queen of the South	A	Scottish League	3–1
1940	Rangers	H	League – Southern Division	0–0

Severe rioting by fans during the game led to the Lord Provost of Glasgow, Sir Patrick Dolan, to state: 'The Chief Constable has powers to prohibit games between Celtic and Rangers until the end of the war, and I have informed him that if he cares to exercise that power, he will have the support of all citizens.' Although the games were not banned, Celtic Park was closed for a month and the club were forced to play home matches at Clyde's Shawfield ground.

| 1946 | Rangers | H | Scottish League | 2–3 |

The decision by the Celtic board to increase admission prices for the game was not a popular one, for both the Celtic and Rangers Supporters Associations found themselves in agreement for once and organised a boycott of the game in protest. As a result, the gate figure of 28,000 was less than half the number that might otherwise have been expected to have attended.

1954	Partick Thistle	A	Glasgow Cup	2–2
1957	Falkirk	A	Scottish League	1–0
1960	Third Lanark	H	Glasgow Cup semi-final replay	3–1
1963	Rangers	A	Scottish League	1–2
1965	Andreas Thom was born.			
1968	Clyde	A	Scottish League	3–0
1974	Clyde	A	Scottish League	4–2
1983	Hibernian	H	League Cup	5–1
1985	Hibernian	A	Scottish League Premier Division	5–0
1988	Honved	A	European Cup 1st round 1st leg	0–1
1991	St Mirren	H	Scottish League Premier Division	0–0
1996	Hibernian	H	Scottish League Premier Division	5–0

SEPTEMBER 8TH

1894	St Mirren	A	Scottish League	3–0
1900	Queen's Park	A	Scottish League	2–0
1906	Partick Thistle	A	Glasgow Cup	2–0
1910	Partick Thistle	A	Glasgow Cup	2–1
1917	Queen's Park	A	Glasgow Cup	2–1
1923	Queen's Park	A	Scottish League	2–0
1928	Kilmarnock	H	Scottish League	3–0
1934	Rangers	H	Scottish League	1–1
1945	Rangers	A	League – 'A' Division	3–5
1947	Dundee	A	League Cup	1–4
1948	Partick Thistle	H	Glasgow Cup	2–1
1951	Motherwell	A	Scottish League	2–2
1956	Queen's Park	H	Scottish League	2–0
1962	Rangers	H	Scottish League	0–1
1971	Clydebank	A	League Cup quarter-final	5–0
1973	Clyde	H	Scottish League	5–0

For the first home game of the season the entire team wore number 8 on their shorts to celebrate winning 8 consecutive Championships.

1979	Dundee United	H	Scottish League Premier Division	2–2
1982	Partick Thistle	H	League Cup quarter-final	4–0
1984	Dumbarton	A	Scottish League Premier Division	1–1
1990	Hibernian	H	Scottish League Premier Division	2–0

SEPTEMBER 9TH

1893	Hearts	A	Scottish League	4–2
1899	Hibernian	H	Scottish League	2–1
1901	Rangers	N	Glasgow International Exhibition Cup final	1–3
1905	Queen's Park	H	Glasgow Cup	3–0
1916	Airdrie	H	Scottish League	3–1
1922	Raith Rovers	H	Scottish League	3–0
1925	Partick Thistle	H	Glasgow Cup	5–1
1933	Rangers	A	Scottish League	2–2

1936	Clyde	H	Scottish League	3–1
1944	Rangers	H	League – Southern Division	0–4
1950	Morton	H	Scottish League	3–4
1954	Partick Thistle	H	Glasgow Cup replay	2–2
1955	Partick Thistle	A	Glasgow Cup semi-final	2–0
1961	Third Lanark	H	Scottish League	1–0
1964	East Fife	A	League Cup quarter-final	0–2
1967	Clyde	H	Scottish League	3–0
1970	Dundee	A	League Cup quarter-final	2–2
1972	Morton	A	Scottish League	2–0
1978	Rangers	H	Scottish League Premier Division	3–1
1989	St Mirren	A	Scottish League Premier Division	0–1

1994 Tommy Burns broke Celtic's transfer record when he paid £1.75 million for Phil O'Donnell from Motherwell.

SEPTEMBER 10TH

1892 Abercorn H Scottish League 3–2

Dan McArthur made his debut in goal. At 5ft 5in he was the shortest goalkeeper ever to play for Celtic and Scotland.

1898	Hibernian	A	Scottish League	1–2
1904	Queen's Park	H	Glasgow Cup	3–0

Alec McNair made his debut for the club.

1921	Aberdeen	A	Scottish League	1–1
1927	Queen's Park	H	Scottish League	3–0
1932	Rangers	H	Scottish League	1–1
1934	Rangers	H	Glasgow Cup	1–2
1938	Rangers	H	Scottish League	6–2
1947	Third Lanark	H	Glasgow Cup semi-final	1–3
1949	Queen of the South	A	Scottish League	2–0
1955	Falkirk	A	Scottish League	1–3
1958	Cowdenbeath	H	League Cup quarter-final	2–0

Bobby Collins scored in his final game for the club. In over 300 games for the club this great forward scored 116 goals. He won 1 Championship medal and 2 Scottish Cup and League Cup winners' medals during his time at the club.

1960	Rangers	H	Scottish League	1–5
1966	Clyde	A	Scottish League	3–0
1969	Aberdeen	A	League Cup quarter-final	0–0
1975	Stenhousemuir	A	League Cup quarter-final	2–0

Roy Aitken came on as a substitute for Shuggie Edvaldson to make his debut.

1977 Rangers A Scottish League Premier Division 2–3

Tom McAdam came on as sub for John Dowie to make his debut.

1983 St Johnstone H Scottish League Premier Division 5–2

1985 Jock Stein died of a heart attack shortly after Scotland drew with Wales 1–1 in a World Cup qualifying match in Cardiff. The most influential man in Celtic's history had virtually ensured Scotland's qualification to the final stages in Mexico.

1994 Partick Thistle A Scottish League 2–1

Phil O'Donnell scored on his debut one day after becoming the club's record buy.

1995	Aberdeen	A	Scottish League Premier Division	3–2
1996	Hamburg	H	UEFA Cup qualifying 1st leg	0–2
1997	Motherwell	H	League Cup 4th round	1–0

SEPTEMBER 11TH

1897	Hearts	A	Scottish League	0–0
1905	Hearts	A	Scottish League	1–1
1909	Morton	A	Scottish League	1–2
1915	Morton	A	Scottish League	1–0
1920	Hamilton Academical	H	Scottish League	2–1
1926	Clyde	A	Scottish League	2–2
1928	Rangers	Dunnoon	Dunnoon Festival	2–3
1929	Clyde	H	Glasgow Cup	6–0
1934	Hibernian	H	Scottish League	4–0
1937	Rangers	A	Scottish League	1–3
1940	Clyde	H	Glasgow Cup semi-final	1–0
1943	Rangers	A	League – Southern Division	1–0
1948	Hibernian	H	League Cup	1–0
1954	Clyde	A	Scottish League	2–2
1957	Third Lanark	H	League Cup quarter-final	6–1
1965	Clyde	H	Scottish League	2–1
1968	Hamilton Academical	H	League Cup quarter-final	10–0
1971	Rangers	A	Scottish League	3–2
1974	Hamilton Academical	H	League Cup quarter-final	2–0
1976	Dundee United	A	Scottish League Premier Division	0–1
1982	St Mirren	A	Scottish League Premier Division	2–1
1993	Raith Rovers	A	Scottish League Premier Division	4–1

SEPTEMBER 12TH

1891	Abercorn	A	Scottish League	5–2
1896	St Bernards	A	Scottish League	2–1
1903	Queen's Park	H	Glasgow Cup	1–1
1908	Queen's Park	H	Glasgow Cup	4–4
1914	Clyde	A	Glasgow Cup	0–2
1925	Cowdenbeath	H	Scottish League	6–1
1931	Queen's Park	H	Scottish League	2–2

Before the game the players and supporters observed a two-minute silence in respect of goalkeeper John Thomson who died tragically a week earlier in the game against Rangers. Whilst 'The Last Post' was played the goal was kept empty as a mark of respect.

1936	Hamilton Academical	A	Scottish League	2–1
1942	Morton	A	League – Southern Division	0–4
1953	Clyde	H	Scottish League	1–0
1956	Dunfermline Athletic	A	League Cup quarter-final	6–0
1958	Bobby Collins was sold to Everton for £23,500.			
1959	Hearts	H	Scottish League	3–4

1964	Clyde	A	Scottish League	1–1
1970	Rangers	H	Scottish League	2–0
1973	Motherwell	A	League Cup	2–1
1978	Burnley	A	Anglo Scottish Cup quarter-final 1st leg	0–1
1980	Roy Aitken made his international debut against Peru in the 1–1 draw at Hampden.			
1981	Morton	H	Scottish League Premier Division	2–1
1987	Falkirk	A	Scottish League Premier Division	1–0
1989	Partizan Belgrade	A	Cup-Winners' Cup 1st round 1st leg	1–2
1992	Hibernian	H	Scottish League Premier Division	2–3

SEPTEMBER 13TH

1890	Third Lanark	A	Scottish League	1–2
1902	Queen's Park	A	Glasgow Cup	2–1
1913	St Mirren	H	Scottish League	0–2
1919	Hearts	A	Scottish League	1–0
1924	St Mirren	H	Scottish League	5–0
1930	Hamilton Academical	A	Scottish League	0–0
1941	Clyde	H	League – Southern Division	5–2
1947	Third Lanark	A	League Cup	2–3

Tommy McDonald scored 2 of Third Lanark's goals and was so impressive he was to join Celtic 4 weeks later.

1949	Rangers	H	Glasgow Cup	1–2
1952	Raith Rovers	A	Scottish League	1–1
1958	Kilmarnock	A	Scottish League	4–1
1967	Ayr United	H	League Cup quarter-final	6–2
1969	Hibernian	H	Scottish League	1–2
1972	Rosenborg	H (Hampden)		
			European Cup 1st round 1st leg	2–1
1975	Motherwell	A	Scottish League Premier Division	1–1
1980	Hearts	A	Scottish League Premier Division	2–0
1986	Dundee United	A	Scottish League Premier Division	2–2
1997	Motherwell	A	Scottish League Premier Division	3–2

SEPTEMBER 14TH

1889	Queen's Park	A	Scottish Cup	1–2
1895	Hearts	H	Scottish League	0–5
1901	Clyde	H	Glasgow Cup	3–1
1907	Kilmarnock	A	Scottish League	0–0
1912	Airdrie	A	Scottish League	4–1
1918	Queen's Park	A	Scottish League	3–0
1929	Airdrie	A	Scottish League	1–0
1932	East Stirlingshire	A	Scottish League	3–1
1935	Albion Rovers	H	Scottish League	4–0
1938	Hamilton Academical	H	Scottish League	1–2
1940	Queen's Park	A	League – Southern Division	1–0
1946	Queen of the South	A	Scottish League	1–3

Joe Baillie made his senior debut for the club.

1957	Third Lanark	A	League Cup quarter-final	3–0
1963	Third Lanark	H	Scottish League	4–4
1966	Dunfermline Athletic	H	League Cup quarter-final	6–3
1968	Rangers	H	Scottish League	2–4
1974	Rangers	H	Scottish League	1–2
1977	Jeunesse Esch	H	European Cup 1st round 1st leg	5–0
1983	Aahrus GF	H	UEFA Cup 1st round 1st leg	1–0
1985	Aberdeen	H	Scottish League Premier Division	2–1
1991	St Johnstone	A	Scottish League Premier Division	0–1
1993	Young Boys Berne	A	UEFA Cup 1st round 1st leg	0–0
1994	Dinamo Batumi	A	Cup-Winners' Cup 1st round 1st leg	3–2
1996	Dundee United	A	Scottish League Premier Division	2–1

SEPTEMBER 15TH

1894	Battlefield	H	Glasgow Cup	2–2
1900	Rangers	H	Glasgow Cup	3–3
1902	Hearts	A	Scottish League	2–1
1906	Hearts	H	Scottish League	3–0
1913	Hearts	A	Scottish League	0–2
1917	Partick Thistle	H	Scottish League	2–1
1923	Rangers	A	Glasgow Cup	0–1
1924	Hibernian	A	Scottish League	3–2
1928	Cowdenbeath	A	Scottish League	1–0
1934	Hamilton Academical	A	Scottish League	2–4
1937	Morton	A	Scottish League	3–2
1945	Hamilton Academical	H	League – 'A' Division	2–0
1948	Queen's Park	A	Glasgow Cup semi-final	3–0
1951	Forfar Athletic	H	League Cup quarter-final	4–1
1956	Dunfermline Athletic	H	League Cup quarter-final	0–3
1961	Mark Reid was born in Kilwinning.			
1962	Clyde	A	Scottish League	3–1
1965	Raith Rovers	A	League Cup quarter-final	8–1
1971	B 1903	A	European Cup 1st round 1st leg	1–2
1973	Rangers	A	Scottish League	1–0
1976	Wisla Krakow	H	UEFA Cup 1st round 1st leg	2–2
1979	Hibernian	A	Scottish League Premier Division	3–1
1982	Ajax Amsterdam	H	European Cup 1st round 1st leg	2–2
1984	Hearts	H	Scottish League Premier Division	1–0
1987	Borussia Dortmund	H	UEFA Cup 1st round 1st leg	2–1
1990	Rangers	A	Scottish League Premier Division	1–1
1992	Cologne	A	UEFA Cup 1st round 1st leg	0–2

1893	Linthouse	A	Glasgow Cup	2–1
1899	Partick Thistle	H	Glasgow Cup	5–0
1901	Hibernian	A	Scottish League	2–1
1905	Falkirk	A	Scottish League	5–0
1911	Dundee	A	Scottish League	1–3
1916	Motherwell	A	Scottish League	4–0
1935	Dunfermline Athletic	H	Scottish League	5–3
1944	Dumbarton	A	League – Southern Division	3–0
1950	Motherwell	H	League Cup quarter-final	1–4
1961	Rangers	A	Scottish League	2–2

Willie Fernie scored on his final appearance for the club. In over 300 games he had scored 74 goals. He won a Championship medal, a Cup winners' medal and 2 League Cup winners' medals. He was later sold to St Mirren for £4000.

1964	East Fife	H	League Cup quarter-final	6–0
1967	Rangers	A	Scottish League	0–1
1970	KPV (Karleby)	H	European Cup 1st round 1st leg	9–0
1972	Rangers	H	Scottish League	3–1
1975	Valur	A	Cup-Winners' Cup 1st round 1st leg	2–0
1978	Hibernian	H	Scottish League Premier Division	0–1
1981	Juventus	H	European Cup 1st round 1st leg	1–0

An own-goal by Sciera helped Celtic to a first-leg lead which they were unable to hang on to. Starring in the Juventus midfield that night was Liam Brady, who was to return to Parkhead as manager a few years later.

1989	Dundee United	A	Scottish League Premier Division	2–2
1995	Motherwell	H	Scottish League Premier Division	1–1
1997	Liverpool	H	UEFA Cup 1st round 1st leg	2–2

SEPTEMBER 17TH

1892	Pollokshaws	A	Glasgow Cup	7–2
1898	Clyde	H	Glasgow Cup	7–0
1900	Hearts	A	Scottish League	2–0

Willie Loney scored on his debut.

1904	St Mirren	A	Scottish League	3–2
1910	Dundee	H	Scottish League	2–1
1921	Partick Thistle	H	Glasgow Cup semi-final	1–1
1923	Hibernian	A	Scottish League	0–0
1927	Dunfermline Athletic	A	Scottish League	1–1
1932	Queen's Park	A	Scottish League	1–1

Bobby Hogg made his debut.

| 1937 | Bertie Thomson died from a heart attack at the age of 30. |

| 1938 | Clyde | A | Scottish League | 4–1 |
| 1949 | Hearts | H | Scottish League | 3–2 |

1952 Jackie Millsop died at the age of 21 after suffering from appendicitis.

| 1955 | Stirling Albion | H | Scottish League | 3–0 |

John McPhail played in what was to be his last game for the club. During his 15 years at the club he made nearly 350 appearances during and after the war, scoring nearly

100 goals.

1958	Cowdenbeath	A	League Cup quarter-final	8–1
1960	Third Lanark	A	Scottish League	0–2
1963	FC Basel	A	Cup-Winners' Cup 1st round 1st leg	5–1
1966	Rangers	H	Scottish League	2–0
1969	FC Basel	A	European Cup 1st round 1st leg	0–0

1973 Bobby Murdoch, after 14 years at the club, was allowed to join Middlesbrough. He played nearly 500 games for Celtic, scoring over 100 goals. He won 8 Championships, 4 Scottish Cup winners' medals and 5 League Cup winners' medals to go with his European Cup medal. He only won 12 caps for Scotland which is a bit of a mystery to all who had the pleasure of seeing Bobby play.

1977	Aberdeen	A	Scottish League Premier Division	1–2
1980	Politechnica Timisoara	H	Cup-Winners' Cup 1st round 1st leg	2–1
1983	Motherwell	A	Scottish League Premier Division	3–0
1986	Shamrock Rovers	A	European Cup 1st round 1st leg	1–0
1988	Aberdeen	H	Scottish League Premier Division	1–3
1994	Kilmarnock	H	Scottish League	1–1
1996	Hearts	A	League Cup	0–1

SEPTEMBER 18TH

1897	Clyde	H	Glasgow Cup	2–1
1899	Hibernian	A	Scottish League	1–1
1909	Hamilton Academical	A	Scottish League	5–1
1915	Dundee	A	Scottish League	2–0

1917 After a short loan period Willie Cringan was signed from Sunderland for £600.

1920	Rangers	H	Glasgow Cup semi-final	2–1
1922	Hibernian	A	Scottish League	0–1
1926	Hamilton Academical	H	Scottish League	2–2
1937	Hearts	H	Scottish League	2–1
1943	Hamilton Academical	H	League – Southern Division	1–0
1948	Clyde	A	League Cup	2–0
1954	Rangers	H	Scottish League	2–0
1965	Rangers	A	Scottish League	1–2

John Divers played his last game for the club. He had played 232 games and scored 102 goals.

1968	AS Saint-Etienne	A	European Cup 1st round 1st leg	0–2
1971	Morton	H	Scottish League	3–1
1974	Olympiakos	H	European Cup 1st round 1st leg	1–1
1976	Hearts	H	Scottish League Premier Division	2–2

1978 Davie Provan was signed for £100,000 from Kilmarnock.

1982	Motherwell	A	Scottish League Premier Division	7–0
1985	Atletico Madrid	A	Cup-Winners' Cup 1st round 1st leg	1–1
1991	Germinal Ekeren	H	UEFA Cup 1st round 1st leg	2–0
1993	Dundee United	H	Scottish League Premier Division	1–1

1891	Kelvinside	H	Glasgow Cup	11–1
1896	Clyde	H	Glasgow Cup	5–1
1898	Hearts	A	Scottish League	2–2
1903	Queen's Park	A	Glasgow Cup	1–0
1904	Hearts	A	Scottish League	0–2
1908	Queen's Park	A	Glasgow Cup	2–1
1910	Hibernian	A	Scottish League	4–0
1914	Hibernian	A	Scottish League	1–1
1921	Hibernian	A	Scottish League	1–2
1925	Dundee United	A	Scottish League	0–1
1931	Morton	A	Scottish League	3–3
1933	Cowdenbeath	H	Scottish League	7–0
1936	Rangers	H	Scottish League	1–1
1942	Motherwell	A	League – Southern Division	1–2
1951	Forfar Athletic	A	League Cup quarter-final	1–1
1953	Rangers	A	Scottish League	1–1
1959	Raith Rovers	A	Scottish League	3–0
1964	Dundee United	H	Scottish League	1–1
1970	Hibernian	A	Scottish League	0–2
1973	TPS Turku	A	European Cup 1st round 1st leg	6–1
1978	Bobby Lennox rejoined the club after a very brief spell with Houston Hurricane.			
1979	Partizani Tirane	A	European Cup 1st round 1st leg	0–1
1981	Rangers	A	Scottish League Premier Division	2–0
1984	Kaa Gent	A	Cup-Winners' Cup 1st round 1st leg	0–1
1987	Aberdeen	H	Scottish League Premier Division	2–2
1992	Falkirk	A	Scottish League Premier Division	5–4
1995	Rangers	H	League Cup	0–1

SEPTEMBER 20TH

1890	Battlefield	H	Glasgow Cup	7–0

Johnny Campbell made his first appearance for the club. Willie Groves scored 6 goals in the game.

1897	St Bernards	A	Scottish League	2–0
1902	Kilmarnock	A	Scottish League	3–1
1909	Hearts	A	Scottish League	2–1
1913	Morton	A	Scottish League	4–0
1919	Queen's Park	H	Glasgow Cup semi-final	3–1
1920	Hibernian	A	Scottish League	3–0
1924	Third Lanark	A	Glasgow Cup semi-final	4–2
1930	Rangers	H	Scottish League	2–0
1932	Clyde	H	Glasgow Cup	3–1
1941	Hamilton Academical	A	League – Southern Division	3–3
1947	Rangers	A	Scottish League	0–2
1950	Motherwell	A	League Cup quarter-final	1–0
1952	Rangers	H	Scottish League	2–1
1958	Raith Rovers	H	Scottish League	3–1

1967	Dinamo Kiev	H	European Cup 1st round 1st leg	1–2
1969	Rangers	A	Scottish League	1–0
1972	Stranraer	A	League Cup	2–1
1975	St Johnstone	A	Scottish League Premier Division	2–1

1978   Paul Wilson was sold to Motherwell for £50,000. In the 11 years he was at the club he played over 200 games, scoring on 50 occasions. He won a League Championship medal, 2 Scottish Cup winners' medals and a League Cup winners' medal.

1980	Airdrie	H	Scottish League Premier Division	1–1
1986	Hibernian	H	Scottish League Premier Division	5–1
1989	Aberdeen	Hampden Park		
			League Cup semi-final	0–1
1997	Aberdeen	H	Scottish League Premier Division	2–0

SEPTEMBER 21ST

1885   Charlie Shaw was born in Twechar.

1895	Linthouse	A	Glasgow Cup	7–1
1901	Morton	H	Scottish League	2–1
1907	Airdrie	H	Scottish League	1–1
1912	Dundee	A	Scottish League	1–3
1929	Dundee	H	Scottish League	1–1
1935	Rangers	A	Scottish League	2–1

This was Celtic's first victory at Ibrox for over 14 years Frank Murphy and Johnny Crum scoring the goals.

1940	Dumbarton	H	League – Southern Division	1–0
1946	Hibernian	A	League Cup	2–4
1954	Partick Thistle	H	Glasgow Cup replay	4–5
1957	Rangers	A	Scottish League	3–2

22 years after their last victory at Ibrox Sammy Wilson scored the winner. Jimmy Sharkey played his last League game for the club.

1963	Falkirk	A	Scottish League	0–1

Jim Brogan made his debut.

1966	Dunfermline Athletic	A	League Cup quarter-final	3–1
1968	Dunfermline Athletic	A	Scottish League	1–1
1974	Motherwell	A	Scottish League	2–1

1983   Paul McStay made his international debut for Scotland in the 2–0 victory over Uruguay at Hampden.

1991	Airdrie	H	Scottish League Premier Division	3–1
1994	Dundee United	H	League Cup	1–0
1996	Dunfermline Athletic	H	Scottish League Premier Division	5–1

SEPTEMBER 22ND

1888	Cowlairs	H	Scottish Cup	8–0

Mick Dunbar became the first Celtic player to score a hat-trick.

1894	Rangers	H	Scottish League	5–3
1900	Rangers	A	Glasgow Cup	3–4
1906	Queen's Park	H	Glasgow Cup semi-final	5–0

| 1917 | Rangers | H | Glasgow Cup semi-final | 0–3 |
| 1923 | Ayr United | A | Scottish League | 2–4 |

Willie Cringan played his last match for the club. He acted as spokesman for the team when asking Willie Maley for more money and was promptly transferred a few weeks later. The centre-half played over 200 games for the club in 6 years.

1928	St Mirren	H	Scottish League	0–3
1934	Aberdeen	H	Scottish League	4–1
1945	Hearts	A	League – 'A' Division	2–2
1951	Rangers	A	Scottish League	1–1
1956	Rangers	H	Scottish League	0–2
1962	Aberdeen	H	Scottish League	1–2
1965	Raith Rovers	H	League Cup quarter-final	4–0

John Kennedy, Jock Stein's first signing for the club, made his one and only appearance.

1971	Clydebank	H	League Cup quarter-final	6–2
1976	Albion Rovers	A	League Cup quarter-final	1–0
1979	Aberdeen	A	Scottish League Premier Division	2–1
1980	Hamilton Academical	A	League Cup	3–1
1982	Partick Thistle	A	League Cup quarter-final	3–0
1984	St Mirren	A	Scottish League Premier Division	2–1
1990	Hearts	H	Scottish League Premier Division	3–0

SEPTEMBER 23RD

1893	Leith Athletic	H	Scottish League	4–1
1899	Clyde	A	Scottish League	5–0
1901	Third Lanark	A	Scottish League	2–0
1905	Partick Thistle	H	Glasgow Cup	4–0
1907	Aberdeen	A	Scottish League	1–2

Willie Orr made his final appearance after injury forced him to retire later on in the season. In 10 years at the club he made over 200 appearances scoring 23 times. He won 4 Championship medals and 3 Scottish Cup winners' medals.

1911	Kilmarnock	A	Scottish League	2–0
1916	Rangers	H	Glasgow Cup semi-final	3–0
1922	Dundee	A	Scottish League	1–0
1933	St Johnstone	A	Scottish League	1–1
1944	Clyde	H	League – Southern Division	2–4
1950	Rangers	H	Scottish League	3–2
1961	Dundee United	H	Scottish League	3–1
1964	Leixos SC	A	Fairs Cup 1st round 1st leg	1–1
1967	St Johnstone	H	Scottish League	1–1
1970	Dundee	H	League Cup quarter-final	5–1

Paul Wilson came on as substitute and scored on his debut.

| 1972 | Dundee | A | Scottish League | 0–2 |
| 1978 | Partick Thistle | A | Scottish League Premier Division | 3–2 |

Davie Provan made his debut.

| 1986 | Motherwell | Hampden Park | | |

			League Cup semi-final	2–2
1989	Motherwell	H	Scottish League Premier Division	1–1
1992	Aberdeen	A	League Cup	0–1
1995	Hearts	A	Scottish League Premier Division	4–0

SEPTEMBER 24TH

1892	Rangers	A	Scottish League	2–2
1898	Rangers	H	Scottish League	0–4
1900	Third Lanark	H	Scottish League	5–1
1904	Partick Thistle	H	Glasgow Cup semi-final	2–0
1906	Third Lanark	H	Scottish League	2–0
1910	Third Lanark	H	Glasgow Cup semi-final	1–0
1917	Third Lanark	A	Scottish League	2–0
1921	Dumbarton	A	Scottish League	5–0
1923	Morton	H	Scottish League	3–0
1927	Clyde	H	Scottish League	3–0
1928	Third Lanark	A	Glasgow Cup semi-final	2–2
1932	Kilmarnock	H	Scottish League	0–1
1938	Raith Rovers	H	Scottish League	6–1
1949	Rangers	A	Scottish League	0–4
1951	Clyde	Hampden Park		
			Glasgow Cup final	1–2
1955	Rangers	A	Scottish League	0–0
1960	Aberdeen	H	Scottish League	0–0
1966	Dundee	A	Scottish League	2–1
1969	Aberdeen	H	League Cup quarter-final	2–1
1975	Stenhousemuir	H	League Cup quarter-final	1–0
1977	Clydebank	H	Scottish League Premier Division	1–0
1980	Hamilton Academical	H	League Cup	4–1
1983	Dundee	A	Scottish League Premier Division	6–2
1988	Dundee	A	Scottish League Premier Division	0–1
1994	Hibernian	H	Scottish League	2–0

John Collins scored on his 200th senior appearance for the club.

| 1996 | Hamburg | A | UEFA Cup qualifying round 2nd leg | 0–2 |

SEPTEMBER 25TH

1897	Clyde	H	Scottish League	6–1
1899	Third Lanark	A	Scottish League	3–0
1905	Third Lanark	A	Scottish League	1–0
1909	Queen's Park	A	Glasgow Cup semi-final	1–1
1911	Partick Thistle	H	Scottish League	3–0
1915	Third Lanark	H	Glasgow Cup semi-final	2–0
1920	Ayr United	H	Scottish League	3–1
1922	Aberdeen	A	Scottish League	1–3
1926	Hibernian	A	Scottish League	2–3
1933	Rangers	H	Glasgow Cup semi-final	1–1

1937	Aberdeen	A	Scottish League	1–1
1943	Hearts	A	League – Southern Division	0–0
1944	Third Lanark	H	Glasgow Cup semi-final	2–1
1948	Rangers	H	League Cup	3–1
1950	Partick Thistle	Hampden Park		
			Glasgow Cup final	1–1
1954	Raith Rovers	A	Scottish League	3–1
1961	Queen's Park	H	Glasgow Cup	4–1
1965	Aberdeen	H	Scottish League	7–1
1968	Hamilton Academical	A	League Cup quarter-final	4–2

Kenny Dalglish came on as sub for Charlie Gallagher to make his debut for the club.

| 1971 | Airdrie | A | Scottish League | 5–0 |

John Hughes came on as substitute (for Jim Craig) in what was to be his last game for the club. In nearly 13 years' service he had made over 400 appearances, scoring 189 goals.

1974	Hamilton Academical	A	League Cup quarter-final	4–2
1976	Kilmarnock	A	Scottish League Premier Division	4–0
1982	Hibernian	H	Scottish League Premier Division	2–0
1990	Dundee United	Hampden Park		
			League Cup semi-final	2–0
1993	Hearts	A	Scottish League Premier Division	0–1

SEPTEMBER 26TH

1891	Dumbarton	H	Scottish League	2–0
1895	St Bernards	A	Scottish League	0–3
1896	St Mirren	H	Scottish League	2–1

Davie Adams made his first senior appearance for the club in goal.

1903	Hibernian	H	Scottish League	1–0
1904	Third Lanark	H	Scottish League	2–1
1908	Rangers	H	Glasgow Cup semi-final	2–2
1910	Partick Thistle	A	Scottish League	1–1

Andy McAtee made his debut.

1914	Dundee	A	Scottish League	3–1
1921	Morton	H	Scottish League	1–0
1925	Falkirk	H	Scottish League	3–1
1927	Third Lanark	H	Glasgow Cup semi-final	7–0
1931	Falkirk	H	Scottish League	4–1
1932	Partick Thistle	A	Glasgow Cup semi-final	0–1
1936	Hearts	A	Scottish League	1–0
1938	Queen's Park	H	Glasgow Cup semi-final	2–1
1942	Hibernian	H	League – Southern Division	0–3
1949	Brentford	H	Friendly	2–2
1953	Aberdeen	H	Scottish League	3–0

Bobby Collins became one of the few players to score a hat-trick of penalties in a game.

| 1955 | Rangers | Hampden Park | | |

			Glasgow Cup final	1–1
1959	Clyde	H	Scottish League	1–1

John Fallon made his debut.

1960	Partick Thistle	Hampden Park		
			Glasgow Cup final	0–2
1962	Valencia	A	Fairs Cup 1st round 1st leg	2–4
1964	Hearts	A	Scottish League	2–4

Duncan MacKay made his last appearance for the club after 9 years' service. He made over 230 appearances, scoring 7 times. Even though he failed to win any major trophies he was capped 14 times by Scotland.

1970	Dundee	H	Scottish League	3–0
1979	Stirling Albion	A	League Cup	2–1
1981	Partick Thistle	H	Scottish League Premier Division	2–0
1987	St Mirren	A	Scottish League Premier Division	1–0
1992	Partick Thistle	H	Scottish League Premier Division	1–2

SEPTEMBER 27TH

1890	Carfin Shamrock	H	Scottish Cup	2–2
1897	Rangers	A	Scottish League	4–0
1898	Hibernian	H	Scottish League	1–2
1902	Third Lanark	H	Scottish League	1–0
1909	Third Lanark	A	Scottish League	1–0
1913	Third Lanark	H	Glasgow Cup	0–0

Willie Loney made his last appearance for the club. The centre-half played over 300 games for the club in his 13 years' service.

1915	Clyde	H	Scottish League	5–0
1919	Clyde	H	Scottish League	3–1
1920	Third Lanark	H	Scottish League	3–0
1924	Motherwell	H	Scottish League	4–0

Jimmy McGrory scored his first hat-trick for the club.

1926	Partick Thistle	H	Glasgow Cup semi-final	3–1
1930	Queen's Park	A	Scottish League	3–3
1937	Rangers	H	Glasgow Cup	1–2
1941	Morton	A	League – Southern Division	3–2
1947	Motherwell	H	Scottish League	0–1
1948	Third Lanark	Hampden Park		
			Glasgow Cup final	3–1
1952	Aberdeen	A	Scottish League	2–2
1958	Aberdeen	A	Scottish League	1–3
1967	Ayr United	A	League Cup quarter-final	2–0

Lou Macari came on as sub for Bertie Auld to make his debut.

1969	Clyde	H	Scottish League	2–1
1972	Rosenborg	A	European Cup 1st round 2nd leg	3–1
1975	Dundee United	H	Scottish League Premier Division	2–1
1978	Burnley	H	Anglo Scottish Cup quarter-final 2nd leg	1–2
1980	Aberdeen	A	Scottish League Premier Division	2–2

1984	Dundee	A	Scottish League Premier Division	3–2
1986	Falkirk	A	Scottish League Premier Division	1–0
1989	Partizan Belgrade	H	Cup-Winners' Cup 1st round 2nd leg	5–4
1997	Dundee United	A	Scottish League Premier Division	2–1

SEPTEMBER 28TH

1895	Dumbarton	A	Scottish League	3–2
1901	Kilmarnock	A	Scottish League	1–0
1903	Third Lanark	A	Scottish League	1–3
1907	Queen's Park	H	Glasgow Cup semi-final	2–0
1908	Third Lanark	H	Scottish League	1–0
1912	Clyde	H	Glasgow Cup semi-final	0–0
1914	Clyde	A(H)	Scottish League	3–0
1918	Falkirk	A	Scottish League	2–1
1921	Partick Thistle	A	Glasgow Cup semi-final	2–0
1925	Rangers	H	Glasgow Cup semi-final	2–2
1929	Ayr United	A	Scottish League	3–1
1931	Rangers	H	Glasgow Cup semi-final	1–1
1935	Hearts	H	Scottish League	2–1
1936	Rangers	A	Glasgow Cup semi-final	1–2
1940	Rangers	A	Glasgow Cup final	1–0
1946	Third Lanark	H	League Cup	0–0
1957	Clyde	Ibrox	League Cup semi-final	4–2
1963	St Mirren	A	Scottish League	1–2
1966	FC Zurich	H	European Cup 1st round 1st leg	2–0
1968	Aberdeen	H	Scottish League	2–1
1974	Ayr United	H	Scottish League	5–3
1977	Jeunesse Esch	A	European Cup 1st round 2nd leg	6–1
1983	Aarhus GF	A	UEFA Cup 1st round 2nd leg	4–1
1985	Dundee	A	Scottish League Premier Division	2–0
1988	Motherwell	H	Scottish League Premier Division	3–1
1991	Hibernian	A	Scottish League Premier Division	1–1
1994	Dinamo Batumi	H	Cup-Winners' Cup 1st round 2nd leg	4–0
1996	Rangers	A	Scottish League Premier Division	0–2

SEPTEMBER 29TH

1902	Hearts	H	Scottish League	2–2
1906	Airdrie	A	Scottish League	2–0
1913	Clyde	H	Scottish League	2–0
1917	Hearts	A	Scottish League	1–0
1919	Third Lanark	A	Scottish League	4–1
1923	Aberdeen	A	Scottish League	2–0
1924	Cowdenbeath	H	Scottish League	3–1
1928	Hamilton Academical	A	Scottish League	1–1
1928	Bertie Peacock was born in Coleraine.			
1930	Clyde	A	Glasgow Cup semi-final	3–1

1934	Albion Rovers	A	Scottish League	1–2
1941	Rangers	Hampden Park		
			Glasgow Cup semi-final	2–3

One of the smallest crowds – just 15,000 – to have witnessed an Old Firm derby turned up at Hampden Park for the Glasgow Cup semi-final. As there had been crowd trouble at the previous meeting between the two sides, the semi-final was made an all-ticket affair.

1945	Queen of the South	H	League – 'A' Division	2–0
1951	Hearts	H	Scottish League	1–3
1956	Motherwell	A	Scottish League	0–1
1962	Raith Rovers	A	Scottish League	2–0
1964	Morton	Ibrox	League Cup semi-final	2–0
1965	Go Ahead Eagles	A	Cup-Winners' Cup 1st round 1st leg	6–0

Bobby Lennox scored a hat-trick.

1971	B 1903	H	European Cup 1st round 2nd leg	3–0
1973	St Johnstone	A	Scottish League	1–2
1976	Wisla Krakow	A	UEFA Cup 1st round 2nd leg	0–2
1979	St Mirren	H	Scottish League Premier Division	3–1
1982	Ajax Amsterdam	A	European Cup 1st round 2nd leg	2–1
1987	Borussia Dortmund	A	UEFA Cup 1st round 2nd leg	0–2
1990	St Mirren	A	Scottish League Premier Division	3–2
1993	Young Boys Berne	H	UEFA Cup 1st round 2nd leg	1–0

SEPTEMBER 30TH

1893	St Mirren	A	Scottish League	2–1
1899	Hearts	H	Scottish League	0–2
1900	Hibernian	A	Scottish League	2–2
1905	Airdrie	H	Scottish League	2–1
1907	Third Lanark	A	Scottish League	3–1
1911	Hearts	A	Scottish League	1–2
1912	Partick Thistle	A	Scottish League	3–2
1916	Hearts	H	Scottish League	1–0

'Sunny Jim' Young played what was to be his last game before injury forced him to retire. His 14 years at the club saw him make over 440 appearances. He won 10 Championship medals and 6 Scottish Cup winners' medals. One of the finest players ever to wear the shirt of Celtic, Young is mentioned in the same breath as Jock Stein, which shows his magnitude when it comes to contribution to the history of the club.

1918	Third Lanark	H	Scottish League	3–1
1929	Queen's Park	H	Glasgow Cup semi-final	3–1
1933	Queen's Park	H	Scottish League	3–1
1935	Third Lanark	H	Glasgow Cup semi-final	1–1
1939	Queen's Park	H	Glasgow Cup semi-final	2–2
1944	Morton	A	League – Southern Division	3–4
1944	Jimmy Johnstone was born in Viewpark.			
1950	Raith Rovers	A	Scottish League	2–1
1961	Falkirk	A	Scottish League	1–3

1967	Stirling Albion	A	Scottish League	4–0
1970	KPV (Karleby)	A	European Cup 1st round 2nd leg	5–0
1972	Ayr United	H	Scottish League	1–0
1978	St Mirren	H	Scottish League Premier Division	2–1
1981	Juventus	A	European Cup 1st round 2nd leg	0–2
1989	Aberdeen	A	Scottish League Premier Division	1–1
1992	Cologne	H	UEFA Cup 1st round 2nd leg	3–0

1993   Stuart Slater was sold to Ipswich for £750,000. He had scored just 3 goals in his 55 games for the club.

1995	Rangers	H	Scottish League Premier Division	0–2
1997	Liverpool	A	UEFA Cup 1st round 2nd leg	0–0

OCTOBER 1ST

1892	Clyde	H	Scottish League	3–1
1898	St Mirren	A	Scottish League	0–4
1904	Queen's Park	A	Scottish League	3–2
1910	Queen's Park	A	Scottish League	1–0
1921	Rangers	Hampden Park		
			Glasgow Cup final	0–1
1927	Dundee	A	Scottish League	4–1
1932	Hearts	A	Scottish League	1–1
1934	Dundee	A	Scottish League	0–0
1938	Albion Rovers	A	Scottish League	8–1
1949	Raith Rovers	H	Scottish League	2–2
1955	Raith Rovers	H	Scottish League	2–0

Jim Sharkey scored on his debut for the club.

1958	Partick Thistle	Ibrox	League Cup semi-final	1–2
1960	Airdrie	A	Scottish League	0–2
1966	St Johnstone	H	Scottish League	6–1
1969	FC Basel	H	European Cup 1st round 2nd leg	2–0
1975	Valur	H	Cup-Winners' Cup 1st round 2nd leg	7–0

George McCluskey came on as sub for Paul Wilson and scored on his full debut.

1977	Hibernian	H	Scottish League Premier Division	3–1
1980	Politechnica Timisoara	A	Cup-Winners' Cup 1st round 2nd leg	0–1
1983	St Mirren	H	Scottish League Premier Division	1–1
1986	Shamrock Rovers	H	European Cup 1st round 2nd leg	2–0
1988	Hibernian	A	Scottish League Premier Division	1–3
1991	Germinal Ekeren	A	UEFA Cup 1st round 2nd leg	1–1

1991   Anton Rogan was sold to Sunderland. He made 169 appearances for the club.

1994	Motherwell	A	Scottish League	1–1

OCTOBER 2ND

1897	St Mirren	A	Scottish League	0–0
1909	Dundee	H	Scottish League	1–0
1911	Raith Rovers	A	Scottish League	2–1
1915	Hibernian	A	Scottish League	4–0

1920	Clyde	H	Glasgow Cup final	1–0
1926	Dundee	H	Scottish League	0–0
1928	Third Lanark	H	Glasgow Cup semi-final	5–1
1937	Clyde	H	Scottish League	3–1
1943	Albion Rovers	H	League – Southern Division	3–2
1948	Hibernian	A	League Cup	2–4
1954	Kilmarnock	H	Scottish League	6–3
1968	AS Saint-Etienne	H	European Cup 1st round 2nd leg	4–0
1971	St Johnstone	H	Scottish League	0–1
1974	Olympiakos	A	European Cup 1st round 2nd leg	0–2
1976	Hibernian	H	Scottish League Premier Division	1–1
1982	Dundee United	A	Scottish League Premier Division	2–2
1985	Atletico Madrid	H	Cup-Winners' Cup 1st round 2nd leg	1–2

1985 As a result of the incident the previous year, Parkhead was empty for this match as the spectator ban was enforced. Without the usual marvellous support, the palyers struggled and the team went down 2–3 on aggregate.

1987 Frank McAvennie was signed for £750,000 from West Ham United.

| 1993 | Kilmarnock | H | Scottish League Premier Division | 0–0 |

OCTOBER 3RD

1891	St Mirren	A	Scottish League	2–1
1896	Dundee	A	Scottish League	2–2
1903	Queen's Park	H	Scottish League	3–0
1908	Rangers	A	Glasgow Cup semi-final replay	2–0
1910	Raith Rovers	A	Scottish League	1–2
1914	Dundee	H	Scottish League	6–0
1925	Airdrie	A	Scottish League	1–3
1931	Kilmarnock	A	Scottish League	3–2
1936	Aberdeen	H	Scottish League	3–2
1942	Partick Thistle	A	League – Southern Division	3–2

1944 Henry 'Harry' Hood was born in Glasgow.

| 1959 | Arbroath | A | Scottish League | 5–0 |

1959 John Clark made his debut. John Hughes signed for the club.

1964 Steve Chalmers scored on his international debut for Scotland in the 2–3 defeat against Wales in Cardiff. Jimmy Johnstone also made the first of 23 appearances for his country in this match.

1970	Dunfermline Athletic	A	Scottish League	2–0
1973	TPS Turku	H	European Cup 1st round 2nd leg	3–0
1979	Partizani Tirane	H	European Cup 1st round 2nd leg	4–1
1981	Dundee	A	Scottish League Premier Division	3–1
1984	Kaa Gent	H	Cup-Winners' Cup 1st round 2nd leg	3–0
1987	Hibernian	H	Scottish League Premier Division	1–1

1987 Frank McAvennie made his debut.

| 1992 | Dundee | A | Scottish League Premier Division | 1–0 |

1890	Carfin Shamrock	H	Scottish Cup	3–1
1902	Queen's Park	A	Scottish League	1–2
1913	Aberdeen	H	Scottish League	2–1
1919	Partick Thistle	H	Glasgow Cup final	1–0
1921	St Mirren	H	Scottish League	2–0
1924	Rangers	A	Glasgow Cup final	1–4
1930	Morton	H	Scottish League	4–1
1941	Motherwell	H	League – Southern Division	1–2

1946 George Patterson left the club for Brentford 20 years after he made his debut. He made nearly 300 Celtic appearances before and during the war, scoring 8 goals.

1947	Aberdeen	A	Scottish League	0–2
1952	Motherwell	H	Scottish League	3–0
1958	Queen of the South	H	Scottish League	3–1

Paddy Crerand made his debut.

1965	Hibernian	Ibrox	League Cup semi-final	2–2
1967	Dinamo Kiev	A	European Cup 1st round 2nd leg	1–1
1969	Raith Rovers	H	Scottish League	7–1
1972	Stranraer	H	League Cup	5–2
1975	Hearts	H	Scottish League Premier Division	3–1
1978	Motherwell	H	League Cup	0–1
1980	Dundee United	H	Scottish League Premier Division	2–0
1986	St Mirren	H	Scottish League Premier Division	2–0
1989	Hibernian	H	Scottish League Premier Division	3–1
1995	Falkirk	A	Scottish League Premier Division	1–0
1997	Kilmarnock	H	Scottish League Premier Division	4–0

OCTOBER 5TH

1889	Rangers	H	Friendly	1–1
1895	Hibernian	H	Scottish League	3–1
1901	Rangers	A	Scottish League	2–2
1907	Hibernian	A	Scottish League	2–1
1912	Morton	H	Scottish League	1–0
1914	Raith Rovers	A	Scottish League	2–2
1918	Rangers	Hampden Park	Glasgow Cup final	0–2
1929	Falkirk	H	Scottish League	7–0
1935	Kilmarnock	A	Scottish League	1–1

1935 Jimmy Delaney made his international debut for Scotland in the 1–1 draw with Wales in Cardiff.

1940	Airdrie	A	League – Southern Division	0–1
1946	Hamilton Academical	A	League Cup	2–2
1963	Dunfermline Athletic	H	Scottish League	2–2
1966	FC Zurich	A	European Cup 1st round 2nd leg	3–0
1968	Dundee United	H	Scottish League	2–0
1974	Dumbarton	A	Scottish League	3–1
1977	Stirling Albion	A	League Cup	2–1

1983	Kilmarnock	H	League Cup	1–1
1985	St Mirren	H	Scottish League Premier Division	2–0
1988	Honved	H	European Cup 1st round 2nd leg	4–0
1991	Hearts	H	Scottish League Premier Division	3–1

OCTOBER 6TH

1894	Clyde	H	Glasgow Cup	4–1
1900	Rangers	H	Scottish League	2–1
1906	Third Lanark	Ibrox	Glasgow Cup final	3–2
1909	Queen's Park	H	Glasgow Cup semi-final	6–1

1922 Jock Stein was born in 1922.

1923	Clyde	H	Scottish League	4–0
1925	Rangers	A	Glasgow Cup semi-final replay	1–1
1928	Queen's Park	A	Glasgow Cup final	2–0
1931	Rangers	A	Glasgow Cup semi-final	2–2
1934	Queen of the South	H	Scottish League	1–2
1945	Partick Thistle	H	League – 'A' Division	4–1

1948 Willie Fernie was signed from Leslie Hearts.

1951 Bertie Peacock made his international debut for Northern Ireland in the 0–3 defeat by Scotland in Belfast.

1956	Clyde	Hampden Park		
			League Cup semi-final	2–0
1962	Kilmarnock	H	Scottish League	1–1
1971	St Mirren	Hampden Park		
			League Cup semi-final	3–0

Willie Wallace played his last game for the club after coming on as substitute. In 5 years he had scored 135 goals in 234 appearances, winning 5 consecutive Championship medals, 3 Scottish Cup winners' and 2 League Cup winners' medals.

1973	Motherwell	H	Scottish League	2–0
1975	Partick Thistle	Hampden Park		
			League Cup semi-final	1–0
1976	Albion Rovers	H	League Cup quarter-final	5–0
1979	Partick Thistle	A	Scottish League Premier Division	0–0
1980	Queen's Park	H	Glasgow Cup semi-final	2–0
1984	Aberdeen	H	Scottish League Premier Division	2–1
1990	St Johnstone	H	Scottish League Premier Division	0–0
1993	St Johnstone	A	Scottish League Premier Division	1–2

Liam Brady resigned as manager after the game.

OCTOBER 7TH

1893	Northern	A	Glasgow Cup	3–2
1899	Rangers	A	Scottish League	3–3
1905	Third Lanark	Hampden Park		
			Glasgow Cup final	3–0
1911	Hamilton Academical	A	Scottish League	0–1
1913	Third Lanark	A	Glasgow Cup	0–1

| 1916 | Clyde | H | Glasgow Cup final | 3–2 |

Peter Johnstone played his last game for the club before he was killed in action during the war. In 8 years he played over 230 games and had scored 19 goals.

1922	Partick Thistle	H	Scottish League	4–3
1931	Rangers	A	Glasgow Cup semi-final	0–1
1933	Aberdeen	A	Scottish League	0–3
1939	Queen's Park	A	Glasgow Cup semi-final replay	0–1
1944	Rangers	Hampden Park		
			Glasgow Cup final	2–3

Jim McKay scored on his debut.

| 1950 | Raith Rovers | H | Scottish League | 2–3 |

1961 10 years after making his international debut Bertie Peacock made his last appearance for Northern Ireland in the 1–6 defeat by Scotland in Belfast. He had scored 2 goals in his 31 appearances, the last 3 whilst he was at Coleraine.

| 1964 | Leixos SC | H | Fairs Cup 1st round 2nd leg | 3–0 |
| 1965 | Go Ahead Eagles | H | Cup-Winners' Cup 1st round 2nd leg | 1–0 |

Jim Craig made his senior debut.

1967	Hibernian	H	Scottish League	4–0
1970	Dumbarton	Hampden Park		
			League Cup semi-final	0–0
1972	Airdrie	H	Scottish League	1–1
1978	Aberdeen	A	Scottish League Premier Division	1–4
1987	Dundee	A	Scottish League Premier Division	1–1
1992	Hearts	H	Scottish League Premier Division	1–1
1995	Partick Thistle	H	Scottish League Premier Division	2–1

OCTOBER 8TH

1898	St Bernards	H	Scottish League	1–0
1904	Rangers	Hampden Park		
			Glasgow Cup final	2–1
1910	Rangers	Hampden Park		
			Glasgow Cup final	1–3
1910	Charlie Napier was born in Bainsford.			
1912	Clyde	A	Glasgow Cup semi-final	4–0
1921	Dundee	A	Scottish League	0–0
1925	Rangers	A	Glasgow Cup semi-final replay	2–0
1927	Rangers	Hampden Park		
			Glasgow Cup final	2–1
1932	St Johnstone	H	Scottish League	5–0
1949	Motherwell	A	Scottish League	2–1
1955	Hearts	A	Scottish League	1–2
1960	St Mirren	H	Scottish League	4–2
1966	Hibernian	A	Scottish League	5–3
1969	Ayr United	Hampden Park		
			League Cup semi-final	3–3
1977	Partick Thistle	A	Scottish League Premier Division	0–1

1980	Partick Thistle	A	League Cup quarter-final	1–0
1983	Dundee United	A	Scottish League Premier Division	1–2
1986	Hearts	H	Scottish League Premier Division	2–0
1988	St Mirren	H	Scottish League Premier Division	7–1
1991	Motherwell	A	Scottish League Premier Division	2–0
1994	Aberdeen	H	Scottish League	0–0

OCTOBER 9TH

1897	Third Lanark	A	Scottish League	1–0
1909	Rangers	Hampden Park		
			Glasgow Cup final	1–0
1915	Rangers	Hampden Park		
			Glasgow Cup final	2–1
1920	Queen's Park	H	Scottish League	5–1
1922	Alec Thomson signed pro forms for the club.			
1926	Rangers	Hampden Park		
			Glasgow Cup final	1–0
1935	Third Lanark	A	Glasgow Cup semi-final replay	1–0
1937	Arbroath	A	Scottish League	0–2
1943	Partick Thistle	H	League – Southern Division	4–5
	Stephen Murray was born.			
1948	Clyde	H	League Cup	3–6
	John McGrory made his debut.			
1954	Aberdeen	A	Scottish League	2–0
1961	Partick Thistle	A	Glasgow Cup semi-final	5–1
1963	FC Basel	H	Cup-Winners' Cup 1st round 2nd leg	5–0
1964	Frank Haffey was sold to Swindon Town for £8,000.			
1965	Hearts	H	Scottish League	5–2
1968	Clyde	Hampden Park		
			League Cup semi-final	1–0
1971	Hibernian	A	Scottish League	1–0
1974	Airdrie	Hampden Park		
			League Cup semi-final	1–0
1982	Aberdeen	H	Scottish League Premier Division	1–3
1993	Dundee	H	Scottish League Premier Division	2–1

OCTOBER 10TH

1891	Partick Thistle	A	Glasgow Cup	3–1
1896	Rangers	H	Scottish League	1–1
1903	Dundee	H	Scottish League	4–2
1908	Dundee	H	Scottish League	2–0
	Joe Dodds made his senior debut.			
1914	Ayr United	A	Scottish League	0–1
1925	Clyde	H	Glasgow Cup final	1–2

Patsy Gallagher played his last game for the club. In over 460 League and cup appearances he scored just under 200 goals and will always be remembered as one of the greatest players to ever represent the club. In all he had won 7 Championship medals, 4 Scottish Cup winners' medals and no less than 15 Glasgow Cup and Charity Cup winners' medals.

1931	Clyde	H	Scottish League	1–1
1936	Queen's Park	A	Scottish League	2–1
1942	St Mirren	H	League – Southern Division	3–2
1951	Morton	A	Scottish League	1–0
1953	Raith Rovers	H	Scottish League	3–0
1959	Aberdeen	H	Scottish League	1–1
1964	Aberdeen	A	Scottish League	3–1
1966	Queen's Park	H	Glasgow Cup semi-final	4–0
1970	St Johnstone	H	Scottish League	1–0
1973	Motherwell	H	League Cup	0–1
1979	Stirling Albion	H	League Cup	2–0
1981	St Mirren	A	Scottish League Premier Division	2–1
1987	Morton	H	Scottish League Premier Division	3–1

OCTOBER 11TH

1902	Clyde	A	Glasgow Cup semi-final	4–1
1913	Aberdeen	A	Scottish League	1–0
1919	Hibernian	H	Scottish League	7–3
1924	Hearts	H	Scottish League	1–0
1924	Peter Shevlin signed pro forms to replace Charlie Shaw for £120 from St Roch.			
1930	Rangers	Hampden Park		
			Glasgow Cup final	2–1
1930	Ronnie Simpson was born.			
1933	Rangers	A	Glasgow Cup semi-final replay	1–2
	George Patterson made his debut.			
1941	Hibernian	A	League – Southern Division	3–1
1947	Morton	H	Scottish League	3–2
	Jim McLaughlin scored on his debut.			
1952	Clyde	A	Scottish League	2–1
1958	Falkirk	H	Scottish League	3–4
1967	Morton	Hampden Park		
			League Cup semi-final	7–1
1969	Airdrie	A	Scottish League	2–0
1972	Dundee	A	League Cup quarter-final	0–1
1975	Aberdeen	A	Scottish League Premier Division	2–1
1978	Motherwell	A	League Cup	4–1
1980	St Mirren	A	Scottish League Premier Division	2–0
1984	Mo Johnstone was signed from Watford.			
1986	Dundee	A	Scottish League Premier Division	3–0

OCTOBER 12TH

1895	Clyde	A	Scottish League	5–1
1901	Third Lanark	H	Glasgow Cup	5–1
1907	Rangers	Hampden Park		

			Glasgow Cup final	2–2
1912	Rangers		Hampden Park	
			Glasgow Cup final	1–3
1918	Kilmarnock	A	Scottish League	1–1
1920	Falkirk	H	Scottish League	4–1
1929	Rangers		Hampden Park	
			Glasgow Cup final	0–0
1935	Rangers	A	Glasgow Cup final	0–2
1938	Queen of the South	H	Scottish League	5–1
1940	Falkirk	H	League – Southern Division	2–2
1946	Hibernian	H	League Cup	1–1
1957	Raith Rovers	H	Scottish League	1–1
1963	Aberdeen	H	Scottish League	3–0
1964	Morton	H	Scottish League	1–0
1968	Hearts	A	Scottish League	1–0
1970	Dumbarton		Hampden Park	
			League Cup semi-final replay	4–3
1974	Arbroath	H	Scottish League	1–0
1985	Hearts	H	Scottish League Premier Division	0–1
1988	Dundee United	H	Scottish League Premier Division	1–0
1991	Dundee United	H	Scottish League Premier Division	4–1
1996	Motherwell	H	Scottish League Premier Division	1–0

OCTOBER 13TH

1888	Albion Rovers	H	Scottish Cup	4–1
1894	Clyde	A	Scottish League	4–2
1900	Queen's Park	H	Scottish League	2–0
1906	Aberdeen	H	Scottish League	2–1
1917	Kilmarnock	H	Scottish League	2–3
1923	Hearts	A	Scottish League	0–0
1925	Queen's Park	H	Scottish League	4–1
1928	Motherwell	A	Scottish League	3–3
1934	Clyde	A	Scottish League	3–0
1945	Third Lanark	A	League – 'A' Division	2–0
1951	Rangers	A	League Cup semi-final	0–3
1956	Falkirk	A	Scottish League	1–0
1962	Motherwell	A	Scottish League	2–0
1969	Ayr United		Hampden Park	
			League Cup semi-final replay	2–1
1973	Dundee	A	Scottish League	1–0
1979	Dundee	H	Scottish League Premier Division	3–0
1981	Queen's Park	A	Glasgow Cup semi-final	2–0
1984	Hibernian	H	Scottish League Premier Division	3–0
	Mo Johnstone made his debut.			
1990	Dunfermline Athletic	A	Scottish League Premier Division	1–1

1893	St Bernards	H	Scottish League	5–2
1899	Linthouse	H	Glasgow Cup semi-final	5–1
1905	Queen's Park	H	Scottish League	5–1
1911	Aberdeen	H	Scottish League	1–0
1916	Falkirk	A	Scottish League	1–1
1922	Motherwell	H	Scottish League	1–0
1938	Clyde	Hampden Park		
			Glasgow Cup final	3–0
1944	Hibernian	H	League – Southern Division	1–1
1950	Aberdeen	A	Scottish League	1–2
1961	Stirling Albion	H	Scottish League	5–0
1967	Partick Thistle	A	Scottish League	5–1

1969 Evan Williams was signed from Wolves as Ronnie Simpson's successor.

1972	Partick Thistle	A	Scottish League	4–0
1978	Dundee United	A	Scottish League Premier Division	0–1
1989	Dundee	A	Scottish League Premier Division	3–1
1995	Hibernian	H	Scottish League Premier Division	2–2
1997	Dunfermline	A	League Cup semi-final	1–0

OCTOBER 15TH

1865 Jimmy Kelly was born in Renton.

1892	Dumbarton	A	Scottish League	3–0
1898	Rangers	A	Glasgow Cup	1–1
1904	Rangers	H	Scottish League	2–2
1910	Hearts	H	Scottish League	0–0
1921	Albion Rovers	H	Scottish League	3–1
1927	Rangers	A	Scottish League	0–1
1932	Clyde	A	Scottish League	2–0
1949	Aberdeen	H	Scottish League	4–2
1955	Motherwell	H	Scottish League	2–2
1960	Hibernian	A	Scottish League	6–0
1962	Rangers	A	Glasgow Cup	2–2
1966	Airdrie	H	Scottish League	3–0
1969	Clyde	H	Glasgow Cup semi-final	4–1
1977	St Mirren	H	Scottish League Premier Division	1–2
1983	Hearts	H	Scottish League Premier Division	1–1

1987 Paul McGugan was sold to Barnsley for £50,000. In 7 years the tall centre-half made just 59 appearances.

| 1994 | Hearts | A | Scottish League | 0–1 |

OCTOBER 16TH

| 1909 | Port Glasgow Athletic | A | Scottish League | 3–2 |

1912 Joe Cassidy was signed aged 16 from Vale of Clyde, after impressing in his trial game against Hibernian in the Inter City League.

| 1915 | Hamilton Academical | A | Scottish League | 3–2 |
| 1920 | Dundee | A | Scottish League | 2–1 |

1926	St Mirren	A	Scottish League	1–3
1929	Rangers		Hampden Park	
			Glasgow Cup final replay	0–4
1937	Queen's Park	H	Scottish League	4–3

Jimmy McGrory played and inevitably scored in his last appearance for the club. One of the greatest ever goalscorers, McGrory notched up an incredible total of 472 goals in 445 games for the club during his 15 years' service – he was top scorer for 12 of those seasons. His total of 49 in season 1926–27 was also the best in Europe. He won 2 Championship medals and 4 Scottish Cup winners' medals, but the greatest mystery of this century is why he only played for Scotland on 7 occasions, scoring 6 goals in that time. The Celtic legend was to return to the club later on as manager.

1943	Airdrie	A	League – Southern Division	3–1
1943	Tommy Gemmell was born in Craigneuk.			
1948	Rangers	A	League Cup	1–2
1954	Queen of the South	H	Scottish League	1–1
	Eric Smith made his debut for the club.			
1965	Falkirk	A	Scottish League	4–3
1971	Dundee	H	Scottish League	3–1
1976	Ayr United	A	Scottish League Premier Division	2–0
1982	Kilmarnock	H	Scottish League Premier Division	2–1
1993	Hibernian	A	Scottish League Premier Division	1–1

OCTOBER 17TH

1891	Hearts	H	Scottish League	3–1
1896	Third Lanark	H	Scottish League	2–0
1903	Rangers	A	Scottish League	0–0
1908	Third Lanark		Hampden Park	
			Glasgow Cup final	1–1
1914	Falkirk	H	Scottish League	1–0
1914	Willie Buchan was born in Grangemouth.			
1925	Rangers	A	Scottish League	0–1
1931	Dundee	A	Scottish League	0–2
1936	Dundee	A	Scottish League	0–0
1942	Third Lanark	A	League – Southern Division	2–4
1953	Queen of the South	A	Scottish League	1–2
1959	Third Lanark	A	Scottish League	2–4
1964	St Mirren	H	Scottish League	4–1
1966	Airdrie		Hampden Park	
			League Cup semi-final	2–0
1970	Airdrie	A	Scottish League	3–1
1981	Dundee United	H	Scottish League Premier Division	1–1
1987	Rangers	A	Scottish League Premier Division	2–2

A typically tense Old Firm derby made more news off the field than anything that had gone on on it, for after Chris Woods, Terry Butcher and Frank McAvennie were sent off, the law courts got in on the act and summoned all three players, together with Graham Roberts, to answer charges of 'behaviour likely to cause a breach of the peace', the case being held the following April.

| 1992 | Motherwell | A | Scottish League Premier Division | 3–1 |

OCTOBER 18TH

1890	Wishaw Thistle	A	Scottish Cup	6–2
1902	Rangers	H	Scottish League	1–1
1913	Dundee	H	Scottish League	1–0

Jimmy McColl made his debut.

| 1919 | Rangers | A | Scottish League | 0–3 |
| 1924 | St Johnstone | A | Scottish League | 0–0 |

Peter Shevlin took over from Charlie Shaw in goal to make his debut.

1930	St Mirren	H	Scottish League	3–1
1941	St Mirren	A	League – Southern Division	2–2
1947	Clyde	A	Scottish League	0–2
1952	Queen of the South	H	Scottish League	1–1
1958	Airdrie	A	Scottish League	4–1
1961	St Johnstone	A	Scottish League	3–0
1965	Hibernian	Ibrox	League Cup semi-final replay	4–0
1967	Racing Club	H	World Club Championship	1–0
1980	Morton	A	Scottish League Premier Division	3–2
1986	Motherwell	H	Scottish League Premier Division	3–1
1997	Hearts	A	Scottish League Premier Division	2–1

OCTOBER 19TH

1895	Cambuslang	H	Glasgow Cup	6–1
1901	Queen's Park	H	Scottish League	1–0
1907	Rangers	Hampden Park		
			Glasgow Cup final replay	0–0
1912	Raith Rovers	A	Scottish League	1–2
1918	Rangers	H	Scottish League	0–3
1929	Queen's Park	H	Scottish League	2–1

Chic Napier made his debut.

| 1935 | Airdrie | H | Scottish League | 4–0 |

Jimmy McGrory's 2 goals helped equal and beat Steve Bloomer's British record for League goals scored.

1940	Motherwell	A	League – Southern Division	1–5
1946	Third Lanark	A (Hampden Park)		
			League Cup	3–2

1946 Willie Miller made his international debut for Scotland in the 1–3 defeat by Wales in Wrexham.

| 1957 | Rangers | Hampden Park | | |
| | | | League Cup final | 7–1 |

One of the most memorable days in the history of the club as Celtic recorded the biggest victory in a Cup final (in Scotland or England).

| 1963 | Dundee United | A | Scottish League | 3–0 |
| 1968 | St Johnstone | H | Scottish League | 2–1 |

1971   John Hughes and Willie Wallace left the club to join Crystal Palace for £30,000.

| 1974 | Hibernian | H | Scottish League | 5–0 |

1975   The home game against Hibernian had to be abandoned after 83 minutes due to fog. Celtic were losing 0–2 at the time.

1977	SW Innsbruck	H	European Cup 2nd round 1st leg	2–1
1983	Sporting Lisbon	A	UEFA Cup 2nd round 1st leg	0–2
1985	Motherwell	A	Scottish League Premier Division	2–1
1991	Falkirk	A	Scottish League Premier Division	3–4
1994	Paris St Germain	A	Cup-Winners' Cup 2nd round 1st leg	0–1

OCTOBER 20TH

1881   Alec Bennett (grandfather of Scottish prop forward Sandy Carmichael) was born.

1894	Dumbarton	H	Scottish League	6–0
1906	Dundee	A	Scottish League	0–0
1917	Rangers	A	Scottish League	2–1
1923	Raith Rovers	H	Scottish League	0–0

1924   Willie Miller was born in Glasgow.

1928	Rangers	H	Scottish League	1–2
1934	Partick Thistle	A	Scottish League	3–1
1945	St Mirren	H	League – 'A' Division	2–2
1951	Dundee	A	Scottish League	1–2
1956	Raith Rovers	H	Scottish League	1–1
1962	Dundee United	H	Scottish League	1–0
1971	Sliema Wanderers	H	European Cup 2nd round 1st leg	5–0
1973	Hibernian	H	Scottish League	1–1
1976	Dundee United	H	Scottish League Premier Division	5–1
1979	Morton	A	Scottish League Premier Division	0–1
1980	Partick Thistle	H	League Cup quarter-final	2–1
1982	Real Sociedad	A	European Cup 2nd round 1st leg	0–2

1982   Jimmy McGrory died aged 78 in Glasgow.

1984	Dundee United	A	Scottish League Premier Division	3–1
1990	Dundee United	H	Scottish League Premier Division	0–0
1992	Borussia Dortmund	A	UEFA Cup 2nd round 1st leg	0–1
1993	Sporting Lisbon	H	UEFA Cup 2nd round 1st leg	1–0
1996	Hearts	A	Scottish League Premier Division	2–2

OCTOBER 21ST

1882   Davie Hamilton was born in Glasgow.

1899	St Mirren	A	Scottish League	2–2
1905	Rangers	A	Scottish League	2–3
1911	Rangers	A	Scottish League	1–3
1916	Morton	H	Scottish League	0–0
1922	Morton	A	Scottish League	1–0
1933	Motherwell	A	Scottish League	1–1
1939	Hamilton Academical	H	League – Western Division	3–4
1944	St Mirren	A	League – Southern Division	1–2

1950	Dundee	H	Scottish League	0–0

1950 Bobby Collins made his international debut for Scotland in the 3–1 victory over Wales in Cardiff.

1961	Hearts	A	Scottish League	1–2
1970	Waterford	Dublin	European Cup 2nd round 1st leg	7–0

Willie Wallace's first goal of his hat-trick, after just 18 seconds, still stands as club record as the fastest ever goal in a European tie. It was also the 100th Celtic goal scored in European competition.

1972	East Fife	H	Scottish League	3–0
1978	Morton	H	Scottish League Premier Division	0–0
1989	Hearts	H	Scottish League Premier Division	2–1
1995	Kilmarnock	A	Scottish League Premier Division	0–0

OCTOBER 22ND

1892	St Mirren	A	Scottish League	3–1
1898	Rangers	H	Glasgow Cup	1–2
1904	Third Lanark	A	Scottish League	2–1
1910	Hamilton Academical	A	Scottish League	1–0
1921	Rangers	A	Scottish League	1–1
1927	Aberdeen	A	Scottish League	1–3
1932	Motherwell	H	Scottish League	4–1

Johnny Crum scored 2 goals on his debut.

1938	Partick Thistle	A	Scottish League	0–0
1949	Dundee	A	Scottish League	0–3
1955	Clyde	A	Scottish League	3–1
1960	Clyde	A	Scottish League	3–0
1964	Paul McStay was born.			
1975	Boavista	A	Cup-Winners' Cup 2nd round 1st leg	0–0
1977	Dundee United	A	Scottish League Premier Division	2–1
1983	Aberdeen	A	Scottish League Premier Division	1–3
1986	Dinamo Kiev	H	European Cup 2nd round 1st leg	1–1
1988	Hearts	A	Scottish League Premier Division	2–0
1991	Neuchatel Xamax	A	UEFA Cup 2nd round 1st leg	1–5
1994	Falkirk	H	Scottish League	0–2

OCTOBER 23RD

1897	Hearts	H	Scottish League	3–2
1909	Queen's Park	H	Scottish League	6–0
1915	St Mirren	H	Scottish League	0–2
1920	Rangers	H	Scottish League	1–2
1926	Aberdeen	H	Scottish League	6–2
1929	Dundee United	A	Scottish League	2–2
1937	St Johnstone	H	Scottish League	6–0
1943	Falkirk	H	League – Southern Division	3–2
1948	Dundee	H	Scottish League	0–1

1948 Bobby Evans won the first of his 48 caps when he played in Scotland's 3–1 victory over Wales in Cardiff.

1959	Bobby Murdoch signed for the club.			
1965	Rangers		Hampden Park	
			League Cup	2–1
1971	Partick Thistle		Hampden Park	
			League Cup final	1–4
1976	Aberdeen	A	Scottish League Premier Division	1–2
1982	Morton	A	Scottish League Premier Division	2–1

OCTOBER 24TH

1891	Vale of Leven	H	Scottish League	6–1
1896	Hearts	A	Scottish League	1–1
1903	Hearts	H	Scottish League	4–0
1908	Third Lanark		Hampden Park	
			Glasgow Cup final replay	2–2
1914	Hamilton Academical	A	Scottish League	1–0
1925	Morton	A	Scottish League	5–0
1931	Ayr United	H	Scottish League	4–2

Joe McGhee scored both goals on his debut.

1936	Hibernian	H	Scottish League	5–1

1936   Richard Beattie was born in Glasgow.

1942	Airdrie	A	League – Southern Division	5–1
1953	Hearts	H	Scottish League	2–0
1959	Motherwell	H	Scottish League	5–1
1962	Valencia	H	Fairs Cup 1st round 2nd leg	2–2
1964	Rangers		Hampden Park	
			League Cup final	1–2
1966	Ayr United	H	Scottish League	5–1
1967	Motherwell	H	Scottish League	4–2
1970	Rangers		Hampden Park	
			League Cup final	0–1
1973	Vejle	H	European Cup 2nd round 1st leg	0–0
1979	Dundalk	H	European Cup 2nd round 1st leg	3–2
1981	Hibernian	A	Scottish League Premier Division	0–1
1984	Rapid Vienna	A	Cup-Winners' Cup 2nd round 1st leg	1–3
1987	Dundee United	H	Scottish League Premier Division	1–2
1992	Airdrie	H	Scottish League Premier Division	2–0

1994   On his 78th international for his country Packy Bonner was named captain in the Republic of Ireland's 4–0 victory over Liechtenstein at Lansdowne Road.

OCTOBER 25TH

1890	Abercorn	A	Scottish League	5–1
1902	Third Lanark	Ibrox	Glasgow Cup final	0–3
1912	Rangers	H	Scottish League	3–2
1913	Rangers	A	Scottish League	2–0
1919	Queen's Park	H	Scottish League	3–1

1919　Patsy Gallagher made his international debut for Ireland in the 1–1 draw with England at Windsor Park, Belfast. Gallagher had reportedly refused to change unless he got paid more than anyone else. Later it was announced he had been paid a record appearance fee.

1924	Rangers	H	Scottish League	0–1
1930	Motherwell	A	Scottish League	3–3
1941	Partick Thistle	H	League – Southern Division	1–1

John McPhail made his debut.

| 1947 | Queen of the South | H | Scottish League | 4–3 |

Tommy McDonald scored on his debut one day after signing from Third Lanark.

1952	Hearts	A	Scottish League	0–1
1958	Third Lanark	H	Scottish League	3–1

1961　Tommy Gemmell signed for the club.

| 1969 | St Johnstone | Hampden Park | | |
| | | League Cup final | | 1–0 |

Bertie Auld scored the winning goal, but the celebrations were soured by the news that Steve Chalmers had broken his leg during the game.

1972	Ujpesti Dozsa	H	European Cup 2nd round 1st leg	2–1
1975	Rangers	Hampden Park		
		League Cup final		0–1

1979　Dominic Sullivan was signed from Aberdeen.

| 1980 | Kilmarnock | H | Scottish League Premier Division | 4–1 |
| 1997 | St Johnstone | H | Scottish League Premier Division | 2–0 |

OCTOBER 26TH

1895	Dundee	H	Scottish League	11–0

The club's record victory in all competitions – unfortunately records do not show the goalscorers on this historic day.

1901	Rangers	Ibrox	Glasgow Cup final	2–2
1907	Rangers	Hampden Park		
		Glasgow Cup final replay		2–1

1913　Malky MacDonald was born in Glasgow.

1918	Dumbarton	A	Scottish League	5–0
1920	Albion Rovers	H	Scottish League	0–2
1929	Rangers	A	Scottish League	0–1
1935	Motherwell	A	Scottish League	2–1
1940	Hibernian	H	League – Southern Division	0–4

Chic Geatons played his last game for the club after making over 350 appearances in all competitions. Pat McAuley made his debut.

| 1946 | Hamilton Academical | H | League Cup | 3–1 |

1948　Leslie Hamilton was signed from Clyde for £12,000 to become Scotland's first player to be sold for £30,000 in accumulated fees.

| 1957 | Third Lanark | A | Scottish League | 2–0 |
| 1963 | Airdrie | H | Scottish League | 9–0 |

John Hughes and John Divers had helped Celtic to a 9–0 lead with a hat-trick apiece when they were awarded a penalty, and allowed goalkeeper Frank Haffey to step up and blast it straight at his opposite number.

| 1968 | Morton | A | Scottish League | 1–1 |

Joe McBride scored on what was to be his last appearance for the club.

1974	Hibernian	Hampden Park		
			League Cup final	6–3
1976	Hearts	Hampden Park		
			League Cup semi-final	2–1
1977	Stirling Albion	H	League Cup	1–1
1983	Hibernian	A	League Cup	0–0
1985	Dundee United	H	Scottish League Premier Division	0–3
1986	Rangers	Hampden Park		
			League Cup final	1–2
1988	SV Werder Bremen	H	European Cup 2nd round 1st leg	0–1
1991	St Mirren	A	Scottish League Premier Division	5–0
1993	Lou Macari was appointed manager.			
1994	Aberdeen	Ibrox	League Cup semi-final	1–0
1996	Hibernian	A	Scottish League Premier Division	4–0

OCTOBER 27TH

1894	Cowlairs	A	Glasgow Cup semi-final	2–0
1900	Kilmarnock	H	Scottish League	1–0
1906	Rangers	H	Scottish League	2–1
1917	Queen's Park	H	Scottish League	3–0
1923	Rangers	A	Scottish League	0–0
1928	Queen's Park	A	Scottish League	4–4
1929	Frank Meechan was born in Condorrat.			
1934	Dunfermline Athletic	H	Scottish League	3–0
1941	John McPhail signed pro forms with the club.			
1945	Falkirk	H	League – 'A' Division	2–1

Malky MacDonald was loaned to Kilmarnock, the club he was later to join in a permanent deal. In his 13 years at Celtic, he played over 340 games before and during the war, scoring over 50 goals.

1951	Hibernian	H	Scottish League	1–1
1956	Partick Thistle	Hampden Park		
			League Cup final	0–0
1962	Airdrie	A	Scottish League	6–1
1965	Dundee	A	Scottish League	2–1
1971	Dunfermline Athletic	A	Scottish League	2–1
1973	Hearts	A	Scottish League	3–1
1979	Rangers	H	Scottish League Premier Division	1–0

Dom Sullivan made his debut.

| 1982 | Dundee United | H | League Cup semi-final | 2–0 |

OCTOBER 28TH

| 1893 | Thistle | A | Glasgow Cup | 7–0 |
| 1899 | St Bernards | H | Scottish League | 5–0 |

1905	Dundee	H	Scottish League	3–1
1908	Third Lanark	Hampden Park		
			Glasgow Cup final replay	0–4
1911	Hibernian	H	Scottish League	3–1
1916	Rangers	H	Scottish League	0–0
1922	Rangers	H	Scottish League	1–3
1933	Hibernian	H	Scottish League	2–1
1939	Clyde	A	League – Western Division	0–2
1944	Airdrie	H	League – Southern Division	4–2
1950	Morton	A	Scottish League	2–0
1961	Dunfermline Athletic	H	Scottish League	2–1
1964	Kilmarnock	A	Scottish League	2–5
1967	Dundee	Hampden Park		
			League Cup final	5–3
1970	Hearts	H	Scottish League	3–2
1978	Hearts	A	Scottish League Premier Division	0–2
1987	Falkirk	H	Scottish League Premier Division	3–2
1989	Dunfermline Athletic	A	Scottish League Premier Division	0–2
1990	Rangers	Hampden Park		
			League Cup final	1–2
1995	Aberdeen	H	Scottish League Premier Division	2–0

OCTOBER 29TH

1892	Partick Thistle	A	Glasgow Cup	2–1
1898	St Bernards	A	Scottish League	3–2
1904	Queen's Park	H	Scottish League	1–1
1910	Rangers	H	Scottish League	0–1
1921	Ayr United	H	Scottish League	2–1
1927	St Mirren	H	Scottish League	6–0
1932	St Mirren	A	Scottish League	1–3
1938	Third Lanark	H	Scottish League	6–1
1949	Hibernian	H	Scottish League	2–2
1955	Dunfermline Athletic	H	Scottish League	4–2
1960	Ayr Utd	H	Scottish League	2–0
1966	Rangers	Hampden Park		
			League Cup final	1–0
1969	Aberdeen	A	Scottish League	3–2
1973	Motherwell	A	League Cup play-off	3–2
1977	Ayr United	H	Scottish League Premier Division	3–2
1983	Hibernian	H	Scottish League Premier Division	5–1
1986	Clydebank	H	Scottish League Premier Division	6–0
1988	Dundee	H	Scottish League Premier Division	2–3

OCTOBER 30TH

1897	Rangers	H	Glasgow Cup	2–1
1909	Rangers	A	Scottish League	0–0

1915	Rangers	A	Scottish League	0–3
1920	Hearts	A	Scottish League	1–0

1931 Goalkeeper Joe Kennaway signed from Canadian team New Bedford.

1943	Hibernian	A	League – Southern Division	2–2
1948	Hibernian	A	Scottish League	2–1

Leslie Hamilton scored twice on his debut.

1954	Falkirk	H	Scottish League	3–1
1965	Stirling Albion	H	Scottish League	6–1
1971	Ayr United	A	Scottish League	1–0
1976	Motherwell	H	Scottish League Premier Division	2–0
1982	Rangers	H	Scottish League Premier Division	3–2
1991	St Johnstone	H	Scottish League Premier Division	4–0
1993	Rangers	A	Scottish League Premier Division	2–1
1994	Rangers	H	Scottish League	1–3

OCTOBER 31ST

1891	Northern	H	Glasgow Cup	6–0
1896	Queen's Park	A	Glasgow Cup semi-final	4–2
1903	Queen's Park	A	Scottish League	0–1
1908	Clyde	A	Scottish League	2–0
1914	Rangers	H	Scottish League	2–1
1925	Dundee	H	Scottish League	0–0
1931	Motherwell	A	Scottish League	2–2

Joe Kennaway made his debut.

1936	Arbroath	A	Scottish League	3–2
1942	Falkirk	H	League – Southern Division	2–2
1953	Dundee	A	Scottish League	1–1
1956	Partick Thistle	Hampden Park		
			League Cup final replay	3–0

Billy McPhail scored 2 of the goals as Celtic won their first Scottish League Cup final.

1959	Hibernian	A	Scottish League	3–3
1964	Airdrie	H	Scottish League	2–1
1970	Motherwell	A	Scottish League	5–0
1973	Aberdeen	H	League Cup quarter-final	3–2
1979	Aberdeen	A	League Cup quarter-final	2–3
1981	Airdrie	A	Scottish League Premier Division	3–1
1987	Aberdeen	A	Scottish League Premier Division	1–0
1992	St Johnstone	A	Scottish League Premier Division	0–0

NOVEMBER 1ST

1902	Kilmarnock	H	Scottish League	3–1
1913	Kilmarnock	H	Scottish League	4–0
1919	Morton	A	Scottish League	2–1
1924	Morton	A	Scottish League	0–1
1930	Partick Thistle	H	Scottish League	5–1

1941	Third Lanark	H	League – Southern Division	3–1
1952	St Mirren	A	Scottish League	2–1
1958	Dundee	A	Scottish League	1–1
1967	Racing Club	A	World Club Championship	1–2

One of the most sickening matches ever played saw the Argentinian side violently battling their way to victory. Ronnie Simpson was injured by a bottle thrown from the crowd before the game in the warm-up and had to be replaced by John Fallon. The rules of the competition meant a replay had to be played to determine the winners, and after consultation it was decided that it was to be played in Montevideo, in neighbouring Uruguay, a few days later. Chairman Bob Kelly had considered pulling out of the game but was put under pressure by Jock Stein to play the game which went ahead after all.

1969	Ayr United	A	Scottish League	4–2
1972	Dundee	H	League Cup quarter-final	3–2
1975	Rangers	H	Scottish League Premier Division	1–1
1980	Rangers	A	Scottish League Premier Division	0–3
1986	Rangers	H	Scottish League Premier Division	1–1

1994 Pat McGinlay was sold back to Hibernian 15 months after he arrived for £420,000, a record for them at the time. He made 61 appearances for the club, scoring 13 goals. The youth team drawn away to Nairn County in the Youth Cup recorded one of the highest scores in the competition, winning 16–0.

| 1997 | Dunfermline | A | Scottish League Premier Division | 2–0 |

NOVEMBER 2ND

| 1901 | Hearts | A | Scottish League | 2–2 |
| 1907 | Port Glasgow Athletic | H | Scottish League | 5–0 |

Davie McLean scored a hat-trick on his debut.

| 1912 | Third Lanark | A | Scottish League | 1–0 |

Johnny Browning made his debut.

1918	St Mirren	H	Scottish League	1–0
1929	Hibernian	H	Scottish League	4–0
1935	Dundee	H	Scottish League	4–2
1946	Falkirk	A	Scottish League	4–1
1957	Kilmarnock	H	Scottish League	4–0
1963	East Stirlingshire	A	Scottish League	5–1
1966	Stirling Albion	H	Scottish League	7–3
1968	Dundee	H	Scottish League	3–1
1974	Aberdeen	H	Scottish League	1–0
1977	SW Innsbruck	A	European Cup 2nd round 2nd leg	0–3

1978 Murdo MacLeod signed for £100,000 from Dumbarton.

1983	Sporting Lisbon	H	UEFA Cup 2nd round 2nd leg	5–0
1985	Aberdeen	A	Scottish League Premier Division	1–4
1988	Aberdeen	A	Scottish League Premier Division	2–2
1991	Rangers	A	Scottish League Premier Division	1–1
1994	Paris St Germain	H	Cup-Winners' Cup 2nd round 2nd leg	0–3

1994 Tosh McKinlay was signed from Hearts for £350,000.

1996	Aberdeen	H	Scottish League Premier Division	1–0

NOVEMBER 3RD

1888	St Bernard's	A	Scottish Cup	4–1
1894	Hearts	H	Scottish League	0–2
1900	Kilmarnock	A	Scottish League	1–2
1906	Hamilton Academical	A	Scottish League	5–2
1917	Airdrie	A	Scottish League	0–2
1923	Airdrie	H	Scottish League	2–2
1928	Raith Rovers	H	Scottish League	3–1
1934	Ayr United	H	Scottish League	7–0

1940 Charlie Gallagher was born in the Gorbals.

1945	Hibernian	A	League – 'A' Division	1–1
1951	Third Lanark	H	Scottish League	2–2

1955 Jim Kennedy signed pro forms.

1956	Dundee	A	Scottish League	1–2
1962	St Mirren	A	Scottish League	7–0
1965	Aarhus GF	A	Cup-Winners' Cup 2nd round 1st leg	1–0
1971	Sliema Wanderers	A	European Cup 2nd round 2nd leg	2–1

Tommy Gemmell played his last game for the club. Described by many as the greatest full-back to play for Celtic, Tommy made 418 appearances for the club, scoring 64 goals. One of the deadliest penalty-takers of his time, he missed just 3 in his entire Celtic career. He will also be remembered for scoring in both of the club's European Cup finals as well as for some great attacking play. He would almost certainly feature in most people's greatest ever Celtic team. In 16 years at Parkhead he won 6 Championship medals, 3 Scottish Cup medals and 4 League Cup medals.

1973	East Fife	H	Scottish League	4–2
1979	Kilmarnock	A	Scottish League Premier Division	0–2
1982	Real Sociedad	H	European Cup 2nd round 2nd leg	2–1
1984	Morton	A	Scottish League Premier Division	1–2
1987	Queen's Park	H	Glasgow Cup semi-final	2–0
1990	Aberdeen	A	Scottish League Premier Division	0–3
1992	Borussia Dortmund	H	UEFA Cup 2nd round 2nd leg	1–2
1993	Sporting Lisbon	A	UEFA Cup 2nd round 2nd leg	0–2

NOVEMBER 4TH

1893	Dundee	H	Scottish League	3–1
1899	Hearts	A	Scottish League	2–3
1905	Partick Thistle	A	Scottish League	3–0
1911	Falkirk	A	Scottish League	1–1

Alex Thomson made his debut.

1916	Dundee	A	Scottish League	2–1
1922	Clyde	A	Scottish League	1–0

Jimmy McStay made his debut.

1933	Partick Thistle	H	Scottish League	2–0
1939	Queen of the South	H	League Western Division	0–3

| 1944 | Motherwell | A | League – Southern Division | 1–2 |

1949 Tommy Docherty was sold to Preston North End. Docherty described it as one of his saddest days in his eventful footballing life. He had made only 9 appearances in his 15 months at the club.

1950	Clyde	A	Scottish League	3–1
1961	Dundee	A	Scottish League	1–2
1967	Racing Club	N	World Club Championship play-off	0–1

After the last encounter and despite moving the game to another country, the tactics and behaviour of the South Americans didn't change and another battle took place. Jimmy Johnstone, Bobby Lennox and John Hughes were sent off and Bertie Auld was also dismissed but refused to leave the field as Celtic went down 0–1. The loss of a major trophy seemed insignificant when compared to the behaviour of the opposition. Fortunately everyone came out unscathed.

1970	Waterford	H	European Cup 2nd round 2nd leg	3–2
1972	Dundee United	H	Scottish League	3–1
1978	Motherwell	H	Scottish League Premier Division	1–2

Murdo MacLeod made his debut.

| 1989 | Rangers | A | Scottish League Premier Division | 0–1 |
| 1995 | Motherwell | A | Scottish League Premier Division | 2–0 |

NOVEMBER 5TH

| 1892 | Hearts | H | Scottish League | 5–0 |

Michael Mulvey scored on his debut.

1898	Clyde	H	Scottish League	9–2
1904	Kilmarnock	A	Scottish League	3–0
1910	St Mirren	H	Scottish League	5–0
1921	Hearts	H	Scottish League	3–0
1927	Airdrie	H	Scottish League	3–2
1932	Partick Thistle	A	Scottish League	0–3
1938	Ayr United	H	Scottish League	3–3
1949	Clyde	H	Scottish League	4–1
1955	East Fife	H	Scottish League	0–0
1960	Raith Rovers	A	Scottish League	2–2
1966	St Mirren	H	Scottish League	1–1

1968 Joe McBride was sold to Hibernian for £15,000. Injury prevented him from possibly being the greatest goalscorer in the club's history when he netted an incredible 86 goals in 94 games.

| 1975 | Boavista | H | Cup-Winners' Cup 2nd round 2nd leg | 3–1 |

UEFA regulations insisted that numbers be worn on the back of players' shirts. This was the first match in the club's history that saw numbers on the Celtic jerseys.

1977	Motherwell	A	Scottish League Premier Division	3–2
1983	Rangers	A	Scottish League Premier Division	2–1
1986	Dinamo Kiev	A	European Cup 2nd round 2nd leg	1–3
1988	Hamilton Academical	A	Scottish League Premier Division	8–0
1994	Dundee United	A	Scottish League	2–2

1887   They day it all began! John Glass, acting as chairman of a meeting held at St Mary's parish hall, voted in the idea of a Catholic football club being formed in Scotland. The rest is history.

1897	Dundee	A	Scottish League	2–1
1909	Hearts	H	Scottish League	1–0
1915	Aberdeen	H	Scottish League	3–1
1920	Dumbarton	A	Scottish League	3–1
1926	Airdrie	A	Scottish League	2–2
1937	Partick Thistle	H	Scottish League	6–0
1943	Motherwell	H	League – Southern Division	2–1
1948	Clyde	A	Scottish League	4–0

John Bonnar made his debut in goal.

1949   Charlie Tully won the first of his 10 international caps for Northern Ireland in the famous 2–9 defeat by England at Maine Road.

1954	St Mirren	A	Scottish League	1–1

1964   Duncan MacKay moved to Third Lanark.

1965	Partick Thistle	H	Scottish League	1–1
1971	Aberdeen	H	Scottish League	1–1
1974	Partick Thistle	A	Scottish League	2–1
1976	Aberdeen	Hampden Park		
		League Cup final		1–2
1982	Dundee	A	Scottish League Premier Division	3–2
1990	Motherwell	H	Scottish League Premier Division	2–1

Mark McNally made his debut.

1991	Neuchatel Xamax	H	UEFA Cup 2nd round 2nd leg	1–0

1991   Tony Mowbray signed in a £1 million deal from Middlesbrough.

1993	Partick Thistle	H	Scottish League Premier Division	3–0

NOVEMBER 7TH

1891	Northern	H	Glasgow Cup	3–2
1896	Abercorn	H	Scottish League	5–0
1903	Clyde	A	Glasgow Cup semi-final	2–0
1908	Partick Thistle	H	Scottish League	3–0
1914	Kilmarnock	A	Scottish League	3–1
1925	Aberdeen	A	Scottish League	4–2
1936	St Mirren	H	Scottish League	3–0
1942	Hearts	H	League – Southern Division	3–0
1953	Hibernian	H	Scottish League	2–2
1959	Ayr Utd	H	Scottish League	2–3
1964	St Johnstone	A	Scottish League	0–3
1966	Partick Thistle	H	Glasgow Cup final	4–0
1970	Cowdenbeath	H	Scottish League	3–0
1979	Dundalk	A	European Cup 2nd round 2nd leg	0–0
1981	Aberdeen	H	Scottish League Premier Division	2–1
1984	Rapid Vienna	H	Cup-Winners' Cup 2nd round 2nd leg	3–0

Once again farcical behaviour by foreign opposition prevented Celtic from progressing in a European competition. This time Rapid Vienna's substitute claimed he had been hit by a bottle as he lay prone for nearly 15 minutes before being carried from the pitch. TV evidence proved later that no object struck the player. Rapid made a complaint the next day to UEFA regarding the result and were awarded a replay.

1984   After a short loan period at Wolverhampton Wanderers, Jim Melrose was sold to Manchester City for £40,000. He scored 11 goals in 48 appearances for the club.

| 1987 | Hearts | A | Scottish League Premier Division | 1–1 |
| 1992 | Rangers | H | Scottish League Premier Division | 0–1 |

NOVEMBER 8TH

1890	Our Boys	A	Scottish Cup	3–1
1913	Queen's Park	A	Scottish League	2–0
1919	Falkirk	H	Scottish League	1–1
1924	Kilmarnock	H	Scottish League	6–0
1930	Hearts	H	Scottish League	2–1
1941	Airdrie	H	League – Southern Division	3–3
1947	Falkirk	H	Scottish League	0–3
1952	Third Lanark	H	Scottish League	5–4
1958	Dunfermline Athletic	A	Scottish League	0–1
1961	Jimmy Johnstone signed pro forms.			
1969	Hearts	H	Scottish League	0–2
1972	Ujpesti Dozsa	A	European Cup 2nd round 2nd leg	0–3
1973	Vejle	A	European Cup 2nd round 2nd leg	1–0
1975	Dundee	A	Scottish League Premier Division	0–1
1978	Montrose	A	League Cup quarter-final	1–1
1980	Aberdeen	H	Scottish League Premier Division	0–2

1980   Bobby Lennox decided to retire from football and immediately became the club's coach. He made over 570 appearances for Celtic and scored 273 goals and holds the post-war record of goals scored which is a great testament to the player as he wasn't even a centre-forward. He won 10 Championship medals, 8 Scottish Cup winners' medals and 4 League Cup winners' medals.

1986	Hamilton Academical	A	Scottish League Premier Division	2–1
1988	SV Werder Bremen	A	European Cup 2nd round 2nd leg	0–0
1995	Raith Rovers	H	Scottish League Premier Division	0–0
1997	Rangers	A	Scottish League Premier Division	0–1

NOVEMBER 9TH

1901	St Mirren	H	Scottish League	3–1
1907	Clyde	A	Scottish League	2–0
1909	Jock Morrison was born in Kilsyth.			
1911	Partick Thistle	H	Glasgow Cup	3–3
1912	Hearts	H	Scottish League	1–0
1918	Hearts	H	Scottish League	1–1
1929	Motherwell	A	Scottish League	1–2
1935	Hibernian	A	Scottish League	5–0

1936   Joe Dodds, Celtic's great left-back of the early part of the century, was appointed assistant trainer.

1940	St Mirren	H	League – Southern Division	0–0
1946	Hibernian	H	Scottish League	4–1
1957	East Fife	A	Scottish League	3–0
1963	Partick Thistle	H	Scottish League	5–2

Bobby Murdoch made his international debut for Scotland in the 1–0 victory over Italy at Hampden Park.

1968	Arbroath	A	Scottish League	5–0
1974	Dundee United	A	Scottish League	0–0
1977	St Mirren	A	League Cup quarter-final	3–1
1983	Airdrie	H	League Cup	0–0
1985	Rangers	A	Scottish League Premier Division	0–3

Mark McGhee made his debut for the club.

1991	Aberdeen	H	Scottish League Premier Division	2–1

Tony Mowbray made his debut.

1993	Aberdeen	A	Scottish League Premier Division	1–1
1994	Partick Thistle	H	Scottish League	0–0

NOVEMBER 10TH

1894	St Bernards	A	Scottish League	2–0
1900	Dundee	A	Scottish League	1–1
1906	Hibernian	H	Scottish League	2–1
1917	Hamilton Academical	H	Scottish League	1–0
1923	Hamilton Academical	A	Scottish League	5–2
1928	Aberdeen	A	Scottish League	2–2
1934	Falkirk	A	Scottish League	2–1
1945	Motherwell	H	League – 'A' Division	3–0
1951	Stirling Albion	A	Scottish League	1–2
1956	East Fife	H	Scottish League	4–0
1962	Queen of the South	H	Scottish League	0–1

1971 Kenny Dalglish won the first of his record-breaking 102 caps for Scotland, in the 1–0 victory over Belgium in the European Championship qualifier at Aberdeen.

1973	Ayr United	A	Scottish League	1–0
1979	Dundee United	A	Scottish League Premier Division	1–0
1982	Dundee United	A	League Cup semi-final	1–2
1984	Dumbarton	H	Scottish League Premier Division	2–0

1988 Chris Morris won the first of his 33 caps for the Republic of Ireland in the 5–0 victory over Israel in Dublin.

1990	Hearts	A	Scottish League Premier Division	0–1

NOVEMBER 11TH

1893	Renton	A	Scottish League	3–0
1899	Rangers	Cathkin Park		
			Glasgow Cup final	1–1
1905	Port Glasgow Athletic	H	Scottish League	0–1
1911	Hamilton Academical	H	Scottish League	2–1

1916	Queen's Park	A	Scottish League	3–1
1922	Ayr United	H	Scottish League	1–4
1933	Cowdenbeath	A	Scottish League	1–0
1939	Morton	A	League – Western Division	1–1
1943	Dan McArthur died aged 66.			
1944	Falkirk	A	League – Southern Division	1–2
1950	Falkirk	H	Scottish League	3–0
1963	Partick Thistle	A	Glasgow Cup	1–1

Frank Haffey broke his ankle in what was to be his last appearance for the club. He made 201 appearances for Celtic.

1967	Airdrie	A	Scottish League	2–0
1972	Motherwell	A	Scottish League	5–0
1978	Rangers	A	Scottish League Premier Division	1–1
1992	Dundee United	A	Scottish League Premier Division	1–1
1995	Partick Thistle	A	Scottish League Premier Division	2–1

NOVEMBER 12TH

1892	Partick Thistle	A	Glasgow Cup	1–1
1904	Hibernian	A	Scottish League	2–2
1910	Airdrie	A	Scottish League	0–0
1921	Kilmarnock	A	Scottish League	3–4
1927	Hearts	A	Scottish League	2–2
1932	East Stirlingshire	H	Scottish League	3–0
1938	Falkirk	A	Scottish League	1–1
1949	Stirling Albion	A	Scottish League	1–2
1955	Dundee	A	Scottish League	2–1
1960	Partick Thistle	H	Scottish League	0–1
1966	Falkirk	A	Scottish League	3–0
1969	Benfica	H	European Cup 2nd round 1st leg	3–0
1975	Ayr United	A	Scottish League Premier Division	7–2
1977	Rangers	H	Scottish League Premier Division	1–1
1980	Dundee United	A	League Cup semi-final	1–1

Mark Reid made his debut for the club.

1983	Motherwell	H	Scottish League Premier Division	4–0
1988	Rangers	H	Scottish League Premier Division	3–1

NOVEMBER 13TH

1897	Rangers	H	Glasgow Cup	2–2
1909	Partick Thistle	A	Scottish League	3–1
1911	Partick Thistle	A	Glasgow Cup	0–3
1915	Hearts	A	Scottish League	0–2
1920	Kilmarnock	H	Scottish League	2–0
1926	Hearts	H	Scottish League	1–0
1937	Third Lanark	A	Scottish League	1–1
1943	St Mirren	H	League – Southern Division	5–0
1948	East Fife	H	Scottish League	0–1

| 1954 | Stirling Albion | H | Scottish League | 7–0 |

1956 Jimmy Walsh was sold to Leicester City. He made over 140 appearances for the club and scored 59 goals.

| 1965 | St Johnstone | A | Scottish League | 4–1 |

1965 Jim Kennedy was sold to Morton. The left-back had made over 240 appearances for the club.

1968	Red Star Belgrade	H	European Cup 2nd round 1st leg	5–1
1971	Dundee United	A	Scottish League	5–1
1982	St Mirren	H	Scottish League Premier Division	5–0
1993	Kilmarnock	A	Scottish League Premier Division	2–2

NOVEMBER 14TH

1896	Rangers	Cathkin Park		
			Glasgow Cup final	1–1
1903	Kilmarnock	A	Scottish League	6–1
1908	Port Glasgow Athletic	H	Scottish League	2–1
1914	Third Lanark	H	Scottish League	1–0
1925	Raith Rovers	A	Scottish League	2–1
1928	Queen's Park	H	Denial Cup	4–0
1928	Queen's Park	H	Denial Cup	4–0
1931	Partick Thistle	H	Scottish League	1–2
1936	Partick Thistle	A	Scottish League	1–1
1942	Albion Rovers	H	League – Southern Division	4–4
1953	East Fife	A	Scottish League	1–4
1959	Dunfermline Athletic	H	Scottish League	4–2
1964	Dundee	H	Scottish League	0–2
1970	Kilmarnock	H	Scottish League	3–0
1976	Ipswich	H	Friendly	1–2
1981	Morton	A	Scottish League Premier Division	1–1
1987	Dundee	H	Scottish League Premier Division	5–0

Joe Miller scored on his debut for the club.

| 1989 | Raith Rovers | A | Friendly | 2–1 |
| 1996 | Rangers | H | Scottish League Premier Division | 0–1 |

NOVEMBER 15TH

1902	Partick Thistle	H	Scottish League	4–1
1913	Dumbarton	A	Scottish League	4–0
1919	Ayr United	A	Scottish League	1–1
1924	Queen's Park	A	Scottish League	1–3
1930	Cowdenbeath	A	Scottish League	1–1
1941	Falkirk	A	League – Southern Division	1–0
1947	Partick Thistle	A	Scottish League	5–3
1952	Partick Thistle	A	Scottish League	0–3
1958	St Mirren	H	Scottish League	3–3
1961	St Mirren	H	Scottish League	7–1

Chalmers, Jackson and Carroll scored 2 goals each as Celtic recorded their highest win of the season.

1967	Kilmarnock	H	Scottish League	3–0
1969	Motherwell	A	Scottish League	2–1
1975	Motherwell	H	Scottish League Premier Division	0–2
1978	Montrose	H	League Cup quarter-final	3–1
1980	Airdrie	A	Scottish League Premier Division	4–1
1986	Dundee United	H	Scottish League Premier Division	1–0
1997	Motherwell	H	Scottish League Premier Division	0–2

NOVEMBER 16TH

1901	Dundee	A	Scottish League	3–2
1907	Queen's Park	H	Scottish League	4–1
1912	Queen's Park	A	Scottish League	1–0
1929	Cowdenbeath	H	Scottish League	2–1

Bertie Thompson made his debut.

1935	Arbroath	H	Scottish League	5–0
1940	Third Lanark	A	League – Southern Division	0–1
1946	Partick Thistle	A	Scottish League	1–4
1957	St Mirren	H	Scottish League	2–2

John Divers scored both goals on his debut.

| 1963 | Hibernian | A | Scottish League | 1–1 |

1966   Joe McBride won the last of his 2 caps for Scotland in the 2–1 victory over Northern Ireland at Hampden. He was joined in the team by 5 other Celtic players Craig, Gemmell, Clark, Chalmers and Lennox.

| 1968 | Raith Rovers | H | Scottish League | 2–0 |
| 1974 | Airdrie | H | Scottish League | 6–0 |

Ronnie Glavin scored on his debut.

| 1977 | St Mirren | H | League Cup quarter-final | 2–0 |

After holding a special meeting concerning Rapid Vienna's protests UEFA decided astonishingly that the game was to be replayed, despite not having any conclusive evidence that Celtic were to blame for any incidents in the game. Both teams were fined and the game was ordered to be replayed more than 100 kilometres from Glasgow. Old Trafford was chosen ahead of Aberdeen's ground. The game would take place on December 12th.

| 1985 | Clydebank | H | Scottish League Premier Division | 2–0 |
| 1991 | Hearts | A | Scottish League Premier Division | 1–3 |

NOVEMBER 17TH

1894	Rangers	Cathkin Park	Glasgow Cup final	2–0
1900	Hearts	H	Scottish League	1–3
1906	Falkirk	A	Scottish League	3–2
1917	Dumbarton	A	Scottish League	2–0
1923	Dundee	H	Scottish League	0–0
1928	Clyde	H	Scottish League	4–0
1934	Airdrie	A	Scottish League	2–1

1945	Kilmarnock	A	League – 'A' Division	1–2
1951	Airdrie	H	Scottish League	3–1
1956	Ayr Utd	A	Scottish League	3–1

1960 Neil Mochan was sold to Dundee United for £1,500. He made over 260 appearances for the club scoring 111 goals.

1962	Dundee	A	Scottish League	0–0
1965	Aarhus GF	H	Cup-Winners' Cup 2nd round 2nd leg	2–0
1973	Partick Thistle	H	Scottish League	7–0

Dixie Deans scored 6 goals and created a post-war record for the number of goals scored by one player in a single game.

1979	Hibernian	H	Scottish League Premier Division	3–0
1984	Hearts	A	Scottish League Premier Division	5–1
1987	Motherwell	A	Scottish League Premier Division	2–0

1989 Polish international Dariusz Wdowczyk was signed for £400,000 from Gwardia Warsaw.

| 1990 | St Mirren | H | Scottish League Premier Division | 4–1 |

NOVEMBER 18TH

1893	Rangers	A	Glasgow Cup	0–1
1899	Rangers	Cathkin Park	Glasgow Cup final replay	0–1
1905	Morton	A	Scottish League	4–0
1911	Hibernian	A	Scottish League	1–1
1916	Partick Thistle	H	Scottish League	0–0
1922	Airdrie	A	Scottish League	0–1
1933	Ayr United	A	Scottish League	1–3
1939	Kilmarnock	H	League – Western Division	1–1
1944	Third Lanark	A	League – Southern Division	2–1
1950	Airdrie	A	Scottish League	4–2

1951 Alec McNair died aged 68 in Larbert.

| 1961 | Airdrie | H | Scottish League | 3–0 |
| 1964 | Barcelona | A | Fairs Cup 2nd round 1st leg | 1–3 |

Ronnie Simpson made his debut.

1967	Falkirk	H	Scottish League	3–0
1972	Hearts	H	Scottish League	4–2
1978	Hibernian	A	Scottish League Premier Division	2–2
1989	Dundee United	H	Scottish League Premier Division	0–1

NOVEMBER 19TH

1892	Partick Thistle	H	Glasgow Cup	8–0
1895	Third Lanark	A	Scottish League	7–0
1898	Dundee	A	Scottish League	4–1
1904	Dundee	H	Scottish League	3–0
1910	Third Lanark	H	Scottish League	0–0
1921	Queen's Park	H	Scottish League	3–1
1927	Cowdenbeath	H	Scottish League	1–1

1932	Cowdenbeath	H	Scottish League	3–0
1938	Motherwell	H	Scottish League	1–3

1948 Bobby Hogg's request for a free transfer was granted after 17 years of service. The great right-back played 216 times for the club.

1949	Third Lanark	H	Scottish League	2–1
1955	St Mirren	H	Scottish League	3–0
1960	Dunfermline Athletic	A	Scottish League	2–2
1966	Dunfermline Athletic	A	Scottish League	5–4
1977	Aberdeen	H	Scottish League Premier Division	3–2
1980	Dundee United	H	League Cup semi-final	0–3
1983	St Mirren	A	Scottish League Premier Division	2–4
1985	Partick Thistle	A	Glasgow Cup	3–2
1986	Hibernian	A	Scottish League Premier Division	1–0
1988	Hibernian	H	Scottish League Premier Division	1–0
1994	Kilmarnock	A	Scottish League	0–0

Gordon Marshall saved Tom Black's penalty kick, the first the Kilmarnock player had missed for 9 years.

1995	Rangers	A	Scottish League Premier Division	3–3
1997	Rangers	H	Scottish League Premier Division	1–1

NOVEMBER 20TH

1897	Rangers	A	Glasgow Cup	1–3
1909	Airdrie	H	Scottish League	3–1
1915	Kilmarnock	H	Scottish League	2–0
1920	Clyde	A	Scottish League	1–2
1926	Dunfermline Athletic	A	Scottish League	6–0
1937	Ayr United	A	Scottish League	1–1

Matt Lynch made his debut.

1943	Third Lanark	A	League – Southern Division	4–3

1945 Jimmy Quinn died in his hometown, Croy, aged 67.

1948	Third Lanark	A	Scottish League	2–3
1954	Partick Thistle	A	Scottish League	2–4

1963 A couple of months short of his 30th birthday, Jim Kennedy made his international debut for Scotland in the 2–1 victory over Wales at Hampden.

1965	Hamilton Academical	H	Scottish League	5–0
1971	Falkirk	H	Scottish League	2–0
1972	Dundee	Hampden Park		
			League Cup quarter-final play-off	4–1
1976	Hearts	A	Scottish League Premier Division	4–3
1982	Motherwell	H	Scottish League Premier Division	3–1
1990	Manchester United	A	Bryan Robson testimonial	3–1
1991	Motherwell	H	Scottish League Premier Division	2–2
1993	Hearts	H	Scottish League Premier Division	0–0

1891	Linthouse	H	Glasgow Cup semi-final	9–2
1895	Partick Thistle	H	Glasgow Cup semi-final	5–1
1896	Rangers	Cathkin Park		
			Glasgow Cup final replay	1–2
1899	John McFarlane was born in Bathgate.			
1903	Third Lanark	Ibrox	Glasgow Cup final	1–1
1908	Airdrie	A	Scottish League	2–1
1914	Ayr United	H	Scottish League	4–0
1931	Hearts	A	Scottish League	1–2
1936	Third Lanark	H	Scottish League	6–3
1942	Dumbarton	A	League – Southern Division	2–4
1953	Airdrie	H	Scottish League	4–1
1959	Stirling Albion	A	Scottish League	2–2
1964	Falkirk	H	Scottish League	3–0
1970	Falkirk	A	Scottish League	0–0
1973	Aberdeen	A	League Cup quarter-final	0–0

1973 Davie Provan came on as substitute to make his international debut in Scotland's 0–2 defeat by Belgium in Brussels.

1981	Rangers	H	Scottish League Premier Division	3–3
1987	Dunfermline Athletic	H	Scottish League Premier Division	4–0
1992	Falkirk	H	Scottish League Premier Division	3–2

NOVEMBER 22ND

1902	Port Glasgow Athletic	H	Scottish League	3–0

1902 Jimmy McMenemy scored on his first appearance for the club.

1913	Hamilton Academical	H	Scottish League	1–0
1919	Partick Thistle	H	Scottish League	0–0
1924	Third Lanark	A	Scottish League	1–1
1928	Willie Fernie was born in Fife.			
1930	Ayr United	A	Scottish League	6–2
1941	Hearts	H	League – Southern Division	4–4
1947	St Mirren	A	Scottish League	2–1
1952	Airdrie	A	Scottish League	0–0
1958	Partick Thistle	A	Scottish League	0–2
1959	Frank McAvennie was born in Glasgow.			
1962	Rangers	H	Glasgow Cup replay	3–2

1968 Tommy Callaghan was signed by Jock Stein from Dunfermline Athletic, where Stein had previously managed him.

1975	St Johnstone	H	Scottish League Premier Division	3–2
1980	St Mirren	H	Scottish League Premier Division	1–2
1986	Falkirk	H	Scottish League Premier Division	4–2
1989	St Mirren	H	Scottish League Premier Division	1–1

1989 Dariusz Wdowczyk made his debut for the club.

1997	Dundee United	H	Scottish League Premier Division	4–0

1895	Hearts	A	Scottish League	4–1
1907	Hearts	A	Scottish League	0–1
1912	Motherwell	H	Scottish League	1–2
1918	Partick Thistle	A	Scottish League	1–0
1929	St Johnstone	A	Scottish League	6–1
1935	Ayr United	A	Scottish League	2–0
1940	Hamilton Academical	A	League – Southern Division	0–1
1946	Motherwell	A	Scottish League	2–1
1957	Hibernian	A	Scottish League	1–0
1963	Kilmarnock	H	Scottish League	5–0
1968	Partick Thistle	A	Scottish League	4–0

Tommy Callaghan made his debut.

1974	Hearts	A	Scottish League	1–1
1983	Nottingham Forest	A	UEFA Cup 3rd round 1st leg	0–0
1985	Hibernian	H	Scottish League Premier Division	1–1
1991	Airdrie	A	Scottish League Premier Division	3–0

NOVEMBER 24TH

1894	Queen's Park	H	Scottish Cup	4–1
1900	Morton	H	Scottish League	4–2
1906	Clyde	H	Scottish League	3–3
1917	Hibernian	H	Scottish League	2–0
1923	St Mirren	A	Scottish League	1–0
1928	Third Lanark	A	Scottish League	2–0
1934	Dundee	H	Scottish League	4–0
1945	Morton	H	League – 'A' Division	2–1
1951	Queen of the South	A	Scottish League	0–4
1956	Partick Thistle	H	Scottish League	1–1

1958 Roy Aitken was born in Irvine. Willie Fernie was sold to St Mirren for £4000.

| 1962 | Partick Thistle | H | Scottish League | 0–2 |

1965 Tommy Boyd was born in Glasgow.

1973	Dumbarton	A	Scottish League	2–0
1976	Rangers	A	Scottish League Premier Division	1–0
1979	Aberdeen	H	League Cup quarter-final	0–1
1984	St Mirren	H	Scottish League Premier Division	7–1

Frank McGarvey's hat-trick meant he was the first player to score 100 goals in the Premier League.

| 1993 | Motherwell | H | Scottish League Premier Division | 2–0 |

NOVEMBER 25TH

1893	Hurlford	H	Scottish Cup	6–0
1899	Dundee	A	Scottish League	2–1
1905	St Mirren	H	Scottish League	2–1
1911	Motherwell	A	Scottish League	2–3
1916	Aberdeen	H	Scottish League	1–0
1922	Third Lanark	H	Scottish League	3–0

1925	Hearts	H	Scottish League	3–0
1933	Third Lanark	H	Scottish League	3–1
1939	Albion Rovers	A	League – Western Division	2–3
1944	Hearts	A	League – Southern Division	0–2
1950	Third Lanark	H	Scottish League	1–1
1961	Aberdeen	A	Scottish League	0–0
1967	Raith Rovers	A	Scottish League	2–0
1972	Falkirk	A	Scottish League	3–2
1978	Partick Thistle	H	Scottish League Premier Division	1–0
1987	St Mirren	H	Scottish League Premier Division	1–0
1989	Motherwell	A	Scottish League Premier Division	0–0
1990	Rangers	H	Scottish League Premier Division	1–2
1995	Hearts	H	Scottish League Premier Division	3–1

NOVEMBER 26TH

1898	Partick Thistle	H	Scottish League	4–0
1904	Airdrie	A	Scottish League	3–1
1910	Dundee	A	Scottish League	0–1
1921	Motherwell	A	Scottish League	1–1
1927	Bo'ness	A	Scottish League	1–0
1932	Third Lanark	A	Scottish League	4–0
1938	Arbroath	A	Scottish League	2–0
1949	Falkirk	A	Scottish League	1–1
1955	Airdrie	A	Scottish League	2–1
1960	St Johnstone	A	Scottish League	1–2
1966	Hearts	H	Scottish League	3–0
1969	Benfica	A	European Cup 2nd round 2nd leg	0–3

After surrendering a 3–0 lead from the 1st leg, Celtic hung on to the scoreline after extra time. The tie was decided by a toss of the coin in which Celtic won and went on to play Fiorentina in the next round.

1983	Dundee	H	Scottish League Premier Division	1–0
1986	Aberdeen	A	Scottish League Premier Division	1–1
1988	St Mirren	A	Scottish League Premier Division	3–2
1996	Barcelona	H	Friendly	0–1

NOVEMBER 27TH

1897	Hibernian	A	Scottish League	2–1
1909	Aberdeen	A	Scottish League	1–0
1914	Peter Somers died aged 36.			
1915	Raith Rovers	H	Scottish League	2–0
1920	Raith Rovers	H	Scottish League	5–0
1926	Dundee United	H	Scottish League	7–2
1937	Falkirk	H	Scottish League	2–0
1943	Clyde	H	League – Southern Division	4–0
1948	Falkirk	H	Scottish League	4–4
1954	Motherwell	A	Scottish League	2–2

| 1965 | Kilmarnock | H | Scottish League | 2–1 |

1967 Jim Craig won his only cap for Scotland in the 3–2 victory over Wales at Hampden. In achieving this it created a new record for the club as it had 14 international players (13 of whom were Scots), which beat the previous best of 13 by Rangers in 1933.

1968	Red Star Belgrade	A	European Cup 2nd round 2nd leg	1–1
1971	Partick Thistle	A	Scottish League	5–1
1972	Aberdeen	Hampden Park		
			League Cup	3–2
1976	Kilmarnock	H	Scottish League Premier Division	2–1
1982	Hibernian	A	Scottish League Premier Division	3–2
1993	Raith Rovers	H	Scottish League Premier Division	2–0
1994	Raith Rovers	Ibrox	League Cup final	2–2

More misery as another trophy eluded the club, this time losing out to First Division opposition (only the second time this has happened). Paul McStay missed the all-important penalty with the score on 5–6.

NOVEMBER 28TH

1891	St Mirren	A	Scottish Cup	4–2
1892	Linthouse	H	Scottish Cup	3–1
1896	Hibernian	H	Scottish League	1–1

Patrick Gilhooly scored on his debut.

1903	Third Lanark	Ibrox	Glasgow Cup final replay	0–1
1908	Queen's Park	H	Scottish League	4–0
1914	Dumbarton	A	Scottish League	4–1
1928	Partick Thistle	N	Denial Cup	1–3
1928	Partick Thistle	N	Denial Cup	1–3
1931	Cowdenbeath	A	Scottish League	2–1
1936	Dunfermline Athletic	H	Scottish League	3–1

1938 Frank Haffey was born in Glasgow.

1942	Queen's Park	H	League – Southern Division	2–1
1953	Partick Thistle	H	Scottish League	2–1
1959	Partick Thistle	A	Scottish League	1–3

1962 John Divers scored 3 goals as a Scottish League team beat a League of Ireland team 11–0 at Parkhead.

1964	Third Lanark	A	Scottish League	3–0
1970	St Mirren	H	Scottish League	3–0
1981	Partick Thistle	A	Scottish League Premier Division	2–0
1987	Hibernian	A	Scottish League Premier Division	1–0
1992	Hibernian	A	Scottish League Premier Division	2–1

NOVEMBER 29TH

1902	Dundee	H	Scottish League	2–2
1913	Airdrie	A	Scottish League	1–0
1919	Aberdeen	A	Scottish League	1–0
1921	Third Lanark	H	Unemployment Cup	2–1

1924	Partick Thistle	H	Scottish League	1–2
1925	St Johnstone	A	Scottish League	3–0
1941	Albion Rovers	A	League – Southern Division	4–4
1948	Davy Adams died in Edinburgh aged 55.			
1958	Hibernian	A	Scottish League	2–3
1969	Morton	A	Scottish League	3–0
1975	Dundee United	A	Scottish League Premier Division	3–1
1980	Dundee United	A	Scottish League Premier Division	3–0
1986	St Mirren	A	Scottish League Premier Division	1–0
1994	Hibernian	A	Scottish League	1–1

NOVEMBER 30TH

1895	St Mirren	A	Scottish League	3–1
1901	Hearts	H	Scottish League	1–2
1912	Clyde	A	Scottish League	1–1
1929	Partick Thistle	A	Scottish League	2–3
1935	Partick Thistle	H	Scottish League	1–1
1940	Morton	H	League – Southern Division	2–0
	Robert Milne made his debut.			
1946	Kilmarnock	H	Scottish League	4–2
1957	Airdrie	A	Scottish League	5–2
1963	Dundee	A	Scottish League	1–1
1966	FC Nantes	A	European Cup 2nd round 1st leg	3–1
1968	Hibernian	A	Scottish League	5–2
1974	Morton	A	Scottish League	1–0
1983	Kilmarnock	A	League Cup	1–0
1987	Nottingham Forest	H	Friendly	1–3
1991	Dunfermline Athletic	H	Scottish League Premier Division	1–0
1993	Dundee United	A	Scottish League Premier Division	0–1
1996	Hearts	H	Scottish League Premier Division	2–2
1997	Dundee United	Ibrox	League Cup final	3–0

DECEMBER 1ST

1900	Partick Thistle	A	Scottish League	6–2
1906	Partick Thistle	H	Scottish League	4–1
	John Mitchell made his debut.			
1917	Morton	A	Scottish League	1–1
1923	Third Lanark	H	Scottish League	3–1
1928	St Johnstone	H	Scottish League	0–0
1934	St Mirren	A	Scottish League	4–2
1945	Clyde	A	League – 'A' Division	3–3
1951	Partick Thistle	H	Scottish League	2–1
1956	Hearts	H	Scottish League	1–1
1962	Hibernian	A	Scottish League	1–1
1969	St Mirren	H	Scottish League	2–0
	Evan Williams made his debut in goal.			

1973	Arbroath	A	Scottish League	2–1
1974	Simon Donnelly was born in Glasgow.			
1979	St Mirren	A	Scottish League Premier Division	1–2
1984	Dundee	H	Scottish League Premier Division	5–1
1990	Hibernian	A	Scottish League Premier Division	3–0

DECEMBER 2ND

1893	Renton	H	Scottish League	3–2
1899	St Bernards	A	Scottish League	1–1
1905	Port Glasgow Athletic	A	Scottish League	1–0
1911	St Mirren	H	Scottish League	3–1

Davie Adams made his final appearance in goal for the club. In 10 years between the posts he made 291 appearances for the club. He was an ever present in the six-in-a-row team and also won 4 Scottish Cup medals. As one legend finished his career another one started as Patsy Gallagher made his debut for the club.

1916	Raith Rovers	A	Scottish League	4–1
1922	Albion Rovers	A	Scottish League	3–2
1933	Airdrie	H	Scottish League	4–2
1939	St Mirren	H	League – Western Division	2–1
1944	Albion Rovers	H	League – Southern Division	5–0
1947	John Campbell died aged 75.			
1950	Partick Thistle	A	Scottish League	1–0
1961	Partick Thistle	H	Scottish League	5–1
1964	Barcelona	H	Fairs Cup 2nd round 2nd leg	0–0
1967	Dundee United	H	Scottish League	1–1
1972	Dumbarton	A	Scottish League	6–1
1989	Aberdeen	H	Scottish League Premier Division	1–0
1992	Aberdeen	H	Scottish League Premier Division	2–2
1995	Kilmarnock	H	Scottish League Premier Division	4–2

DECEMBER 3RD

1898	Partick Thistle	A	Scottish League	8–3
1904	Motherwell	H	Scottish League	4–2
1910	Motherwell	H	Scottish League	3–0
1921	Airdrie	H	Scottish League	1–0
1927	Motherwell	H	Scottish League	1–2
1930	Willie Walsh was born in Glasgow.			
1932	Airdrie	A	Scottish League	3–0
1938	Hibernian	H	Scottish League	5–4
1949	Partick Thistle	H	Scottish League	1–0
1955	Stirling Albion	A	Scottish League	3–0
1962	Partick Thistle	A	Glasgow Cup semi-final	3–1
1966	Kilmarnock	A	Scottish League	0–0
1983	St Johnstone	A	Scottish League Premier Division	3–0
1986	Hearts	A	Scottish League Premier Division	0–1
1988	Motherwell	A	Scottish League Premier Division	3–1

| 1994 | Motherwell | H | Scottish League | 2–2 |

DECEMBER 4TH

| 1897 | Third Lanark | H | Scottish League | 4–0 |

Peter Somers scored on his debut.

1909	Kilmarnock	H	Scottish League	2–1
1915	Queen's Park	H	Scottish League	6–2
1920	Falkirk	A	Scottish League	3–1
1926	Motherwell	A	Scottish League	1–0
1937	Motherwell	A	Scottish League	2–1
1943	Morton	A	League – Southern Division	1–1
1948	Partick Thistle	A	Scottish League	2–1
1951	Jock Stein signed pro forms with the club.			
1954	East Fife	H	Scottish League	2–2
1963	Dinamo Zagreb	H	Cup-Winners' Cup 2nd round 1st leg	3–0
1971	Kilmarnock	H	Scottish League	5–1
1982	Rangers	Hampden Park		
			League Cup final	2–1
1991	Hibernian	H	Scottish League Premier Division	0–0
1993	St Johnstone	H	Scottish League Premier Division	1–0

DECEMBER 5TH

1896	Third Lanark	A	Scottish League	3–0
1903	Morton	A	Scottish League	1–0
1908	Motherwell	A	Scottish League	2–1
1914	Aberdeen	A	Scottish League	1–0
1925	Clydebank	H	Scottish League	1–1
1931	Third Lanark	H	Scottish League	5–0
1936	Falkirk	A	Scottish League	3–0
1942	Hamilton Academical	A	League – Southern Division	1–2

Pat McDonald scored on his debut for the club.

1953	Stirling Albion	A	Scottish League	1–2
1959	Dundee	H	Scottish League	2–3
1962	Willie Lyon died aged 50 in Manchester.			
1970	Dundee United	A	Scottish League	2–1
1973	Rangers	Hampden Park		
			League Cup semi-final	3–1
1981	Dundee	H	Scottish League Premier Division	3–1
1987	Morton	A	Scottish League Premier Division	4–0
1992	Partick Thistle	A	Scottish League Premier Division	3–2

DECEMBER 6TH

| 1902 | Partick Thistle | A | Scottish League | 0–0 |
| 1913 | Third Lanark | H | Scottish League | 3–0 |

Ebenezer Owers scored on his debut.

| 1919 | Motherwell | H | Scottish League | 5–0 |

1924	Ayr United	H	Scottish League	2–0
1930	Airdrie	A	Scottish League	2–1

John Morrison made his debut.

1941	Dumbarton	H	League – Southern Division	4–2

1945 Tommy Callaghan was born in Cowdenbeath.

1947	Dundee	H	Scottish League	1–1
1952	Hibernian	A	Scottish League	1–1

1966 Willie Wallace was signed from Hearts for a club record fee of £28,000.

1975	Hearts	A	Scottish League Premier Division	1–0
1980	Partick Thistle	A	Scottish League Premier Division	1–0
1986	Dundee	H	Scottish League Premier Division	2–0
1989	Ajax Amsterdam	H	Friendly	1–0

Tommy Burns made his final appearance as a player for the club. In his 16 years he played 500 games and scored 81 goals. He won 6 Championship medals, 4 Cup winners' medals and a League Cup winners' medal. He was to return to the club later as manager.

1994	Liverpool	A	Ian Rush testimonial	0–6
1997	Kilmarnock	A	Scottish League Premier Division	0–0

DECEMBER 7TH

1895	St Bernards	H	Scottish League	2–1
1901	Queen's Park	A	Scottish League	2–3
1907	St Mirren	H	Scottish League	4–0
1912	Hamilton Academical	H	Scottish League	2–1
1918	Motherwell	A	Scottish League	1–3
1929	St Mirren	H	Scottish League	3–0
1935	Third Lanark	A	Scottish League	3–1
1940	Hearts	A	League – Southern Division	1–2
1946	Morton	A	Scottish League	1–2
1957	Dundee	H	Scottish League	0–0
1963	St Johnstone	H	Scottish League	3–1
1966	FC Nantes	H	European Cup 2nd round 2nd leg	3–2
1968	St Mirren	H	Scottish League	5–0

A couple of goals by Steve Chalmers secured Celtic's 6th straight victory in the League in which they had scored 24 goals.

1969	Dundee	H	Scottish League	1–0
1974	Dunfermline Athletic	H	Scottish League	2–1
1983	Nottingham Forest	H	UEFA Cup 3rd round 2nd leg	1–2
1991	Dundee United	A	Scottish League Premier Division	1–1
1996	Motherwell	A	Scottish League Premier Division	1–2

DECEMBER 8TH

1888	Clyde	H	Scottish Cup	9–2
1917	Clydebank	H	Scottish League	3–0
1923	Kilmarnock	A	Scottish League	1–1
1928	Falkirk	A	Scottish League	0–3

1934	Motherwell	H	Scottish League	3–2
1945	Queen's Park	H	League – 'A' Division	3–3
1951	St Mirren	H	Scottish League	2–1

Jock Stein made his debut.

1956	St Mirren	A	Scottish League	2–0
1962	Hearts	H	Scottish League	2–2

1962 Players wore black armbands in memory of Willie Lyon the great skipper who passed away 3 days before.

1963 Brian McClair was born in Airdrie.

1967 Joe Miller signed from Aberdeen.

1973	Dundee United	H	Scottish League	3–3
1984	Aberdeen	A	Scottish League Premier Division	2–4
1990	Dundee United	A	Scottish League Premier Division	1–3

DECEMBER 9TH

1899	St Mirren	H	Scottish League	3–1
1905	Aberdeen	H	Scottish League	1–0
1911	Queen's Park	A	Scottish League	4–1

John Mulrooney made his debut in goal.

1916	Ayr United	H	Scottish League	5–0
1922	Falkirk	H	Scottish League	1–1
1933	Dundee	A	Scottish League	2–3

1933 Peter Scarff died after suffering from TB at the age of 25.

1939	Partick Thistle	A	League Western Division	2–4
1944	Queen's Park	A	League – Southern Division	2–0
1950	St Mirren	A	Scottish League	0–0
1967	Hearts	H	Scottish League	3–1
1972	Hibernian	Hampden Park		
			League Cup final	1–2
1978	Aberdeen	H	Scottish League Premier Division	0–0
1985	SV Hamburg	H	Friendly	1–2
1989	Hibernian	A	Scottish League Premier Division	3–0
1995	Hibernian	A	Scottish League Premier Division	4–0
1997	Aberdeen	A	Scottish League Premier Division	2–0

DECEMBER 10TH

1904	Morton	A	Scottish League	1–0
1910	Clyde	A	Scottish League	2–0
1921	Ayr United	A	Scottish League	0–0

1926 Mike Haughney was born in Paisley.

1927	St Johnstone	A	Scottish League	5–3
1932	Dundee	H	Scottish League	3–2
1938	St Johnstone	A	Scottish League	1–1
1949	St Mirren	H	Scottish League	0–0
1955	Kilmarnock	H	Scottish League	0–2
1960	Dundee United	H	Scottish League	1–1

| 1966 | Motherwell | H | Scottish League | 4–2 |

Willie Wallace made his debut for the club.

1975	Hibernian	H	Scottish League Premier Division	1–1
1977	Partick Thistle	H	Scottish League Premier Division	3–0
1983	Aberdeen	H	Scottish League Premier Division	0–0
1988	Aberdeen	H	Scottish League Premier Division	0–0

DECEMBER 11TH

1897	Partick Thistle	A	Scottish League	6–3
1909	St Mirren	H	Scottish League	1–1
1915	Ayr United	A	Scottish League	4–0
1920	Partick Thistle	H	Scottish League	1–0
1926	St Johnstone	H	Scottish League	4–0
1943	Queen's Park	H	League – Southern Division	2–0
1948	St Mirren	A	Scottish League	1–1
1954	Hibernian	A	Scottish League	5–0

1958 John Fallon signed pro forms.

1963	Dinamo Zagreb	A	Cup-Winners' Cup 2nd round 2nd leg	1–2
1965	Hibernian	H	Scottish League	2–0
1971	East Fife	H	Scottish League	2–1
1974	Benfica	H	Friendly (UNICEF benefit)	3–3

Billy McNeill missed the deciding penalty in the shoot-out.

1982	Aberdeen	A	Scottish League Premier Division	2–1
1990	Ayr United	A	Ian McAllister testimonial	2–1
1993	Dundee	A	Scottish League Premier Division	1–1

DECEMBER 12TH

1880 Jimmy 'Dun' Hay was born in Beith.

1891	Clyde	Cathkin Park	Glasgow Cup final	7–1
1896	Clyde	H	Scottish League	4–1
1903	Airdrie	H	Scottish League	3–0
1908	Hibernian	H	Scottish League	2–0
1914	Queen's Park	H	Scottish League	5–1
1925	St Mirren	A	Scottish League	2–0
1931	Airdrie	H	Scottish League	6–1
1936	Motherwell	H	Scottish League	3–2
1942	Clyde	H	League – Southern Division	1–1
1953	St Mirren	H	Scottish League	4–0
1959	Airdrie	H	Scottish League	0–0
1964	Partick Thistle	A	Scottish League	4–2
1970	Aberdeen	H	Scottish League	0–1

John Fallon made his last appearance for the club in front of 63,000 fans. The likeable goalkeeper had made over 180 appearances with nearly a third of these keeping a clean sheet.

| 1984 | Rapid Vienna | Old Trafford |

Cup-Winners' Cup 2nd round replay   0–1

The team couldn't quite live up to the tremendous support on the night as they lost to an early goal by Pacult. During the second half a fan ran on to the pitch and attacked the Rapid goalkeeper and at the end of the game Pacult was also attacked. Once again another fine was imposed and Celtic were ordered to play their next European tie behind closed doors.

1987	Hearts	H	Scottish League Premier Division	2–2
1992	Dundee	H	Scottish League Premier Division	1–0
1995	Manchester United	H	Paul McStay testimonial	3–1

A crowd of over 37,000 saw a couple of goals from Van Hooijdonk and Hay give Celtic victory over the English Premier Division runners-up.

DECEMBER 13TH

1890	Royal Albert	A (Ibrox)	Scottish Cup	2–0
1902	St Mirren	A	Scottish League	1–3
1913	Raith Rovers	A	Scottish League	2–1
1919	Airdrie	A	Scottish League	0–0
1921	Rangers	A	Unemployment Cup	0–2
1921	Rangers	Hampden Park		
			Lord Provosts' Rent Relief Fund Cup final	0–2
1924	Hearts	A	Scottish League	1–3
1930	Leith Athletic	H	Scottish League	4–0
1941	Queen's Park	A	League – Southern Division	1–1
1947	Hibernian	A	Scottish League	1–1
1952	Dundee	H	Scottish League	5–0
1958	Stirling Albion	H	Scottish League	7–3

John Colraine scored a hat-trick.

1961	Cowdenbeath	H	Scottish Cup	5–1
1975	Aberdeen	H	Scottish League Premier Division	0–2
1978	Rangers	Hampden Park		
			League Cup semi-final	2–3
1980	Hearts	H	Scottish League Premier Division	3–2
1986	Motherwell	A	Scottish League Premier Division	1–1
1997	Hearts	H	Scottish League Premier Division	1–0

DECEMBER 14TH

1895	Rangers	H	Scottish League	6–2
1901	Hibernian	H	Scottish League	2–2
1907	Hamilton Academical	A	Scottish League	4–2
1912	Morton	A	Scottish League	2–1
1918	Dumbarton	H	Scottish League	2–0
1929	Kilmarnock	A	Scottish League	1–1
1935	Dunfermline Athletic	A	Scottish League	0–1
1940	Albion Rovers	H	League – Southern Division	2–0
1946	Clyde	H	Scottish League	3–3
1957	Clyde	A	Scottish League	6–3

1963	Hearts	A	Scottish League	1–1
1968	Falkirk	A	Scottish League	0–0
1969	St Johnstone	A	Scottish League	4–1
1974	Dundee	A	Scottish League	6–0
1985	Hearts	A	Scottish League Premier Division	1–1
1991	St Mirren	H	Scottish League Premier Division	4–0

DECEMBER 15TH

1888	East Stirlingshire	A	Scottish Cup	2–1
1894	Hibernian	A	Scottish Cup	0–2
1900	St Mirren	H	Scottish League	3–0
1906	St Mirren	A	Scottish League	3–0
1914	Rangers	Firhill Park		
			Belgian Relief War Fund Shield semi-final	1–2
1917	Motherwell	A	Scottish League	4–3
1923	Motherwell	H	Scottish League	2–1
1928	Hearts	H	Scottish League	1–0
1934	Hibernian	A	Scottish League	2–3
1945	Aberdeen	A	League – 'A' Division	1–1
1951	East Fife	A	Scottish League	1–3
1956	Dunfermline Athletic	H	Scottish League	3–1
1962	Third Lanark	A	Scottish League	0–2
1973	Dundee	Hampden Park		
			League Cup final	0–1

Celtic suffered their 5th Scottish League Cup final defeat. One of the lowest attendances, 27,974, watched the final due to severe weather conditions of snow and ice. The match also kicked off at the unusual time of 1.30pm due to power crisis which meant that the floodlights could not be used.

1979	Partick Thistle	H	Scottish League Premier Division	5–1
1984	Hibernian	A	Scottish League Premier Division	1–0
1990	Dunfermline Athletic	H	Scottish League Premier Division	1–2

DECEMBER 16TH

1893	Albion Rovers	H	Scottish Cup	7–0
1895	Queen's Park	Ibrox	Glasgow Cup final	6–3
1899	Kilmarnock	H	Scottish League	3–3
1905	Motherwell	A	Scottish League	4–0
1911	Third Lanark	A	Scottish League	0–1
1916	Hamilton Academical	A	Scottish League	4–0
1922	Hearts	A	Scottish League	3–0
1939	Third Lanark	H	League – Western Division	1–2
1944	Hamilton Academical	H	League – Southern Division	5–3
1950	East Fife	H	Scottish League	6–2
1956	Tommy Burns was born in Glasgow.			
1961	Hibernian	H	Scottish League	4–3
1967	Dundee	A	Scottish League	5–4

1972	Arbroath	A	Scottish League	2–1
1978	Dundee United	H	Scottish League Premier Division	1–1
1989	Dundee	H	Scottish League Premier Division	4–1
1995	Falkirk	H	Scottish League Premier Division	1–0

DECEMBER 17TH

1892	Fifth Kirkudbright Rovers	H	Scottish Cup	7–0
1898	Hearts	H	Scottish League	3–2
1904	Partick Thistle	H	Scottish League	2–2
1910	Kilmarnock	H	Scottish League	2–0
1921	Clydebank	H	Scottish League	6–0
1927	Partick Thistle	H	Scottish League	0–0
1932	Ayr United	A	Scottish League	1–0
1938	St Mirren	H	Scottish League	3–2
1949	East Fife	A	Scottish League	1–5
1955	Partick Thistle	H	Scottish League	5–1
1960	Hearts	A	Scottish League	1–2
1966	Partick Thistle	H	Scottish League	6–2
1969	Dundee United	H	Scottish League	7–2
1971	Tommy Gemmell was sold to Nottingham Forest for £40,000.			
1977	St Mirren	A	Scottish League Premier Division	3–3
1983	Hearts	A	Scottish League Premier Division	3–1
1988	Dundee United	A	Scottish League Premier Division	0–1

DECEMBER 18TH

1897	St Bernards	H	Scottish League	5–1
1909	Motherwell	A	Scottish League	3–1
1915	Partick Thistle	H	Scottish League	4–0
1920	Airdrie	H	Scottish League	2–1
1926	Partick Thistle	A	Scottish League	3–0
1937	Hibernian	A	Scottish League	3–0
1943	Dumbarton	A	League – Southern Division	1–1
1948	Motherwell	H	Scottish League	3–2
1954	Dundee	H	Scottish League	4–1
	Jimmy Rowan scored his only goal on his debut. He was to play in only one more game.			
1965	Dunfermline Athletic	A	Scottish League	2–0
1971	Motherwell	A	Scottish League	5–1
1976	Ayr United	H	Scottish League Premier Division	3–0
1982	Kilmarnock	A	Scottish League Premier Division	4–0
1993	Hibernian	H	Scottish League Premier Division	1–0

DECEMBER 19TH

1891	Kilmarnock Athletic	H	Scottish Cup	3–0
1896	Rangers	A	Scottish League	0–2
1903	Partick Thistle	A	Scottish League	4–0

1908	Aberdeen	A	Scottish League	2–0
1914	Airdrie	A	Scottish League	1–0
1925	Airdrie	H	Scottish League	3–2
1931	Leith Athletic	H	Scottish League	6–0

Jimmy McGrory scored 4 of the goals, his 3rd hat-trick of the season, as Peter Scarff made his last appearance for the club. In 5 years Scarff had played 112 times, scoring 55 goals.

1936	Queen of the South	A	Scottish League	0–1
1942	Motherwell	H	League – Southern Division	3–2
1959	St Mirren	A	Scottish League	3–0
1964	Dunfermline Athletic	H	Scottish League	1–2
1967	Paul Wilson signed pro forms with the club shortly after his 17th birthday.			
1970	Ayr United	A	Scottish League	2–1
1987	Aberdeen	H	Scottish League Premier Division	0–0
1992	Hearts	A	Scottish League Premier Division	0–1

DECEMBER 20TH

1890	Dumbarton	A	Scottish Cup quarter-final	0–3
1890	Alexander 'Duke' McMahon was signed from Hibernian.			
1902	Morton	H	Scottish League	1–1
1913	Motherwell	H	Scottish League	0–0
1919	Dumbarton	A	Scottish League	0–0
1924	Hamilton Academical	H	Scottish League	0–2
1930	Kilmarnock	A	Scottish League	3–0
1941	Hamilton Academical	H	League – Southern Division	2–1
1947	Airdrie	H	Scottish League	0–0
1952	Falkirk	A	Scottish League	3–2
1956	Willie McGonagle died aged 52 in Gloucester.			
1958	Hearts	A	Scottish League	1–1
1969	Kilmarnock	H	Scottish League	3–1
1975	Hibernian	A	Scottish League Premier Division	3–1
1980	Airdrie	H	Scottish League Premier Division	2–1
1986	Aberdeen	H	Scottish League Premier Division	1–1
1997	Hibernian	H	Scottish League Premier Division	5–0

DECEMBER 21ST

1895	Dumbarton	H	Scottish League	3–0
1907	Kilmarnock	H	Scottish League	4–1
1912	Dundee	H	Scottish League	2–0
1918	Hamilton Academical	A	Scottish League	2–1
1929	Hearts	A	Scottish League	3–1
1935	Aberdeen	H	Scottish League	5–3

Jimmy McGrory scored his 4th hat-trick in his record-breaking season. He was to go on and complete 7 League hat-tricks and score 50 goals in total.

1940	Dumbarton	A	League – Southern Division	3–2
1946	Hearts	A	Scottish League	1–2
1957	Partick Thistle	H	Scottish League	2–3

1963	Motherwell	H	Scottish League	2–1
1968	Kilmarnock	H	Scottish League	1–1
1974	St Johnstone	H	Scottish League	3–1
1996	Dundee United	H	Scottish League Premier Division	1–0

DECEMBER 22ND

1893	Dumbarton	A	Scottish League	5–4
1894	St Mirren	H	Scottish League	2–2
1900	Dundee	H	Scottish League	1–2
1906	Port Glasgow Athletic	H	Scottish League	4–0
1917	Dumbarton	H	Scottish League	3–0
1923	Dundee	A	Scottish League	1–2
1928	Airdrie	A	Scottish League	1–0
1934	Kilmarnock	A	Scottish League	3–2
1945	Hamilton Academical	A	League – 'A' Division	1–0

Pat McDonald played his last game for the club. The left-back had made 90 appearances for the club during wartime.

1951	Motherwell	H	Scottish League	2–2
1956	Airdrie	A	Scottish League	7–3
1973	Falkirk	H	Scottish League	6–0
1979	Morton	H	Scottish League Premier Division	3–1
1984	Rangers	H	Scottish League Premier Division	1–1
1987	Falkirk	A	Scottish League Premier Division	2–0
1990	St Johnstone	A	Scottish League Premier Division	2–3

DECEMBER 23RD

1899	Dundee	H	Scottish League	1–1
1905	Morton	H	Scottish League	4–0
1911	Morton	H	Scottish League	1–1
1916	Partick Thistle	A	Scottish League	2–0
1922	Kilmarnock	H	Scottish League	1–2
1933	Queen of the South	H	Scottish League	0–1
1939	Dumbarton	A	League – Western Division	5–1
1944	Clyde	A	League – Southern Division	3–0
1961	Raith Rovers	A	Scottish League	4–0
1963	Partick Thistle	H	Glasgow Cup replay	2–1
1967	Morton	A	Scottish League	4–0

Joe McBride scored a hat-trick.

1972	Hibernian	H	Scottish League	1–1
1978	Morton	A	Scottish League Premier Division	0–1
1985	Dundee United	A	Scottish League Premier Division	0–1

DECEMBER 24TH

1904	St Mirren	H	Scottish League	1–0
1910	Morton	A	Scottish League	1–1
1921	Falkirk	H	Scottish League	0–0

1927	Hibernian	A	Scottish League	2–2
1932	Aberdeen	A	Scottish League	0–1
1938	Aberdeen	A	Scottish League	1–3
1949	Queen of the South	H	Scottish League	3–0
1955	Hibernian	A	Scottish League	3–2
1960	Motherwell	H	Scottish League	1–0
1966	Aberdeen	A	Scottish League	1–1
1977	Dundee United	H	Scottish League Premier Division	1–0

DECEMBER 25TH

1897	Clyde	A	Scottish League	9–1
1909	Kilmarnock	A	Scottish League	1–0
1911	Belfast Celtic	Belfast	Friendly	1–0
1915	Airdrie	H	Scottish League	6–0
1920	St Mirren	A	Scottish League	2–0
1926	Kilmarnock	H	Scottish League	4–0
1933	Queen's Park	A	Scottish League	3–2
1934	Queen's Park	H	Scottish League	4–1
1937	Kilmarnock	H	Scottish League	8–0
1943	Hamilton Academical	A	League – Southern Division	3–3
1946	Queen's Park	H	Scottish League	1–0
1947	Hearts	H	Scottish League	4–2
1948	Aberdeen	H	Scottish League	3–0
1954	Clyde	H	Scottish League	2–2
1957	Queen of the South	H	Scottish League	1–2
1965	Morton	H	Scottish League	8–1

Joe McBride scored a hat-trick.

1971	Hearts	H	Scottish League	3–2

DECEMBER 26TH

1883 Alec McNair was born in Bo'ness.

1891	St Mirren	H	Scottish League	2–1
1903	Port Glasgow Athletic	H	Scottish League	4–1
1908	Clyde	H	Scottish League	0–1
1914	Hamilton Academical	H	Scottish League	3–1
1925	Cowdenbeath	A	Scottish League	1–1
1931	Dundee United	A	Scottish League	0–1
1932	Queen's Park	H	Scottish League	2–0
1936	Albion Rovers	H	Scottish League	4–0

1936 Stephen Chalmers was born in Glasgow.

1942	Morton	H	League – Southern Division	0–2
1953	Clyde	A	Scottish League	7–1
1955	Rangers	Hampden Park	Glasgow Cup final replay	5–3
1959	Kilmarnock	A	Scottish League	1–2
1960	Dundee	H	Scottish League	2–1

1962	Dunfermline Athletic	H	Scottish League	2–1
1964	Motherwell	H	Scottish League	2–0
1970	Morton	A	Scottish League	3–0
1976	Aberdeen	H	Scottish League Premier Division	2–2
1987	Dundee United	A	Scottish League Premier Division	2–1
1988	Red Star Belgrade	H	Friendly	2–2
1989	Hearts	A	Scottish League Premier Division	0–0
1992	Dundee United	H	Scottish League Premier Division	0–1
1994	Aberdeen	A	Scottish League	0–0

A record that the club would have liked not to create: failure to win meant they had gone 11 consecutive League games without a win, something they had managed to avoid in the previous 106 years.

| 1996 | Aberdeen | A | Scottish League Premier Division | 2–1 |

DECEMBER 27TH

1913	Ayr United	H	Scottish League	6–0
1919	Third Lanark	H	Scottish League	2–1
1923	John McPhail was born in Lambhill.			
1924	Raith Rovers	A	Scottish League	2–2
1930	Falkirk	H	Scottish League	3–0
1941	Morton	H	League – Southern Division	3–0
1947	Queen's Park	A	Scottish League	2–3
1952	Raith Rovers	H	Scottish League	0–1
1954	John McMaster died in Greenock aged 60.			
1958	Clyde	H	Scottish League	3–1
1969	Partick Thistle	H	Scottish League	8–1
1975	Ayr United	H	Scottish League Premier Division	3–1
1980	Aberdeen	A	Scottish League Premier Division	1–4
1982	Morton	H	Scottish League Premier Division	5–1
1983	Dundee United	H	Scottish League Premier Division	1–1
1986	Clydebank	A	Scottish League Premier Division	1–1
1997	St Johnstone	A	Scottish League Premier Division	0–1

DECEMBER 28TH

1893	Third Lanark	A	Scottish League	3–1
1901	Kilmarnock	H	Scottish League	4–2
1907	Airdrie	A	Scottish League	0–0
1912	St Mirren	A	Scottish League	3–1
1918	Hibernian	H	Scottish League	2–0
1929	Morton	H	Scottish League	0–1
1935	Hamilton Academical	H	Scottish League	2–0
1940	Queen's Park	H	League – Southern Division	5–1
1946	Hamilton Academical	H	Scottish League	2–1
1957	Hearts	H	Scottish League	0–2
1963	Queen of the South	A	Scottish League	2–0
1968	Airdrie	A	Scottish League	0–0

1974	Kilmarnock	A	Scottish League	1–0
1985	Clydebank	H	Scottish League Premier Division	2–0
1991	Aberdeen	A	Scottish League Premier Division	2–2
1996	Dunfermline Athletic	H	Scottish League Premier Division	4–2

DECEMBER 29TH

1894	Hibernian	A	Scottish Cup	2–0
1899	Hibernian	A	Inter City League	0–1
1906	Kilmarnock	A	Scottish League	2–2
1917	Ayr United	A	Scottish League	2–1
1928	Dundee	H	Scottish League	2–1
1945	Hearts	H	League – 'A' Division	3–5
1951	Aberdeen	A	Scottish League	4–3
1956	Hibernian	A	Scottish League	3–3
1962	Falkirk	H	Scottish League	2–1
1973	Dunfermline Athletic	H	Scottish League	6–0

Dixie Deans, Harry Hood and Kenny Dalglish scored 2 goals apiece.

1979	Rangers	A	Scottish League Premier Division	1–1
1984	Dundee United	H	Scottish League Premier Division	1–2
1990	Hearts	H	Scottish League Premier Division	1–1

DECEMBER 30TH

1905	Hibernian	A	Scottish League	1–0
1911	Airdrie	A	Scottish League	0–0
1916	Falkirk	H	Scottish League	2–0
1922	Raith Rovers	A	Scottish League	3–0
1933	Falkirk	A	Scottish League	0–2
1939	Motherwell	H	League Western Division	2–2
1944	Dumbarton	H	League – Southern Division	2–1
1950	Hearts	H	Scottish League	2–2

John McAlindon scored both goals on his debut.

1961	Charlie Nicholas was born in Cowcaddens.			
1967	Dunfermline Athletic	H	Scottish League	3–2
1989	Dunfermline Athletic	H	Scottish League Premier Division	0–2

DECEMBER 31ST

1898	Third Lanark	A	Scottish League	4–2
1904	Kilmarnock	H	Scottish League	3–1
1906	Airdrie	H	Scottish League	2–1
1910	Raith Rovers	H	Scottish League	5–0
1921	Hamilton Academical	A	Scottish League	3–1
1932	Hamilton Academical	H	Scottish League	0–3
1938	Hearts	H	Scottish League	2–2
1949	Hearts	A	Scottish League	2–4
1955	Queen of the South	A	Scottish League	3–1
1960	Kilmarnock	H	Scottish League	3–2

1966	Dundee United	A	Scottish League Premier Division	2–3
1977	Ayr United	A	Scottish League Premier Division	1–2
1983	Hibernian	A	Scottish League Premier Division	1–0
1988	Hearts	H	Scottish League Premier Division	4–2
1994	Falkirk	H	Scottish League Premier Division	2–0